Sociological Thought

Nature, Development and the Social Context

SOCIOLOGICAL THOUGHT

Nature, Development and the Social Context

C.R. Romesh

CENTRUM PRESS
NEW DELHI-110002 (INDIA)

CENTRUM PRESS
H.O.: 4360/4, Ansari Road, Daryaganj,
New Delhi-110002 (India)
Tel: 23278000, 23261597, 23255577, 23286875
B.O.: No. 1015, Ist Main Road, BSK IIIrd Stage,
IIIrd Phase, IIIrd Block, Bengaluru-560085 (INDIA)
Tel: 080-41723429
Email: centrumpress@gmail.com
Visit us at: www.centrumpress.com

Sociological Thought: Nature, Development and the Social Context

First Edition, 2012

ISBN 978-93-81293-56-0

PRINTED IN INDIA

Printed at Tarun Offset, Delhi

Contents

Preface

Social thought provides general theories to explain actions and behaviour of society as a whole, encompassing sociological, political, and philosophical ideas. Social theory is used to make distinctions and generalizations among different types of societies, and to analyse modernity as it has emerged in the past few centuries. Classical social theory has generally been presented from a perspective of Western philosophy, and often regarded as Eurocentric. Eastern philosophy includes the various philosophies of Asia, including Chinese philosophy, Indian philosophy, Iranian philosophy, Japanese philosophy and Korean philosophy. The term can also sometimes include Babylonian philosophy and Islamic philosophy, though these may also be considered Western philosophies.

For sociology especially, the private is becoming a popular object of concern as the discipline's anxiety over the significance of the public realm increases. The mutuality of the private and the public, their co-determination as a set of powerful discourses and the changing ways they constitute each other at the moment is emerging as an object of attention. The relevance of the public/private distinction, the pressing of it into sociological service, is becoming familiar. Mills' mission to connect 'the personal troubles of the milieu' with 'the public issues of the social structure' was one of the defining rhetorical flourishes of post-war Anglophone sociology. However, current, and particularly powerful, sociological accounts of contemporary social change seen as a pattern of 'reflexive modernisation' with an associated form of politics strain even more towards a social science which addresses personal and individual experience within an envelope of a public realm in flux. We now see an advocacy for the private which is a reversal of an earlier stress in all the social disciplines, not least in sociology, on the public realm as the primary locus of social value. A view of the intellectual history of the public/private dichotomy as a seesaw in which, to caricature, the ancient Greek priority of the public gave way to a Romantic stress on the private to be followed by a swing back to a social welfarist public and now to a new privatism may be a useful starting point.

The discipline of sociology studies social life, social change, and social causes and consequences of human behaviour. The parameters of sociology include an investigation of the structure of groups, organizations, and societies, and how people intermingle within these spaces; thereby generating channels for scientific assessment. Human beings are social animals; and so, they are shaped by social factors. The subject matter of sociology covers from the intimate family to the hostile mob; from organized criminalities to religious denominations; from race, gender and social class to the shared beliefs of a common culture; and from the sociology of work to the sociology of sports. Sociology like anthropology and other areas within the Social Sciences provide plethora perspectives on the world, while generating new ideas and reviewing the old. Despite the subject matter, the field offers a range of research techniques that can be applied to virtually any aspect of social life: street crimes, prostitution, teenage pregnancy, wellbeing of the people, fertility, delinquency, corporate downsizing, how people express emotions, stress, education reform, how families differ and flourish, or issues of peace and war, and how social systems work.

The present work on Sociological Thought provides an authentic, up-to-date and thought. The book would be of great value for the students as well as the teachers.

—Editor

1

Social Thought

Social thought provides general theories to explain actions and behaviour of society as a whole, encompassing sociological, political, and philosophical ideas. Social theory is used to make distinctions and generalizations among different types of societies, and to analyze modernity as it has emerged in the past few centuries. Classical social theory has generally been presented from a perspective of Western philosophy, and often regarded as Eurocentric.

BACKGROUND OF GREEK PHILOSOPHY

Ancient Greek philosophers, including Aristotle and Plato, did not see a distinction between politics and society. The concept of society did not come until much later, during the Enlightenment period. The term, *societe*, was probably first used as key concept by Rousseau in discussion of social relations.

Ibn Khaldun

Ibn Khaldun, an influential Muslim scholar, is famous for writing the *Muqaddimah (Introduction to History)*, the first part of his universal history book, *Al-Aitibar*. The *Muqaddimah* was possibly the first work dealing with the subjects of sociology, historiography, and the social sciences in general. Ibn Khaldun mainly dealt with two types of societies: (1) the city or town-dweller and (2) the mobile, nomadic societies.

The concept of "Asabiyyah" is one of the most well-known aspects of the *Muqaddimah*. Ibn Khaldun uses the term *Asabiyyah* to describe the bond of cohesion among humans in a group forming community. The bond, Asabiyyah, exists at any level of civilization, from nomadic society to states and empires. Asabiyyah is most strong in the nomadic phase, and decreases as civilization advances. As this Asabiyyah declines, another more compelling Asabiyyah may take its place; thus, civilizations rise and fall, and history describes these cycles of Asabiyyah as they play out.

Montesquieu

Montesquieu, in *The Spirit of Laws*, was possibly the first to suggest a universal explanation for history. Another innovative aspect of Montesquieu's thinking was that he included changes in mores and manners as part of his explanation of political and historic events.

Enlightenment

Many philosophers, including Jean-Jacques Rousseau, Voltaire, and Denis Diderot, developed new social ideas during the Enlightenment period that were based on reason and methods of scientific inquiry. These ideas did not draw on ideas of the past from classical thinkers, nor involved "blindly" following religious teachings and authority of the monarch. An important idea was that with new discoveries challenging the status quo way of thinking, scientists were required to find new normativity. This process allowed scientific knowledge and society to progress. French thought during this period focused on moral critique and criticisms of the monarchy. Modernity arose during the Enlightenment period, with the emergence of the world economy and exchange among diverse societies, bringing sweeping changes and new challenges for society. During the Eighteenth century, many French and Scottish intellectuals and philosophers embraced the idea of progress and ideas of modernity.

Adam Smith addressed the question of whether vast inequalities of wealth represented progress. He explained that the wealthy often demand convenience, employing numerous others to carry out labour to meet their demands. He argued that this allows wealth to be redistributed among inhabitants, and for all to share in progress of society. Smith explained that social forces could regulate the market economy with social objectivity and without need for government intervention. Smith regarded the division of labour as an important factor for economic progress. John Millar suggested that improved status of women was important for progress of society. Millar also advocated for abolition of slavery, suggesting that personal liberty makes people more industrious, ambitious, and productive.

Voltaire's *Lettres Philosophiques* presented new scientific and philosophical ideas developed by Isaac Newton, John Locke, and others, introducing them to the French. Methods used to study scientific phenomenon were extended to study social and moral issues. David Hume used this approach in his *Treatise of Human Nature.*

Social Questions

Philosophical questions addressed by social thinkers often centered around modernity, including:

- Can human reason make sense of the social world and shape it for the better?
- Did the development of modern societies, with vast inequalities in wealth among citizens, constitute progress?
- How do particular government interventions and regulations impact natural social processes?
- Should the economy/market be regulated or not?

Other issues relating to modernity that were addressed by social thinkers include social atomization, alienation, loneliness, social disorganization, and secularization.

European Social Thought

Adam Ferguson, Montesquieu, and John Millar, among others, were the first to study society as distinct from political institutions and processes. In the nineteenth century, the scientific method was introduced into study of society, which was a significant advance leading to development of sociology as a discipline. At the time of the Enlightenment, European societies were still largely rural, with minimal involvement of government in everyday life of citizens. With industrialization and urbanization, societies were significantly transformed, and new ways of thinking about society arose.

In the 19th century, questions involving social order gained importance. The French Revolution freed French society of control by the monarchy, with no effective means of maintaining social order until Napoleon came to power.

French Social Thought

- Claude Henri Saint-Simon
- Auguste Comte
- Emile Durkheim.

British Social Thought

British social thought, with thinkers such as Herbert Spencer, addressed questions and ideas relating to political economy and social evolution. The political ideals of John Ruskin were a precursor of social economy.

German Social Thought

Important German philosophers and social thinkers included Immanuel Kant, Georg Wilhelm Friedrich Hegel, Karl Marx, Max Weber, and Georg Simmel.

Italian Sociology

Important Italian social scientists include Antonio Gramsci, Gaetano Mosca, and Umberto Eco.

Chicago School

The Chicago school developed in the 1920s, through the work of Albion Woodbury Small, W. I. Thomas, Ernest W. Burgess, Robert E. Park, Ellsworth Faris, and other sociologists at the University of Chicago. The Chicago school included focus on patterns and arrangement of social phenomenon across time and place, and within context of other social variables. George Herbert Mead, a member of the Philosophy department at the University of Chicago, was also influential.

Theories of Positivism

Auguste Comte, Herbert Spencer, Emile Durkheim, and Vilfredo Pareto were aligned with the positivist perspective, which favored use of rigorous scientific methodology in developing and testing theories. This approach incorporated determinism and empiricism in formulating theories.

Critical Theory

Critical theorists including Hegel and Marx and rejected the "objective", scientific approach. They sought to frame theories within ideologies of human freedom.

Marxism

Karl Marx wrote and theorized about the importance of political economy on society, and focused on the "material conditions" of life.

Other Perspectives

Other theories include:

- Social constructionist theory
- Rational choice theory
- Structural functionalism-influenced by Spencer and Durkheim
- Action theory-influenced by Weber and Pareto
- Conflict theory-influenced by Marx, Simmel
- Symbolic interaction-influenced by George Herbert Mead.

Postmodernism

Postmodernism was defined by Jean-François Lyotard as "incredulity towards metanarratives" and contrasted that with modern which he described as "any science that legitimates itself with reference to a metadiscourse... making an explicit appeal to some grand narrative, such as the dialectics of Spirit the hermeneutics of meaning, the emancipation of the rational or working subject, or the creation of wealth.

SOME MEANINGS OF 'THE PRIVATE' IN SOCIOLOGICAL THOUGHT

What does 'the private' mean in sociology now? There has been a relatively recent increase in interest in the sociological significance accorded, variously, to issues of intimacy, the emotions, the everyday, individualism, the self, the personal and the domestic. These topics, with their own separate research traditions and agendas, none the less refer to a common dimension of social life that seems to be intellectually distinctive and is becoming increasingly significant in the self-construction of sociology. This, by contrast with a familiarly used and well-grounded 'public' realm, can be called the 'private.' It refers to subjectivity and interiority as sociological topics no less significant than the forms of social institutions and organisations that are the more conventional remit of the discipline. This concern with the private is not only true for sociology. The sources, character and social construction of individualism, privatism and the self are an increasing interest in the social sciences generally; for instance, in political philosophy, with its interest in citizenship, rights and political identity, in feminism with its deconstruction of the domestic and the familial, in social history with its uncovering of the social variability of the intimate and even in economics with its occasional reconsideration of the meaning of 'interests'.

For sociology especially, the private is becoming a popular object of concern as the discipline's anxiety over the significance of the public realm increases. The mutuality of the private and the public, their co-determination as a set of powerful discourses and the changing ways they constitute each other at the moment is emerging as an object of attention. The relevance of the public/private distinction, the pressing of it into sociological service, is becoming familiar. Mills' mission to connect 'the personal troubles of the milieu' with 'the public issues of the social structure' was one of the defining rhetorical flourishes of post-war Anglophone sociology.

However, current, and particularly powerful, sociological accounts of contemporary social change seen as a pattern of 'reflexive modernisation' with an associated form of politics strain even more towards a social science which addresses personal and individual experience within an envelope of a public realm in flux. We now see an advocacy for the private which is a reversal of an earlier stress in all the social disciplines, not least in sociology, on the public realm as the primary locus of social value. A view of the intellectual history of the public/private dichotomy as a seesaw in which, to caricature, the ancient Greek priority of the public gave way to a Romantic stress on the private to be followed by a swing back to a social welfarist public and now to a new privatism may be a useful starting point.

The aim of this paper is to address the under-theorisation of the private in sociological thought. It argues that the recent frequently noted lessening of social science confidence in the public realm provides a context for re-examining the somewhat neglected importance of the public/private distinction in the formation of sociological thought. Current interest in the private usually focuses on the familial and the domestic, but the paper suggests that a more inclusive and fruitful approach might be to see the sociological private as composed of three interrelated dimensions — intimacy, the self and the unconscious — which are the developing objects of theorisation and research in sociology now and which indicate directions for further development. Public and private discourses are seen as always locked together and the forms of the private suggested here are associated with characteristic public versions. Finally, it is proposed that the privileging of the public in sociological and political discourse may be being challenged by the concern with the private.

Context: A Turn from the Public

There is a coincidence between the general anxieties of our time and the debates in the discipline which is detectable in the sociological energy now spent on the private. The sense of a historic shift in late or post-modern society from a public world of the state, the market, civil society and community and generally the realm of formal organisations is palpable. It has a number of obvious dimensions.

The sense of a decline in the vitality of public life, the disillusionment and disengagement from politics and the civic, the collapse of appealing political and cultural utopias, the loss of faith in internationalism, the declining confidence in collectivities and even in social solidarity itself and the sense of danger and of 'endism' are often remarked on. The list could be extended. Although formal political activity is the focus for much of this concern there is a n increasing parallel concentration on difficulties in civil society and with the possibility and substance of community. Perhaps the most obvious sense of a shift from a confidence in the public realm is in the variety of debates on postmodernity and globalisation. The former is saturated with descriptions of a world beyond the reach of the conventional public institutions and organisations of social control, notably the state and the market. The latter emphasises the terminal enfeeblement of the most public of all social structures, the nation state, at precisely the moment when potentially colossal risks of global damage evade all mechanisms of control which need necessarily to operate at the nation-state scale. The status of the public realm as the locus of the levers of social change is at least in question.

The simultaneous increase in interest in the private is not necessarily the other side of this coin. But it is conjunctive. A concern with the self, with identity, with inwardness and feeling and with intimacy and with all the subjective and expressive discontents (and sometimes the pleasures) that come with this territory are equally obvious features of contemporary sociological writing as well as general culture.

It may be that these versions of the private have come to fill the gap left by an exhausted or evacuated public realm or that they are the implicitly promised versions of the good life inherited from the modern public political and economic order. But the concern with some forms of the private — subjectivity, imagination, the intimate, the inner, the unconscious — has been a notable modern preoccupation and is now certainly a late modern one.

This general rebalancing, a tilting away from a dominant concern with the public within social thought, and especially within sociological theory, has a particularly charged quality. Sociology as a discipline, especially in its British and American formations, has been organised to privilege the public realm, to understand and manage social change through the public institutions which could use its knowledge. Hence the degree of self-doubt we now see concerning its function in a world which displays increasing unmanageability.

Public and private are the common referents to deep and basic domains of social experience. They denote fundamental ordering categories in everyday life and they also connote anxieties, choices and diagnoses for sociologists and for those they study. They are part of that set of basic and generative ordering principles (such as culture/nature; female/male; structure/agency) that sociological thought rests, trades upon and constantly reflexively questions. They form a complex and often apparently unstable unity in which each requires a form of the other, but their general dimensions can be unpacked.

THEMES IN CONFUCIAN THOUGHT

Humanity is core in Confucianism. A simple way to appreciate Confucian thought is to consider it as being based on varying levels of honesty, and a simple way to understand Confucian thought is to examine world by using logic of humanity. In practice, the elements of Confucianism accumulated over time. There is classical Wuchang consisting of five elements: Ren (Humanity), Yi (Righteousness), Li (Ritual), Zhi (Knowledge), Xin (Integrity), and there is also classical Sizi with four elements: Zhong (Loyalty), Xiao (Filial piety), Jie (Continency), Yi (Righteousness). There are still many other elements, such as Cheng, Shu (kindness and forgiveness), Lian (honesty and cleanness), Chi (shame, judge and sense of right and wrong), Yong (bravery), Wen (kind and gentle), Liang (good, kindhearted), Gong (respectful, reverent), Jian(frugal), Rang (modestly, self-effacing). Among all elements, Ren (Humanity) and Yi (Righteousness) are fundamental. Sometimes morality is interpreted as the phantom of Humanity and Righteousness.

Humanity

Ritual and filial piety are indeed the ways in which one should act towards others, but from an underlying attitude of humaneness. Confucius' concept of humaneness is probably best expressed in the Confucian version of the Ethic of reciprocity, or the *Golden Rule*: "do not do unto others what you would not have them do unto you."

Confucius never stated whether man was born good or evil, noting that 'By nature men are similar; by practice men are wide apart'-implying that whether good or bad, Confucius must have perceived all men to be born with intrinsic similarities, but that man is conditioned and infuenced by study and practise. Xunzi's opinion is that men originally just want what they instinctively want despite positive or negative results it may bring, so cultivation is needed. In Mencius' view, all men are born to share goodness such as compassion and good heart, although they may become wicked. The Three Character Classic begins with "People at birth, are naturally good (kind-hearted)", with root from Mencius' idea. All the views eventually lead to recognize the importance of human education and cultivation.

Ren also has a political dimension. If the ruler lacks *Ren*, Confucianism holds, it will be difficult if not impossible for his subjects to behave humanely. *Ren* is the basis of Confucian political theory: it presupposes an autocratic ruler, exhorted to refrain from acting inhumanely towards his subjects. An inhumane ruler runs the risk of losing the "Mandate of Heaven", the right to rule. A ruler lacking such a mandate need not be obeyed. But a ruler who reigns humanely and takes care of the people is to be obeyed strictly, for the benevolence of his dominion shows that he has been mandated by heaven. Confucius himself had little to say on the will of the people, but his leading follower Mencius did state on one occasion that the people's opinion on certain weighty matters should be considered.

Ritual

In Confucianism the term "ritual" was soon extended to include secular ceremonial behaviour, and eventually referred also to the propriety or politeness which colours everyday life. Rituals were codified and treated as a comprehensive system of norms. Confucius himself tried to revive the etiquette of earlier dynasties. After his death, people regarded him as a great authority on ritual behaviours. It is important to note that "ritual" has developed a specialized meaning in Confucianism, as opposed to its usual religious meanings. In Confucianism, the acts of everyday life are considered ritual. Rituals are not necessarily regimented or arbitrary practices, but the routines that people often engage in, knowingly or unknowingly, during the normal course of their lives. Shaping the rituals in a way that leads to a content and healthy society, and to content and healthy people, is one purpose of Confucian philosophy.

The Rites

Translations from the 17th century to the present have varied widely. Comparison of these many sources is needed for a true "general consensus" of what message Confucius meant to imply. Confucius argued that under law, *external* authorities administer punishments *after* illegal actions, so people generally behave well without understanding reasons why they should; whereas with ritual, patterns of behaviour are *internalized* and exert their influence *before* actions are taken, so people behave properly because they fear shame and want to avoid losing face. In this sense, "rite" is an ideal form of social norm.

The Chinese character for "rites", or "ritual", previously had the religious meaning of "sacrifice". Its Confucian meaning ranges from politeness and propriety to the understanding of each person's correct place in society. Externally, ritual is used to distinguish between people; their usage allows people to know at all times who is the younger and who the elder, who is the guest and who the host and so forth. Internally, rites indicate to people their duty amongst others and what to expect from them.

Internalization is the main process in ritual. Formalized behaviour becomes progressively internalized, desires are channelled and personal cultivation becomes the mark of social correctness. Though this idea conflicts with the common saying that "the cowl does not make the monk," in Confucianism sincerity is what enables behaviour to be absorbed by individuals. Obeying ritual with sincerity makes ritual the most powerful way to cultivate oneself: Respectfulness, without the Rites, becomes labourious bustle; carefulness, without the Rites, become timidity; boldness, without the Rites, becomes insubordination; straightforwardness, without the Rites, becomes rudeness.

Ritual can be seen as a means to find the balance between opposing qualities that might otherwise lead to conflict. It divides people into categories, and builds hierarchical relationships through protocols and ceremonies, assigning everyone a place in society and a proper form of behaviour. Music, which seems to have played a significant role in Confucius' life, is given as an exception, as it transcends such boundaries and "unifies the hearts". Although the Analects heavily promote the rites, Confucius himself often behaved other than in accord with them.

Loyalty

Loyalty is the equivalent of filial piety on a different plane.

It is particularly relevant for the social class to which most of Confucius' students belonged, because the only way for an ambitious young scholar to make his way in the Confucian Chinese world was to enter a ruler's civil service. Like filial piety, however, loyalty was often subverted by the autocratic regimes of China. Confucius had advocated a sensitivity to the realpolitik of the class relations in his time; he did not propose that "might makes right", but that a superior who had received the "Mandate of Heaven" should be obeyed because of his moral rectitude. In later ages, however, emphasis was placed more on the obligations of the ruled to the ruler, and less on the ruler's obligations to the ruled.

Loyalty was also an extension of one's duties to friends, family, and spouse. Loyalty to one's family came first, then to one's spouse, then to one's ruler, and lastly to one's friends. Loyalty was considered one of the greater human virtues. Confucius also realized that loyalty and filial piety can potentially conflict.

Filial Piety

"Filial piety" is considered among the greatest of virtues and must be shown towards both the living and the dead (including even remote ancestors). The term "filial" (meaning "of a child") characterizes the respect that a child, originally a son, should show to his parents. This relationship was extended by analogy to a series of *five relationships*:

The Five Bonds

- Ruler to Ruled
- Father to Son
- Husband to Wife
- Elder Brother to Younger Brother
- Friend to Friend.

Specific duties were prescribed to each of the participants in these sets of relationships. Such duties were also extended to the dead, where the living stood as sons to their deceased family. This led to the veneration of ancestors. The only relationship where respect for elders wasn't stressed was the Friend to Friend relationship. In all other relationships, high reverence was held for elders. The idea of Filial piety influenced the Chinese legal system: a criminal would be punished more harshly if the culprit had committed the crime against a parent, while fathers often exercised enormous power over their children. It's differentiated in other relationships much as the same. At the time it lean overly to parent side. Now filial piety is also built into law. People have responsibility to provide for their elder parents according to law.

The main source of our knowledge of the importance of filial piety is *The Book of Filial Piety*, a work attributed to Confucius and his son but almost certainly written in the 3rd century BCE. The Analects, the main source of the Confucianism of Confucius, actually has little to say on the matter of filial piety and some sources believe the concept was focused on later thinkers as a response to Mohism. Filial piety has continued to play a central role in Confucian thinking to the present day.

Relationships

Relationships are central to Confucianism. Particular duties arise from one's particular situation in relation to others. The individual stands simultaneously in several different relationships with different people: as a junior in relation to parents and elders, and as a senior in relation to younger siblings, students, and others. While juniors are considered in Confucianism to owe their seniors reverence, seniors also have duties of benevolence and concern toward juniors.

This theme of mutuality is prevalent in East Asian cultures even to this day. Social harmony—the great goal of Confucianism—therefore results in part from every individual knowing his or her place in the social order, and playing his or her part well. When Duke Jing of Qi asked about government, by which he meant proper administration so as to bring social harmony, Confucius replied:

There is government, when the prince is prince, and the minister is minister; when the father is father, and the son is son. Mencious says: "When being a child, yearn for and love your parents; when growing mature, yearn for and love your lassie; when having wife and child(ren), yearn for and love your wife and child(ren); when being an official (or a staffer), yearn for and love your sovereign (and/or boss)."

The Gentleman

The term *junzi* is crucial to classical Confucianism. Confucianism exhorts all people to strive for the ideal of a "gentleman" or "perfect man". A succinct description of the "perfect man" is one who "combines the qualities of saint, scholar, and gentleman." In modern times the masculine translation in English is also traditional and is still frequently used. Elitism was bound up with the concept, and gentlemen were expected to act as moral guides to the rest of society.

They were to:

- cultivate themselves morally;
- show filial piety and loyalty where these are due;
- cultivate humanity, or benevolence.

The great exemplar of the perfect gentleman is Confucius himself. Perhaps the tragedy of his life was that he was never awarded the high official position which he desired, from which he wished to demonstrate the general well-being that would ensue if humane persons ruled and administered the state. The opposite of the *Junzi* was the *Xiaoren*. The character in this context means petty in mind and heart, narrowly self-interested, greedy, superficial, or materialistic.

2

Indian Sociological Thought

BENOY KUMAR SARKAR

Benoy Kumar Sarkar (sometimes Binoy Kumar Sarkar) (1887–1949) was an Indian social scientist, professor, and nationalist. He founded several institutes in Calcutta, including: the Bengali Institute of Sociology, Bengali Asia Academy, Bengali Dante Society, and Bengali Institute of American Culture.

Sarkar graduated from the University of Calcutta in 1905 with dual degrees in English and history. The following year he received his master's degree. In 1925 Sarkar started as a lecturer at the Department of Economics of University of Calcutta. In 1947 he became a professor and head of the department. He died on a trip to the United States in Washington, DC, in November 1949.

Selected Publications

Sarker published a large volume of work on a variety of topics, including 53 books in English. A complete list of his publications is contained in Bandyopadhyay's book *The Political Ideas of Benoy Kumar Sarkar*.

- 1914/1921 *The Positive Background of Hindu Sociology*
- 1916 *The beginning of Hindu culture as world-power (A.D. 300-600)*
- 1916 *Chinese Religion Through Hindu Eyes*
- 1918 *Hindu achievements in exact science a study in the history of scientific development.*

PROFESSOR G.S. GHURYE (1893-1983)

No one can dispute the fact that Professor Govind Sadashiv Ghurye is the founding father of Sociology in India. Even in the last decade of his life when he was over eighty years old, he continued to make his intellectual presence felt as an incisive social thinker, highly innovative and equally at ease with Vedic India and contemporary India.

One great advantage that Professor Ghurye had in his studies of India was his thorough grounding in the Sanskrit literature and in the high traditions of Hindu civilization. In 1921, Professor Ghurye was awarded a scholarship by the University of Bombay to study Sociology in England. Ghurye received his sociological training in Cambridge University from where he earned the degree of Ph.D under the guidance of Professor W.H.R. Rivers. For a short time after the untimely death of Rivers in 1922, Ghurye was put under the guidance of Professor A C Haddon. Rivers was then considered as a leading intellectual of Britain. He had already become eminent as a psychologist with his own 'school'.

He had established his reputation as an anthropologist with his study of the Todas of Nilgris in 1906 which at that point of time was considered as a model of intensive investigation. Professor Haddon, the other great luminary with whom Ghurye came in close contact in England, was senior to Professor Rivers and had become famous as an Anthropologist with his original works like *The Races of Man* and The Wanderings of Peoples. This was the kind of academic ethos and milieu in which Professor Ghurye had the privilege of receiving his sociological training

On his return from Cambridge, where he wrote his doctoral dissertation under W.H.R. Rivers and later A.C.Haddon, Ghurye succeeded Sir Patric Geddes as Head of Department of Sociology in the University of Bombay in 1924. He continued to head the Department until his retirement in 1959. After retirement, he was designated the first Emeritus Professor in the University of Bombay. Thus, besides his own outstanding achievements in the field of sociological and anthropological research, Ghurye became internationally known with his clear half a century's record as a post-graduate teacher. With his inspiring leadership and guidance, Professor Ghurye produced a generation of great sociologists some of whom are household names in the field of sociology today, like M N Srinivas, I P Desai and K P Kapadia.

Thus while developing himself as a sociologist, Ghurye was also supremely conscious of his role as a teacher, a 'Guru' in the best of Indian tradition. Kindling the research interests of his colleagues and students was part of his self-chosen and self-imposed duties. Ever conscious of his 'pupil coverage', he attracted brilliant students from different corners of India. He expected them to work like him and gradually created an academic milieu in which writing a paper or a book came to be looked upon as a very natural thing to do for all research students and staff members. In the concluding paragraph of his autobiographical account, Professor Ghurye has written 'So far 80 dissertations have been successfully completed and accepted by the University for appropriate degrees, 25 for the M A. and 55 for the Ph.D. Of these 38 have been published as books and one is in press'. Very often Ghurye helped his students to find out publishers for their works and this was highly necessary and relevant at a time when sociology had neither substantial government support nor private munificence.

Ghurye's contribution to the development of sociology and anthropology in India was enormous and multi-faceted. A Brilliant scholar in Sanskrit, Indology, Anthropology and History, his invaluable and original contributions to the sociological literature on a wide range of subjects both Indian and foreign, were based on profound scholarship, painstaking research and lucid analysis. A prolific writer, Ghurye wrote 32 books and scores of papers, which cover such wide-ranging themes as kinship and marriage, urbanization, ascetic traditions, tribal life, demography, architecture and literature. He has rightly earned a place with world famous social scientists like Rivers, Morgan and Maine.

Ghurye played a key role in the professionalization of sociology by founding the Indian Sociological Society and its journal 'Sociological Bulletin'. In addition, as noted earlier, he encouraged and trained a large number of talented students who, in turn, advanced the frontiers of sociological and anthropological research in the country. With his own voluminous output and through the researches of his able students Ghurye embarked on an ambitious project of mapping out the ethnographic landscape of India.

Let me now turn to the great works of Professor Ghurye. In my view Professor Ghurye's greatest work was 'Caste and Race in India' which was published in England as a part of the History of Civilization Series edited by C.K.Ogden in 1932. For 76 years, this has remained a basic work for students of Indian sociology and anthropology, and has been acclaimed by teachers and reviewers as a sociological classic.

The relationship between caste and politics, which he had briefly dealt with in the 1932 edition, was subsequently developed in a more detailed manner in the 1969 edition. In this revised edition, Professor Ghurye came out with a provocative and thorough-going analysis of caste and politics in Tamil Nadu from early times to the present day. In the concluding chapter of this great work, Professor Ghurye gave an incisive analysis of contemporary India and rightly apprehended in 1969 that India will develop into a plural society and not a casteless one, which was a dream of the architects of her Constitution.

Closely linked with the study of Caste was Professor Ghurye's well-known analysis of the Scheduled Tribe problem. His anthropological inclinations naturally brought the tribes close to his heart, and a start was made when one of his pupils studied the tribe of Katkaris in 1930. Other pupils followed it with studies on the Warlis and Agris, all of them on the Western coast, quite close to Bombay. Inspired by the work of his students, Professor Ghurye wrote on the grand theme of '*Integration of Tribals*' in 1943 and it was essentially in reply to the 'isolationist' approach of Verrier Elwin, which formed the basis of the British colonial policy. Professor Ghurye viewed that the only solution to the problem was their progressive assimilation with the farmers and peasants of the adjoining districts. He had the vision to conclude that the major problems of the tribals were never different from the problems of poor rural people in general. In the subsequent editions of the book '*The Scheduled Tribes*', Professor Ghurye was critical of independent India's government policies which sowed the seeds of disintegration by its internally contradicting steps of laying down the integrationist approach in the Constitution and on the other hand promoting fission by giving importance to the idea of Scheduled Areas. The comprehensive manner in which Ghurye studied the problem 65 years ago led to a methodological contribution as well. In the words of Dr. N.Datta-Majumdar, he raised the study of the tribals from the pure plain of Anthropology to that of Sociology.

Professor Ghurye published a study titled *'The Mahadev Kolis'* in 1957 based on field data from three districts of Maharashtra. This was the first major attempt to deal with a problem at the micro level. The kind of attention he paid to even minor details of the life of the Mahadev Kolis brings to life the ethnographer in him but he is not lost in ethnography, for the mould into which he casts his material is sociological. We can easily see the stamp of this approach in other studies done under his guidance: the Coorgs, Thakurs, Newars and Meities at different periods. The study of the Coorgs by M.N.Srinivas, sub-titled 'A socio-ethnic study' became internationally famous.

Ghurye's basic concern with social process, culture and civilization led to his writing three books dealing with some aspects of these themes. The first book, '*Social Process*' published in 1938 reviewed the topic in the light of a century of sociology since August Compte christened it so in the fourth volume of his great work, *Philosophie Positive*, published in 1838. *Nature*, the well-known scientific journal of London gave an abstract of Ghurye's book in these words: 'Social Process, Ghurye considers, has two aspects: the nature of Cultural Development as reflected in the trend of thought about man as a living entity, and the process by which the individual is assimilating into the cultural flow of the times... Scientifically, proper planning of a good life must rest on the understanding of life, and the psychological study of the individual and society should precede the study of man as a political and moral being'.

The comparative study of ancient civilization and culture Ghurye thought was a required background for students of sociology, and he instituted a compulsory paper on it at the M.A. level. His own views led to the publication of his second connected work *Culture and Society* in 1947 in which he discussed the difference between civilization and culture. He said, 'Culture is what we are; it is the individual's participation or cultural endeavour that makes the collective enterprise called civilization possible'. In 1949, he published his third book titled Occidental Civilization. The birth centenary of Professor Ghurye was celebrated in a befitting manner by the Department of Sociology in the University of Bombay in 1993-94. A national seminar in commemoration of the centenary year was organized by the Department on November 22-23, 1994. In 1997 a landmark book titled *Indian Sociology Through Ghurye: A Dictionary* was published. It was authored by S. Devadas Pillai. This volume makes an academic 'journey' through the themes and thoughts of Prof. Dr.G.S. Ghurye. This is probably the first time that an Indian thinker has been honored with a dictionary on the lines of those on Karl Marx, Emerson and others.

Professor Ghurye often spoke of the dignity of learning: 'of the need to keep scholarship pure, to protect it from its three greatest enemies: amateurism, journalistic prostitution, and obsession with doctrine'. Yes. He was a great Sociologist.

INDOLOGICAL APPROACH OF G.S.GHURYE

Ghurye's rigor and discipline is legendary in Indian sociological circles. In the application of theories to empirical exercises or in the use of methodologies for data collection he was not dogmatic. He seems to have believed in practicing and encouraging disciplined eclecticism in theory and methodology. It would be appropriate to characterize Ghurye as a practitioner of theoretical pluralism. Basically interested in inductive empirical exercises and depicting Indian social reality using any source material –primarily Indological – his theoretical position bordered on laissez-faire. Ghurye's flexible approach to theory and methodology in sociology and social anthropology in sociology and social anthropology was born of his faith in intellectual freedom which is reflected in the diverse theoretical and methodological approaches.

Ghurye was initially influenced by the reality of diffusionist approach of British social anthropology but subsequently he switched on to the studies of Indian society from indological and anthropological perspectives. He emphasized on Indological approach in the study of social and cultural life in India and the elsewhere. Ghurye utilized literature in sociological studies with his profound knowledge of Sanskrit literature, extensively quoted from Vedas, Shastras, epics and poetry of Kalidasa or Bhavabhuti to shed light on the social and cultural life in India. He made use of the literature of modern writers like Bankimchandra Chatterjee as well.

Now-a-days sociology tends to be taken for granted in India, like most established things. But this was not always so. In the early days, it was not clear at all what an Indian sociology would look like, and indeed, whether India really needed something like sociology. In the first quarter of the 20th century, those who became interested in the discipline had to decide for themselves what role it could play in India. In this chapter, you are going to be introduced to some of the founding figures of Indian sociology. These scholars have helped to shape the discipline and adapt it to our historical and social context. The specificity of the Indian context raised many questions. First of all, if western sociology emerged as an attempt to make sense of modernity, what would its role be in a country like India? India, too, was of course experiencing the changes brought about by modernity but with an important difference — it was a colony. The first experience of modernity in India was closely intertwined with the experience of colonial subjugation. Secondly, if social anthropology in the west arose out of the curiosity felt by European society about primitive cultures, what role could it have in India, which was an ancient and advanced civilisation, but which also had 'primitive' societies within it? Finally, what useful role could sociology have in a sovereign, independent India, a nation about to begin its adventure with planned development and democracy?

The pioneers of Indian sociology not only had to find their own answers to questions like these, they also had to formulate new questions for themselves. It was only through the experience of 'doing' sociology in an Indian context that the questions took shape — they were not available 'readymade'. As is often the case, in the beginning Indians became sociologists and anthropologists mostly by accident. For example, one of the earliest and best known pioneers of social anthropology in India, L.K. Ananthakrishna Iyer (1861-1937), began his career as a clerk, moved on to become a school teacher and later a college teacher in Cochin state in present day Kerala. In 1902, he was asked by the Dewan of Cochin to assist with an ethnographic survey of the state. The British government wanted similar surveys done in all the princely states as well as the presidency areas directly under its control. Ananthakrishna Iyer did this work on a purely voluntary basis, working as a college teacher in the Maharajah's College at Ernakulam during the week, and functioning as the unpaid Superintendent of Ethnography in the weekends. His work was much appreciated by British anthropologists and administrators of the time, and later he was also invited to help with a similar ethnographic survey in Mysore state. Ananthakrishna Iyer was probably the first self-taught anthropologist to receive national and international recognition as a scholar and an academician. He was invited to lecture at the University of Madras, and was appointed as Reader at the University of Calcutta, where he helped set up the first post-graduate anthropology department in India. He remained at the University of Calcutta from 1917 to 1932. Though he had no formal qualifications in anthropology, he was elected President of the Ethnology section of the Indian Science Congress. He was awarded an honorary doctorate by a German university during his lecture tour of European universities. He was also conferred the titles of Rao Bahadur and Dewan Bahadur by Cochin state.

The lawyer Sarat Chandra Roy (1871-1942) was another 'accidental anthropologist' and pioneer of the discipline in India. Before taking his law degree in Calcutta's Ripon College, Roy had done graduate and postgraduate degrees in English. Soon after he had begun practising law, he decided to go to Ranchi in 1898 to take up a job as an English teacher at a Christian missionary school. This decision was to change his life, for he remained in Ranchi for the next fortyfour years and became the leading authority on the culture and society of the tribal peoples of the Chhotanagpur region (present day Jharkhand). Roy's interest in anthropological matters began when he gave up his school job and began practising law at the Ranchi courts, eventually being appointed as official interpreter in the court. Roy became deeply interested in tribal society as a byproduct of his professional need to interpret tribal customs and laws to the court. He travelled extensively among tribal communities and did intensive fieldwork among them. All of this was done on an 'amateur' basis, but Roy's diligence and keen eye for detail resulted in valuable monographs and research articles. During his entire career, Roy published more than one hundred articles in leading Indian and British academic journals in addition to his famous monographs on the Oraon, the Mundas and the Kharias. Roy soon became very well known amongst anthropologists in India and Britain and was recognised as an authority on Chhotanagpur. He founded the journal *Man in India* in 1922, the earliest journal of its kind in India that is still published.

Both Ananthakrishna Iyer and Sarat Chandra Roy were true pioneers. In the early 1900s, they began practising a discipline that did not yet exist in India, and which had no institutions to promote it. Both Iyer and Roy were born, lived and died in an India that was ruled by the British. The four Indian sociologists you are going to be introduced in this chapter were born one generation later than Iyer and Roy. They came of age in the colonial era, but their careers continued into the era of independence, and they helped to shape the first formal institutions that established Indian sociology. G.S. Ghurye and D.P. Mukerji were born in the 1890s while A.R. Desai and M.N. Srinivas were about fifteen years younger, having been born in the second decade of the 20th century. Although they were all deeply influenced by western traditions of sociology, they were also able to offer some initial answers to the question that the pioneers could only begin to ask : what shape should a specifically Indian sociology take?

G.S. Ghurye can be considered the founder of institutionalised sociology in India. He headed India's very first post-graduate teaching department of Sociology at Bombay University for thirty-five years. He guided a large number of research scholars, many of whom went on to occupy prominent positions in the discipline. He also founded the Indian Sociological Society as well as its journal *Sociological Bulletin*. His academic writings were not only prolific, but very wide-ranging in the subjects they covered. At a time when financial and institutional support for university research was very limited, Ghurye managed to nurture sociology as an increasingly Indian discipline. Ghurye's Bombay University department was the first to successfully implement two of the features which were later enthusiastically endorsed by his successors in the discipline. These were the active combining of teaching and research within the same institution, and the merger of social anthropology and sociology into a composite discipline.

Best known, perhaps, for his writings on caste and race, Ghurye also wrote on a broad range of other themes including tribes; kinship, family and society.

WORK OF GOVIND SADASHIV GHURYE (1893-1983)

G. S. Ghurye was born on 12 December 1893 in Malvan, a town in the Konkan coastal region of western India. His family owned a trading business which had once been prosperous, but was in decline.

1913: Joined Elphinstone College in Bombay with Sanskrit Honours for the B.A. degree which he completed in 1916. Received the M.A. degree in Sanskrit and English from the same college in 1918.

1919: Selected for a scholarship by the University of Bombay for training abroad in sociology. Initially went to the London School of Economics to study with L.T. Hobhouse, a prominent sociologist of the time. Later went to Cambridge to study with W.H.R. Rivers, and was deeply influenced by his diffusionist perspective.

1923: Ph.D. submitted under A.C. Haddon after River's sudden death in 1922. Returned to Bombay in May. *Caste and Race in India,* the manuscript based on the doctoral dissertation, was accepted for publication in a major book series at Cambridge.

1924: After brief stay in Calcutta, was appointed *Reader* and *Head* of the Department of Sociology at Bombay University in June. He remained as *Head* of the Department at Bombay University for the next 35 years.

1936: Ph.D. Programme was launched at the Bombay Department; the first Ph.D. in Sociology at an Indian university was awarded to G.R. Pradhan under Ghurye's supervision. The M.A. course was revised and made a full-fledged 8-course programme in 1945.

1951: Ghurye established the Indian Sociological Society and became its founding President. The journal of the Indian Sociological Society, *Sociological Bulletin* was launched in 1952.

1959: Ghurye retired from the University, but continued to be active in academic life, particularly in terms of publication — 17 of his 30 books were written after retirement.

G.S. Ghurye died in 1983, at the age of 90. marriage; culture, civilisation and the historic role of cities; religion; and the sociology of conflict and integration. Among the intellectual and contextual concerns which influenced Ghurye, the most prominent are perhaps diffusionism, Orientalist scholarship on Hindu religion and thought, nationalism, and the cultural aspects of Hindu identity.

One of the major themes that Ghurye worked on was that of 'tribal' or 'aboriginal' cultures. In fact, it was his writings on this subject, and specially his debate with Verrier Elwin which first made him known outside sociology and the academic world. In the 1930s and 1940s there was much debate on the place of tribal societies within India and how the state should respond to them. Many British administrator-anthropologists were specially interested in the tribes of India and believed them to be primitive peoples with a distinctive culture far from mainstream Hinduism. They also believed that the innocent and simple tribals would suffer exploitation and cultural degradation through contact with Hindu culture and society. For this reason, they felt that the state had a duty to protect the tribes and to help them sustain their way of life and culture, which were facing constant pressure to assimilate with mainstream Hindu culture. However, nationalist Indians were equally passionate about their belief in the unity of India and the need for modernising Indian society and culture. They believed that attempts to preserve tribal culture were misguided and resulted in maintaining tribals in a backward state as 'museums' of primitive culture. As with many features of Hinduism itself which they felt to be backward and in need of reform, they felt that tribes, too, needed to develop. Ghurye became the best-known exponent of the nationalist view and insisted on characterising the tribes of India as 'backward Hindus' rather than distinct cultural groups. He cited detailed evidence from a wide variety of tribal cultures to show that they had been involved in constant interactions with Hinduism over a long period. They were thus simply further behind in the same process of assimilation that all Indian communities had gone through. This particular argument — namely, that Indian tribals were hardly ever isolated primitive communities of the type that was written about in the classical anthropological texts — was not really disputed. The differences were in how the impact of mainstream culture was evaluated. The 'protectionists' believed that assimilation would result in the severe exploitation and cultural extinction of the tribals. Ghurye and the nationalists, on the other hand, argued that these ill-effects were not specific to tribal cultures, but were common to all the backward and downtrodden sections of Indian society. These were the inevitable difficulties on the road to development.

Ghurye on Caste and Race

G.S. Ghurye's academic reputation was built on the basis of his doctoral dissertation at Cambridge, which was later published as *Caste and Race in India* (1932). Ghurye's work attracted attention because it addressed the major concerns of Indian anthropology at the time. In this book, Ghurye provides a detailed critique of the then dominant theories about the relationship between race and caste. Herbert Risley, a British colonial official who was deeply interested in anthropological matters, was the main proponent of the dominant view. This view held that human beings can be divided into distinct and separate races on the basis of their physical characteristics such as the circumference of the skull, the length of the nose, or the volume (size) of the cranium or the part of the skull where the brain is located.

Risley and others believed that India was a unique 'labouratory' for studying the evolution of racial types because caste strictly prohibits intermarriage among different groups, and had done so for centuries. Risley's main argument was that caste must have originated in race because different caste groups seemed to belong to distinct racial types. In general, the higher castes approximated Indo-Aryan racial traits, while the lower castes seemed to belong to non-Aryan aboriginal, Mongoloid or other racial groups. On the basis of differences between groups in terms of average measurements for length of nose, size of cranium etc., Risley and others suggested that the lower castes were the original aboriginal inhabitants of India. They had been subjugated by an Aryan people who had come from elsewhere and settled in India. Ghurye did not disagree with the basic argument put forward by Risley but believed it to be only partially correct. He pointed out the problem with using averages alone without considering the variation in the distribution of a particular measurement for a given community.

Ghurye believed that Risley's thesis of the upper castes being Aryan and the lower castes being non-Aryan was broadly true only for northern India. In other parts of India, the inter-group differences in the anthropometric measurements were not very large or systematic. This suggested that, in most of India except the Indo-Gangetic plain, different racial groups had been mixing with each other for a very long time. Thus, 'racial purity' had been preserved due to the prohibition on inter-marriage only in 'Hindustan proper' (north India). In the rest of the country, the practice of endogamy (marrying only within a particular caste group) may have been introduced into groups that were already racially varied. Today, the racial theory of caste is no longer believed, but in the first half of the 20th century it was still considered to be true. There are conflicting opinions among historians about the Aryans and their arrival in the subcontinent. However, at the time that Ghurye was writing these were among the concerns of the discipline, which is why his writings attracted attention.

Ghurye is also known for offering a comprehensive definition of caste. His definition emphasises six features.

(i) Caste is an institution based on *segmental division*. This means that caste society is divided into a number of closed, mutually exclusive segments or compartments. Each caste is one such compartment. It is closed because caste is decided by birth — the children born to parents of a particular caste will always belong to that caste. On the other hand, there is no way other than birth of acquiring caste membership. In short, a person's caste is decided by birth at birth; it can neither be avoided nor changed.

(ii) Caste society is based on *hierarchical division*. Each caste is strictly unequal to every other caste, that is, every caste is either higher or lower than every other one. In theory (though not in practice), no two castes are ever equal.

(iii) The institution of caste necessarily involves *restrictions on social interaction*, specially the sharing of food. There are elabourate rules prescribing what kind of food may be shared between which groups. These rules are governed by ideas of purity and pollution. The same also applies to social interaction, most dramatically in the institution of untouchability, where even the touch of people of particular castes is thought to be polluting.

(iv) Following from the principles of hierarchy and restricted social interaction, caste also involves *differential rights and duties* for different castes. These rights and duties pertain not only to religious practices but extend to the secular world. As ethnographic accounts of everyday life in caste society have shown, interactions between people of different castes are governed by these rules.

(v) Caste *restricts the choice of occupation*, which, like caste itself, is decided by birth and is hereditary. At the level of society, caste functions as a rigid form of the division of labour with specific occupations being allocated to specific castes.

(vi) Caste involves *strict restrictions on marriage*. Caste 'endogamy', or marriage only within the caste, is often accompanied by rules about 'exogamy', or whom one may not marry. This combination

DHURJATI PRASAD MUKERJI (1894-1961)

D.P. Mukerji was born on 5 October 1894 in a middle class Bengali brahmin family with a long tradition of involvement in higher education. Undergraduate degree in science and postgraduate degrees in History and Economics from Calcutta University.

1924: Appointed Lecturer in the Department of Economics and Sociology at Lucknow University

1938: 41 Served as Director of Information under the first Congress-led government of the United Provinces of British India (present day Uttar Pradesh).

1947: Served as a Member of the U.P. Labour Enquiry Committee.

1949: Appointed Professor (by special order of the Vice Chancellor) at Lucknow University.

1953: Appointed Professor of Economics at Aligarh Muslim University

1955: Presidential Address to the newly formed Indian Sociological Society

1956: Underwent major surgery for throat cancer in Switzerland Died on 5 December 1961.

Ghurye's definition helped to make the study of caste more systematic. His conceptual definition was based on what the classical texts prescribed. In actual practice, many of these features of caste were changing, though all of them continue to exist in some form. Ethnographic fieldwork over the next several decades helped to provide valuable accounts of what was happening to caste in independent India.

Between the 1920s and the 1950s, sociology in India was equated with the two major departments at Bombay and Lucknow. Both began as combined departments of sociology and economics. While the Bombay department in this period was led by G.S. Ghurye, the Lucknow department had three major figures, the famous 'trinity' of Radhakamal Mukerjee (the founder), D.P. Mukerji, and D.N. Majumdar. Although all three were well known and widely respected, D.P. Mukerji was perhaps the most popular. In fact, D.P. Mukerji — or D.P. as he was generally known — was among the most influential scholars of his generation not only in sociology but in intellectual and public life beyond the academy. His influence and popularity came not so much from his scholarly writings as from his teaching, his speaking at academic events, and his work in the media, including newspaper articles and radio programmes. D.P. came to sociology via history and economics, and retained an active interest in a wide variety of subjects ranging across literature, music, film, western and Indian philosophy, Marxism, political economy, and development planning. He was strongly influenced by Marxism, though he had more faith in it as a method of social analysis than as a political programme for action. D.P. wrote many books in English and Bengali. His

Introduction to Indian Music is a pioneering work, considered a classic in its genre.

D.P. Mukerji on Tradition and Change

It was through his dissatisfaction with Indian history and economics that D.P. turned to sociology. He felt very strongly that the crucial distinctive feature of India was its social system, and that, therefore, it was important for each social science to be rooted in this context. The decisive aspect of the Indian context was the social aspect: history, politics and economics in India were less developed in comparison with the west; however, the social dimensions were 'over-developed'. As D.P. wrote, "... my conviction grew that India had society, and very little else. In fact, she had too much of it. Her history, her economics, and even her philosophy, I realised, had always centred in social groups, and at best, in socialised persons."

Given the centrality of society in India, it became the first duty of an Indian sociologist to study and to know the social traditions of India. For D.P. this study of tradition was not oriented only towards the past, but also included sensitivity to change. Thus, tradition was a living tradition, maintaining its links with the past, but also adapting to the present and thus evolving over time. As he wrote, "...it is not enough for the Indian sociologist to be a sociologist. He must be an Indian first, that is, he is to share in the folk-ways, mores, customs and traditions, for the purpose of understanding his social system and what lies beneath it and beyond it." In keeping with this view, he believed that sociologists should learn and be familiar with both 'high' and 'low' languages and cultures — not only Sanskrit, Persian or Arabic, but also local dialects.

D.P. argued that Indian culture and society are not individualistic in the western sense. The average Indian individual's pattern of desires is more or less rigidly fixed by his sociocultural group pattern and he hardly deviates from it. Thus, the Indian social system is basically oriented towards group, sect, or caste-action, not 'voluntaristic' individual action. Although 'voluntarism' was beginning to influence the urban middle classes, its appearance ought to be itself an interesting subject of study for the Indian sociologist. D.P. pointed out that the root meaning of the word tradition is to transmit. Its

Sanskrit equivalents are either *parampara*, that is, succession; or *aitihya*, which comes from the same root as *itihas* or history. Traditions are thus strongly rooted in a past that is kept alive through the repeated recalling and retelling of stories and myths. However, this link with the past does not rule out change, but indicates a process of adaptation to it. Internal and external sources of change are always present in every society. The most commonly cited internal source of change in western societies is the economy, but this source has not been as effective in India. Class conflict, D.P. believed, had been "smoothed and covered by caste traditions" in the Indian context, where new class relations had not yet emerged very sharply. Based on this understanding, he concluded that one of the first tasks for a dynamic Indian sociology would be to provide an account of the internal, non-economic causes of change.

D.P. believed that there were three principles of change recognised in Indian traditions, namely; *shruti, smriti* and *anubhava*. Of these, the last — *anubhava* or personal experience — is the revolutionary principle. However, in the Indian context personal experience soon flowered into collective experience. This meant that the most important principle of change in Indian society was generalised *anubhava,* or the collective experience of groups. The high traditions were centred in *smriti* and *sruti*, but they were periodically challenged by the collective experience of groups and sects, as for example in the *bhakti* movement. D.P. emphasised that this was true not only of Hindu but also of Muslim culture in India. In Indian Islam, the Sufis have stressed love and experience rather than holy texts, and have been important in bringing about change. Thus, for D.P., the Indian context is not one where discursive reason (*buddhi-vichar*) is the dominant force for change; *anubhava* and *prem* (experience and love) have been historically superior as agents of change.

Conflict and rebellion in the Indian context have tended to work through collective experiences. But the resilience of tradition ensures that the pressure of conflict produces change in the tradition without breaking it. So we have repeated cycles of dominant orthodoxy being challenged by popular revolts which succeed in transforming orthodoxy, but are eventually reabsorbed into this transformed tradition. This process of change — of rebellion contained within the limits of an overarching tradition — is typical of a caste society, where the formation of classes and class consciousness has been inhibited. D.P.'s views on tradition and change led him to criticise all instances of unthinking borrowing from western intellectual traditions, including in such contexts as development planning. Tradition was neither to be worshipped nor ignored, just as modernity was needed but not to be blindly adopted.

D.P. was INDIAN SOCIOLOGISTS 93 simultaneously a proud but critical inheritor of tradition, as well as an admiring critic of the modernity that he acknowledged as having shaped his own intellectual perspective.

AKSHAY RAMANLAL DESAI (1915-1994)

A. R. Desai was born in 1915. Early education in Baroda, then in Surat and Bombay.

1934-39: Member of Communist Party of India; involved with Trotskyite groups.

1946: Ph.D. submitted at Bombay under the supervision of G.S. Ghurye.

1948: Desai's Ph.D. dissertation is published as the book: *Social Background of Indian Nationalism.*

1951: Joins the faculty of the Department of Sociology at Bombay University

1953-1981: Member of Revolutionary Socialist Party.

1961: *Rural Transition in India* is published.

1967: Appointed *Professor* and *Head* of Department.

1975: *State and Society in India: Essays in Dissent* is published.

1976: Retired from Department of Sociology.

1979: *Peasant Struggles in India* is published.

1986: *Agrarian Struggles in India after Independence* is published.

Died on 12 November 1994.

Interested A.R. Desai. As always, his approach to this issue was from a Marxist perspective. In an essay called "The myth of the welfare state", Desai provides a detailed critique of this notion and points to it many shortcomings. After considering the prominent definitions available in the sociological literature, Desai identifies the following unique features of the welfare state:

(i) A welfare state is a positive state. This means that, unlike the 'laissez faire' of classical liberal political theory, the welfare state does not seek to do only the minimum necessary to maintain law and order. The welfare state is an interventionist state and actively uses its considerable powers to design and implement social policies for the betterment of society.

(ii) The welfare state is a democratic state. Democracy was considered an essential condition for the emergence of the welfare state. Formal democratic institutions, specially multi-party elections, were thought to be a defining feature of the welfare state. This is why liberal thinkers excluded socialist and communist states from this definition.

(iii) A welfare state involves a mixed economy. A 'mixed economy' means an economy where both private capitalist enterprises and state or publicly owned enterprises co-exist. A welfare state does not seek to eliminate the capitalist market, nor does it prevent public investment in industry and other fields. By and large, the state sector concentrates on basic goods and social infrastructure, while private industry dominates the consumer goods sector.

Desai then goes on to suggest some test criteria against which the performance of the welfare state can be measured. These are:

(i) Does the welfare state ensure freedom from poverty, social discrimination and security for all its citizens?

(ii) Does the welfare state remove inequalities of income through measures to redistribute income from the rich to the poor, and by preventing the concentration of wealth?

(iii) Does the welfare state transform the economy in such a way that the capitalist profit motive is made subservient to the real needs of the community?

(iv) Does the welfare state ensure stable development free from the cycle of economic booms and depressions?

(v) Does it provide employment for all?

Using these criteria, Desai examines the performance of those states that are most often described as welfare states, such as Britain, the USA and much of Europe, and finds their claims to be greatly exaggerated. Thus, most modern capitalist states, even in the most developed countries, fail to provide minimum levels of economic and social security to all their citizens. They are unable to reduce economic inequality and often seem to encourage it. The so-called welfare states have also been unsuccessful at enabling stable development free from market fluctuations. The presence of excess economic capacity and high levels of unemployment are yet another failure. Based on these arguments, Desai concludes that the notion of the welfare state is something of a myth.

A.R. Desai also wrote on the Marxist theory of the state. In these writings we can see that Desai does not take a one-sided view but openly criticises the shortcomings of Communist states. He cites many Marxist thinkers to emphasise the importance of democracy even under communism, arguing strongly that political liberties and the rule of law must be upheld in all genuinely socialist states.

MYSORE NARASIMHACHAR SRINIVAS (1916-1999)

M.N. Srinivas was Born 16 November 1916. in an Iyengar brahmin family in Mysore. It's father was a landowner and worked for the Mysore power and light department. His early education was at Mysore University, and he later went to Bombay to do an MA under G.S. Ghurye

1942: M.A. thesis on Marriage and Family Among the Coorgs published as book.

1944: Ph.D. thesis (in 2 volumes) submitted to Bombay University under the supervision of G.S. Ghurye.

1945: Leaves for Oxford; studies first under Radcliffe-Brown and then under Evans-Pritchard.

1947: Awarded D.Phil. degree in Social Anthropology from Oxford; returns to India.

1948: Appointed Lecturer in Indian Sociology at Oxford; spends 1948 doing fieldwork in Rampura.

1951: Resigns from Oxford to take up Professorship at Maharaja Sayaji Rao University in Baroda to found its sociology department.

1959: Takes up Professorship at the Delhi School of Economics to set up the sociology department there.

1971: Leaves Delhi University to co-found the Institute of Social and Economic Change at Bangalore.

Died 30 November 1999.

Short visits to villages to conduct surveys and interviews, it was not until he did field work for a year at a village near Mysore that he really acquired first hand knowledge of village society. The experience of field work proved to be decisive for his career and his intellectual path. Srinivas helped encourage and coordinate a major collective effort at producing detailed ethnographic accounts of village society during the 1950s and 1960s. Along with other scholars like S.C. Dube and D.N. Majumdar, Srinivas was instrumental in making village studies the dominant field in Indian sociology during this time.

Srinivas' writings on the village were of two broad types. There was first of all ethnographic accounts of fieldwork done in villages or discussions of such accounts. A second kind of writing included historical and conceptual discussions about the Indian village as a unit of social analysis. In the latter kind of writing, Srinivas was involved in a debate about the usefulness of the village as a concept. Arguing against village studies, some social anthropologists like Louis Dumont thought that social institutions like caste were more important than something like a village, which was after all only a collection of people living in a particular place. Villages may live or die, and people may move from one village to another, but their social institutions, like caste or religion, follow them and go with them wherever they go. For this reason, Dumont believed that it would be misleading to give much importance to the village as a category. As against this view, Srinivas believed that the village was a relevant social entity. Historical evidence showed that villages had served as a unifying identity and that village unity was quite significant in rural social life. Srinivas also criticised the British administrator anthropologists who had put forward a picture of the Indian village as unchanging, self-sufficient, "little republics". Using historical and sociological evidence, Srinivas showed that the village had, in fact, experienced considerable change. Moreover, villages were never self-sufficient, and had been involved in various kinds of economic, social and political relationships at the regional level.

The village as a site of research offered many advantages to Indian sociology. It provided an opportunity to illustrate the importance of ethnographic research methods. It offered eye-witness accounts of the rapid social change that was taking place in the Indian countryside as the newly independent nation began a programme of planned development. These vivid descriptions of village India were greatly appreciated at the time as urban Indians as well as policy makers were able to form impressions of what was going on in the heartland of India. Village studies thus provided a new role for a discipline like sociology in the context of an independent nation. Rather than being restricted to the study of 'primitive' peoples, it could also be made relevant to a modernising society.

RABINDRANATH TAGORE

Rabindranath Tagore (7 May 1861 – 7 August 1941), also known by the sobriquet Gurudev, was a Bengali poet, Brahmo Samaj philosopher, visual artist, playwright, novelist, and composer whose works reshaped Bengali literature and music in the late 19th and early 20th centuries. He became Asia's first Nobel laureate when he won the 1913 Nobel Prize in Literature. A Pirali Bengali Brahmin from Calcutta, Tagore first wrote poems at the age of eight.

At the age of sixteen, he published his first substantial poetry under the pseudonym *Bhanushingho* ("Sun Lion") and wrote his first short stories and dramas in 1877. His home schooling, life in Shilaidaha, and travels made Tagore a nonconformist and pragmatist. Tagore strongly protested against the British Raj and gave his support to the Indian Independence Movement and Mahatma Gandhi. Tagore's life was tragic—he lost virtually his entire family and was devastated to witness Bengal's decline—but his life's work endured, in the form of his poetry and the institution he founded, Visva-Bharati University.

Tagore wrote novels, short stories, songs, dance-dramas, and essays on political and personal topics. *Gitanjali* (*Song Offerings*), *Gora* (*Fair-Faced*), and *Ghare-Baire* (*The Home and the World*) are among his best-known works. His verse, short stories, and novels, which often exhibited rhythmic lyricism, colloquial language, meditative naturalism, and philosophical contemplation, received worldwide acclaim. Tagore was also a cultural reformer and polymath who modernised Bengali art by rejecting strictures binding it to classical Indian forms. Two songs from his *rabindrasangeei* canon are now the national anthems of Bangladesh and India: the *Amar Shonar Bangla* and the *Jana Gana Mana*.

EARLY LIFE

Tagore (nicknamed "Rabi") was born the youngest of thirteen surviving children in the Jorasanko mansion in Calcutta (now Kolkata, India) of parents Debendranath Tagore and Sarada Devi. After undergoing his *upanayan* (the *sacred thread* ceremony, a coming-of-age rite) at age eleven, Tagore and his father left Calcutta on 14 February 1873 to tour India for several months, visiting his father's Santiniketan estate and Amritsar before reaching the Himalayan hill station of Dalhousie. There, Tagore read biographies, studied history, astronomy, modern science, and Sanskrit, and examined the classical poetry of Klidsa. In 1877, he rose to notability when he composed several works, including a long poem set in the Maithili style pioneered by Vidyapati. As a joke, he maintained that these were the lost works of BhnusiCha, a newly discovered 17th-century VaicGava poet. He also wrote "Bhikharini" (1877; "The Beggar Woman"—the Bengali language's first short story) and *Sandhya Sangit* (1882) —including the famous poem "Nirjharer Swapnabhanga" ("The Rousing of the Waterfall").

Seeking to become a barrister, Tagore enrolled at a public school in Brighton, England in 1878. He studied law at University College London, but returned to Bengal in 1880 without a degree. On 9 December 1883 he married Mrinalini Devi (born Bhabatarini, 1873–1902); they had five children, two of whom later died before reaching adulthood. In 1890, Tagore began managing his family's estates in Shilaidaha, a region now in Bangladesh; he was joined by his wife and children in 1898. Known as "Zamindar Babu", Tagore travelled across the vast estate while living out of the family's luxurious barge, the *Padma*, to collect (mostly token) rents and bless villagers; in return, appreciative villagers held feasts in his honour. These years, which composed Tagore's *Sadhana* period (1891–1895; named for one of Tagore's magazines), were among his most fecund. More than half the stories of the three-volume and eighty-four-story *Galpaguchchha* written. With irony and emotional weight, they depicted a wide range of Bengali lifestyles, particularly village life.

SANTINIKETAN

In 1901, Tagore left Shilaidaha and moved to Santiniketan (West Bengal) to found an ashram, which would grow to include a marble-floored prayer hall ("The Mandir"), an experimental school, groves of trees, gardens, and a library. There, Tagore's wife and two of his children died. His father died on 19 January 1905, and he began receiving monthly payments as part of his inheritance. He received additional income from the Maharaja of Tripura, sales of his family's jewellery, his seaside bungalow in Puri, and mediocre royalties (Rs. 2,000) from his works. These works gained him a large following among Bengali and foreign readers alike, and he published such works as *Naivedya* (1901) and *Kheya* (1906) while translating his poems into free verse. On 14 November 1913, Tagore learned that he had won the 1913 Nobel Prize in Literature. According to the Swedish Academy, it was given due to the idealistic and—for Western readers—accessible nature of a small body of his translated material, including the 1912 *Gitanjali: Song Offerings*. In 1915, Tagore also accepted knighthood from the British Crown.

In 1921, Tagore and agricultural economist Leonard Elmhirst set up the Institute for Rural Reconstruction in Surul, a village near the ashram at Santiniketan. Through it, Tagore sought to provide an alternative to Gandhi's symbol-and protest-based *Swaraj* movement, which he denounced. He recruited scholars, donors, and officials from many countries to help the Institute use schooling to "free village[s] from the shackles of helplessness and ignorance" by "vitaliz[ing] knowledge". In the early 1930s, he also grew more concerned about India's "abnormal caste consciousness" and untouchability, lecturing on its evils, writing poems and dramas with untouchable protagonists, and appealing to authorities at the Guruvayoor Temple to admit Dalits.

TWILIGHT YEARS

In his last decade, Tagore remained in the public limelight, publicly upbraiding Gandhi for stating that a massive 15 January 1934 earthquake in Bihar constituted divine retribution for the subjugation of Dalits. He also mourned the incipient socioeconomic decline of Bengal and the endemic poverty of Calcutta; he detailed the latter in an unrhymed hundred-line poem whose technique of searing double-vision would foreshadow Satyajit Ray's film *Apur Sansar*. Tagore also compiled fifteen volumes of writings, including the prose-poems works *Punashcha* (1932), *Shes Saptak* (1935), and *Patraput* (1936). He continued his experimentations by developing prose-songs and dance-dramas, including *Chitrangada* (1914), *Shyama* (1939), and *Chandalika* (1938), and wrote the novels *Dui Bon* (1933), *Malancha* (1934), and *Char Adhyay* (1934). Tagore took an interest in science in his last years, writing *Visva-Parichay* (a collection of essays) in 1937. His exploration of biology, physics, and astronomy impacted his poetry, which often contained extensive naturalism that underscored his respect for scientific laws. He also wove the process of science (including narratives of scientists) into many stories contained in such volumes as *Se* (1937), *Tin Sangi* (1940), and *Galpasalpa* (1941).

Tagore's last four years were marked by chronic pain and two long periods of illness. These began when Tagore lost consciousness in late 1937; he remained comatose and near death for an extended period. This was followed three years later in late 1940 by a similar spell, from which he never recovered. The poetry Tagore wrote in these years is among his finest, and is distinctive for its preoccupation with death. After extended suffering, Tagore died on 7 August 1941 (22 Shravan 1348) in an upstairs room of the Jorasanko mansion in which he was raised; his death anniversary is still mourned in public functions held across the Bengali-speaking world.

EDUCATIONAL IDEAS

Rabindranath Tagore's role in the innovation of educational ideas has been eclipsed by his fame as a poet. He was a pioneer in the field of education. For the last forty years of his life he was content to be a schoolmaster in humble rural surroundings, even when he had achieved fame such as no Indian had known before. He was one of the first, in India, to think out for himself and put in practice principles of education which have now become commonplace of educational theory, if not yet of practice. Today we all know that what the child imbibes at home and in school is far more important than what he studies at college, that the teaching is more easily and naturally communicated through the child's mother-tongue than through an alien medium, that learning through activity is more real than through the written word, that wholesome education consists in training of all the senses along with the mind instead of cramming the brain with memorized knowledge, that culture is something much more than academic knowledge.

But few of Rabindranath's countrymen took notice of him when he made his first experiments in education in 1901 with less than half a dozen pupils. A poet's whim, thought most of them. Even today few of his countrymen understand the significance of these principles in their national life. The schoolmaster is still the most neglected member of our community, despite the fact that Rabindranath attached more merit to what he taught to children in his school than to the Hibbert lectures he delivered before the distinguished audience at Oxfoard. Mahatma Gandhi adopted the scheme of teaching through crafts many years after Rabindranath had worked it out at Santiniketan. In fact the Mahatma imported his first teachers for his basic School from Santiniketan.

If Rabindranath had done nothing else, what he did at Santiniketan and Sriniketan would be sufficient to rank him as one of the India's greatest nation-builders. With the years, Rabindranath had won the world and the world in turn had won him. He sought his home everywhere in the world and would bring the world to his home. And so the little school for children at Santiniketan became a world university, Visva-Bharati, a centre for Indian Culture, a seminary for Eastern

Studies and a meeting-place of the East and West. The poet selected for its motto an ancient Sanskrit verse, *Yatra visvam bhavatieka nidam*, which means, "Where the whole world meets in a single nest."

"Visva-Bharati", he declared, " *represents India where she has her wealth of mind which is for all. Visva-Bharati acknowledges India's obligation to offer to others the hospitality of her best culture and India's right to accept from others their best.*"

In 1940 a year before he died, he put a letter in Gandhi's hand, *"Visva-Bharati is like a vessel which is carrying the cargo of my life's best treasure, and I hope it may claim special care from my countrymen for its preservation."*

SCIENCE AND THE PEOPLE

Gandhi and Tagore severely clashed over their totally different attitudes toward science. In January 1934, Bihar was struck by a devastating earthquake, which killed thousands of people. Gandhi, who was then deeply involved in the fight against untouchability (the barbaric system inherited from India's divisive past, in which "lowly people" were kept at a physical distance), extracted a positive lesson from the tragic event. "A man like me," Gandhi argued, "cannot but believe this earthquake is a divine chastisement sent by God for our sins" — in particular the sins of untouchability. "For me there is a vital connection between the Bihar calamity and the untouchability campaign." Tagore, who equally abhorred untouchability and had joined Gandhi in the movements against it, protested against this interpretation of an event that had caused suffering and death to so many innocent people, including children and babies. He also hated the epistemology implicit in seeing an earthquake as caused by ethical failure. "It is," he wrote, "all the more unfortunate because this kind of unscientific view of [natural] phenomena is too readily accepted by a large section of our countrymen."

The two remained deeply divided over their attitudes toward science. However, while Tagore believed that modern science was essential to the understanding of physical phenomena, his views on epistemology were interestingly heterodox. He did not take the simple "realist" position often associated with modern science. The report of his conversation with Einstein, published in The New York Times in 1930, shows how insistent Tagore was on interpreting truth through observation and reflective concepts.

To assert that something is true or untrue in the absence of anyone to observe or perceive its truth, or to form a conception of what it is, appeared to Tagore to be deeply questionable. When Einstein remarked, "If there were no human beings any more, the Apollo Belvedere no longer would be beautiful?" Tagore simply replied, "No." Going further—and into much more interesting territory—Einstein said, "I agree with regard to this conception of beauty, but not with regard to truth." Tagore's response was: "Why not? Truth is realized through men."

Tagore's epistemology, which he never pursued systematically, would seem to be searching for a line of reasoning that would later be elegantly developed by Hilary Putnam, who has argued: "Truth depends on conceptual schemes and it is nonetheless 'real truth.'" Tagore himself said little to explain his convictions, but it is important to take account of his heterodoxy, not only because his speculations were invariably interesting, but also because they illustrate how his support for any position, including his strong interest in science, was accompanied by critical scrutiny.

NATIONALISM AND COLONIALISM

Tagore was predictably hostile to communal sectarianism (such as a Hindu orthodoxy that was antagonistic to Islamic, Christian, or Sikh perspectives). But even nationalism seemed to him to be suspect. Isaiah Berlin summarizes well Tagore's complex position on Indian nationalism: Tagore stood fast on the narrow causeway, and did not betray his vision of the difficult truth. He condemned romantic overattachment to the past, what he called the tying of India to the past "like a sacrificial goat tethered to a post," and he accused men who displayed it-they seemed to him reactionary-of not knowing what true political freedom was, pointing out that it is from English thinkers and English books that the very notion of political liberty was derived. But against cosmopolitanism he maintained that the English stood on their own feet, and so must Indians. In 1917 he once more denounced the danger of 'leaving everything to the unalterable will of the Master,' be he brahmin or Englishman.

The duality Berlin points to is well reflected also in Tagore's attitude toward cultural diversity. He wanted Indians to learn what is going on elsewhere, how others lived, what they valued, and so on, while remaining interested and involved in their own culture and heritage. Indeed, in his educational writings the need for synthesis is strongly stressed. It can also be found in his advice to Indian students abroad.

In 1907 he wrote to his son-in-law Nagendranath Gangulee, who had gone to America to study agriculture: To get on familiar terms with the local people is a part of your education. To know only agriculture is not enough; you must know America too. Of course if, in the process of knowing America, one begins to lose one's identity and falls into the trap of becoming an Americanised person contemptuous of everything Indian, it is preferable to stay in a locked room.

Tagore was strongly involved in protest against the Raj on a number of occasions, most notably in the movement to resist the 1905 British proposal to split in two the province of Bengal, a plan that was eventually withdrawn following popular resistance. He was forthright in denouncing the brutality of British rule in India, never more so than after the Amritsar massacre of April 13, 1919, when 379 unarmed people at a peaceful meeting were gunned down by the army, and two thousand more were wounded. Between April 23 and 26, Rabindranath wrote five agitated letters to C.F. Andrews, who himself was extremely disturbed, especially after he was told by a British civil servant in India that thanks to this show of strength, the "moral prestige" of the Raj had "never been higher."

A month after the massacre, Tagore wrote to the Viceroy of India, asking to be relieved of the knighthood he had accepted four years earlier: The disproportionate severity of the punishments inflicted upon the unfortunate people and the methods of carrying them out, we are convinced, are without parallel in the history of civilized governments, barring some conspicuous exceptions, recent and remote. Considering that such treatment has been meted out to a population, disarmed and resourceless, by a power which has the most terribly efficient organisation for destruction of human lives, we must strongly assert that it can claim no political expediency, far less moral justification.... The universal agony of indignation roused in the hearts of our people has been ignored by our rulers-possibly congratulating themselves for imparting what they imagine as salutary lessons.... I for my part want to stand, shorn of all special distinctions, by the side of those of my countrymen who for their so-called insignificance are liable to suffer a degradation not fit for human beings.

Both Gandhi and Nehru expressed their appreciation of the important part Tagore took in the national struggle. It is fitting that after independence, India chose a song of Tagore ("Jana Gana Mana Adhinayaka," which can be roughly translated as "the leader of people's minds") as its national anthem. Since Bangladesh would later choose another song of Tagore ("Amar Sonar Bangla") as its national anthem, he may be the only one ever to have authored the national anthems of two different countries. Tagore's criticism of the British administration of India was consistently strong and grew more intense over the years. This point is often missed, since he made a special effort to dissociate his criticism of the Raj from any denigration of British—or Western—people and culture. Mahatma Gandhi's well-known quip in reply to a question, asked in England, on what he thought of Western civilization ("It would be a good idea") could not have come from Tagore's lips. He would understand the provocations to which Gandhi was responding-involving cultural conceit as well as imperial tyranny. D.H. Lawrence supplied a fine example of the former: "I become more and more surprised to see how far higher, in reality, our European civilization stands than the East, Indian and Persian, ever dreamed of.... This fraud of looking up to them—this wretched worship-of-Tagore attitude is disgusting." But, unlike Gandhi, Tagore could not, even in jest, be dismissive of Western civilization.

Even in his powerful indictment of British rule in India in 1941, in a lecture which he gave on his last birthday, and which was later published as a pamphlet under the title *Crisis in*

Civilization, he strains hard to maintain the distinction between opposing Western imperialism and rejecting Western civilization. While he saw India as having been "smothered under the dead weight of British administration" (adding "another great and ancient civilization for whose recent tragic history the British cannot disclaim responsibility is China"), Tagore recalls what India has gained from "discussions centred upon Shakespeare's drama and Byron's poetry and above all...the large-hearted liberalism of nineteenth-century English politics." The tragedy, as Tagore saw it, came from the fact that what "was truly best in their own civilization, the upholding of dignity of human relationships, has no place in the British administration of this country." "If in its place they have established, baton in hand, a reign of 'law and order,' or in other words a policeman's rule, such a mockery of civilization can claim no respect from us."

PATRIOTISM AND ITS CRITICS

Rabindranath rebelled against the strongly nationalist form that the independence movement often took, and this made him refrain from taking a particularly active part in contemporary politics. He wanted to assert India's right to be independent without denying the importance of what India could learn—freely and profitably—from abroad. He was afraid that a rejection of the West in favor of an indigenous Indian tradition was not only limiting in itself; it could easily turn into hostility to other influences from abroad, including Christianity, which came to parts of India by the fourth century; Judaism, which came through Jewish immigration shortly after the fall of Jerusalem, as did Zoroastrianism through Parsi immigration later on (mainly in the eighth century), and, of course—and most importantly—Islam, which has had a very strong presence in India since the tenth century.

Tagore's criticism of patriotism is a persistent theme in his writings. As early as 1908, he put his position succinctly in a letter replying to the criticism of Abala Bose, the wife of a great Indian scientist, Jagadish Chandra Bose: "Patriotism cannot be our final spiritual shelter; my refuge is humanity. I will not buy glass for the price of diamonds, and I will never allow patriotism to triumph over humanity as long as I live." His novel *Ghare Baire* (The Home and the World) has much to say about this theme. In the novel, Nikhil, who is keen on social reform, including women's liberation, but cool toward nationalism, gradually loses the esteem of his spirited wife, Bimala, because of his failure to be enthusiastic about anti-British agitations, which she sees as a lack of patriotic commitment. Bimala becomes fascinated with Nikhil's nationalist friend Sandip, who speaks brilliantly and acts with patriotic militancy, and she falls in love with him. Nikhil refuses to change his views: "I am willing to serve my country; but my worship I reserve for Right which is far greater than my country. To worship my country as a god is to bring a curse upon it."

As the story unfolds, Sandip becomes angry with some of his countrymen for their failure to join the struggle as readily as he thinks they should ("Some Mohamedan traders are still obdurate"). He arranges to deal with the recalcitrants by burning their meager trading stocks and physically attacking them. Bimala has to acknowledge the connection between Sandip's rousing nationalistic sentiments and his sectarian-and ultimately violent-actions. The dramatic events that follow (Nikhil attempts to help the victims, risking his life) include the end of Bimala's political romance.

This is a difficult subject, and Satyajit Ray's beautiful film of *The Home and the World* brilliantly brings out the novel's tensions, along with the human affections and disaffections of the story. Not surprisingly, the story has had many detractors, not just among dedicated nationalists in India. Georg Lukács found Tagore's novel to be "a petit bourgeois yarn of the shoddiest kind," "at the intellectual service of the British police," and "a contemptible caricature of Gandhi." It would, of course, be absurd to think of Sandip as Gandhi, but the novel gives a "strong and gentle" warning, as Bertolt Brecht noted in his diary, of the corruptibility of nationalism, since it is not even-handed. Hatred of one group can lead to hatred of others, no matter how far such feeling may be from the minds of large-hearted nationalist leaders like Mahatma Gandhi.

ADMIRATION AND CRITICISM OF JAPAN

Tagore's reaction to nationalism in Japan is particularly telling. As in the case of India, he saw the need to build the self-confidence of a defeated and humiliated people, of people left behind by developments elsewhere, as was the case in Japan before its emergence during the nineteenth century. At the beginning of one of his lectures in Japan in 1916 ("Nationalism in Japan"), he observed that "the worst form of bondage is the bondage of dejection, which keeps men hopelessly chained in loss of faith in themselves."

Tagore shared the admiration for Japan widespread in Asia for demonstrating the ability of an Asian nation to rival the West in industrial development and economic progress. He noted with great satisfaction that Japan had "in giant strides left centuries of inaction behind, overtaking the present time in its foremost achievement." For other nations outside the West, he said, Japan "has broken the spell under which we lay in torpor for ages, taking it to be the normal condition of certain races living in certain geographical limits."

But then Tagore went on to criticize the rise of a strong nationalism in Japan, and its emergence as an imperialist nation. Tagore's outspoken criticisms did not please Japanese audiences and, as E.P. Thompson wrote, "the welcome given to him on his first arrival soon cooled." Twenty-two years later, in 1937, during the Japanese war on China, Tagore received a letter from Rash Behari Bose, an anti-British Indian revolutionary then living in Japan, who sought Tagore's approval for his efforts there on behalf of Indian independence, in which he had the support of the Japanese government. Tagore replied: Your cable has caused me many restless hours, for it hurts me very much to have to ignore your appeal.

I wish you had asked for my cooperation in a cause against which my spirit did not protest. I know, in making this appeal, you counted on my great regard for the Japanese for I, along with the rest of Asia, did once admire and look up to Japan and did once fondly hope that in Japan Asia had at last discovered its challenge to the West, that Japan's new strength would be consecrated in safeguarding the culture of the East against alien interests. But Japan has not taken long to betray that rising hope and repudiate all that seemed significant in her wonderful, and, to us symbolic, awakening, and has now become itself a worse menace to the defenceless peoples of the East.

How to view Japan's position in the Second World War was a divisive issue in India. After the war, when Japanese political leaders were tried for war crimes, the sole dissenting voice among the judges came from the Indian judge, Radhabinod Pal, a distinguished jurist. Pal dissented on various grounds, among them that no fair trial was possible in view of the asymmetry of power between the victor and the defeated. Ambivalent feelings in India toward the Japanese military aggression, given the unacceptable nature of British imperialism, possibly had a part in predisposing Pal to consider a perspective different from that of the other judges. More tellingly, Subhas Chandra Bose (no relation of Rash Behari Bose), a leading nationalist, made his way to Japan during the war via Italy and Germany after escaping from a British prison; he helped the Japanese to form units of Indian soldiers, who had earlier surrendered to the advancing Japanese army, to fight on the Japanese side as the "Indian National Army." Rabindranath had formerly entertained great admiration for Subhas Bose as a dedicated nonsectarian fighter for Indian independence. But their ways would have parted when Bose's political activities took this turn, although Tagore was dead by the time Bose reached Japan. Tagore saw Japanese militarism as illustrating the way nationalism can mislead even a nation of great achievement and promise. In 1938 Yone Noguchi, the distinguished poet and friend of Tagore (as well as of Yeats and Pound), wrote to Tagore, pleading with him to change his mind about Japan. Rabindranath's reply, written on September 12, 1938, was altogether uncompromising: It seems to me that it is futile for either of us to try to convince the other, since your faith in the infallible right of Japan to bully other Asiatic nations into line with your Government's policy is not shared by me.... Believe me, it is sorrow and shame, not anger, that prompt me to write to you. I suffer intensely not only because the reports of Chinese suffering batter against my heart, but because I can no longer point out with pride the example of a great Japan.

He would have been much happier with the postwar emergence of Japan as a peaceful power. Then, too, since he was not free of egotism, he would also have been pleased by the attention paid to his ideas by the novelist Yasunari Kawabata and others.

INTERNATIONAL CONCERNS

Tagore was not invariably well-informed about international politics. He allowed himself to be entertained by Mussolini in a short visit to Italy in May-June 1926, a visit arranged by Carlo Formichi, professor of Sanskrit at the University of Rome. When he asked to meet Benedetto Croce, Formichi said, "Impossible! Impossible!" Mussolini told him that Croce was "not in Rome." When Tagore said he would go "wherever he is," Mussolini assured him that Croce's whereabouts were unknown.

Such incidents, as well as warnings from Romain Rolland and other friends, should have ended Tagore's flirtation with Mussolini more quickly than it did. But only after he received graphic accounts of the brutality of Italian fascism from two exiles, Gaetano Salvemini and Gaetano Salvadori, and learned more of what was happening in Italy, did he publicly denounce the regime, publishing a letter to the *Manchester Guardian* in August. The next month, Popolo d'Italia, the magazine edited by Benito Mussolini's brother, replied: "Who cares? Italy laughs at Tagore and those who brought this unctuous and insupportable fellow in our midst."

With his high expectations of Britain, Tagore continued to be surprised by what he took to be a lack of official sympathy for international victims of aggression. He returned to this theme in the lecture he gave on his last birthday, in 1941: While Japan was quietly devouring North China, her act of wanton aggression was ignored as a minor incident by the veterans of British diplomacy. We have also witnessed from this distance how actively the British statesmen acquiesced in the destruction of the Spanish Republic.

But distinguishing between the British government and the British people, Rabindranath went on to note "with admiration how a band of valiant Englishmen laid down their lives for Spain."

Tagore's view of the Soviet Union has been a subject of much discussion. He was widely read in Russia. In 1917 several Russian translations of *Gitanjali* (one edited by Ivan Bunin, later the first Russian Nobel Laureate in Literature) were available, and by the late 1920s many of the English versions of his work had been rendered into Russian by several distinguished translators. Russian versions of his work continued to appear: Boris Pasternak translated him in the 1950s and 1960s. When Tagore visited Russia in 1930, he was much impressed by its development efforts and by what he saw as a real commitment to eliminate poverty and economic inequality. But what impressed him most was the expansion of basic education across the old Russian empire. In Letters from Russia, written in Bengali and published in 1931, he unfavorably compares the acceptance of widespread illiteracy in India by the British administration with Russian efforts to expand education: In stepping on the soil of Russia, the first thing that caught my eye was that in education, at any rate, the peasant and the working classes have made such enormous progress in these few years that nothing comparable has happened even to our highest classes in the course of the last hundred and fifty years.... The people here are not at all afraid of giving complete education even to Turcomans of distant Asia; on the contrary, they are utterly in earnest about it.

When parts of the book were translated into English in 1934, the under-secretary for India stated in Parliament that it was "calculated by distortion of the facts to bring the British Administration in India into contempt and disrepute," and the book was then promptly banned. The English version would not be published until after independence.

POLITICS AND NATIONALISM

Once Tagore acquired an image in the West, those in Bengal who were previously censorious of his work suddenly began to hold him in esteem, leaders such as Gandhi sought his comradeship. He had achieved his objective. Thereby he quickly acquired a nationalistic image which held sway all over India, and eventually he allowed himself to be viewed as a religio-political leader of a stature almost comparable to Gandhi. This image, which had its origins in his Western image, further reinforced the latter, through nationalistic propaganda. All major Indian political leaders felt called upon to comment on his life and work; of these judgments we examine only the most salient, made by the most eminent. Dr. Sarvepalli Radhakrishnan who, being a Tamil, did not possess a knowledge of Tagore's work comparable to that possessed by any ordinary educated Bengali, summarised Tagore's oeuvre as follows:

"In all Rabindranath's work three features are striking : (1) The ultimateness of spiritual values to be obtained by inward honesty and cultivation of inner life; (2) the futility of mere negation or renunciation and the need for a holy or a whole development of life; and (3) the positive attitude of sympathy for all, even the lowly and the lost. It is a matter for satisfaction to find an Indian leader insisting on these real values of life at a time when so many old things are crumbling away and a thousand new ones are springing up." This verdict almost defies comment; so vast is its scope, and so vague is the sense in which the words have been used, that one might employ this very summary in characterising the work not of Tagore but of any one amongst Gandhi, Vivekananda and Aurobindo Ghose. No Westerner, who has not read Tagore, can guess from this statement that he was primarily a composer of Bengali songs and poetry.

Jawaharlal Nehru's judgment is, of course, frankly political, and he too was unable to read even a single page of *Gitabitaan* in the original Bengali : "... Rabindranath Tagore has given to our nationalism the outlook of internationalism and has enriched it with art and music and the magic of his words, so that it has become the full-blooded emblem of INDIA'S awakened spirit." (Emphasis mine)

Perhaps Nehru the intellectual (as opposed to the politician) had the perspicacity to see, though he found it imprudent to state, that it was far easier for Tagore to reach out to the Bengali-speaking people of (the erstwhile) East Pakistan through his songs and thereby become an emblem, whether full-blooded or not, of its awakening spirit, which was to lead to the creation of Bangladesh merely seven years after his decease, than to enthrall entire populations of the speakers of Tamil, Telugu, Kannada, Malayalam, Marathi, Gujarati et al who, knowing no Bengali, had no access to his songs and poetry at all.

And Gandhi proclaimed, "I regard the poet as a sentinel warning us against the approach of enemies called Bigotry, Lethargy, Intolerance, Ignorance, Inertia and other memebers of that brood." From all this emerges an image of a religio-political leader, always on the road, addressing hortatory speeches and sermons to great masses of people; its superficiality can be seen by any educated Bengali.

But if such be the utterances of non-Bengali Indians who, on account of their exalted political positions, were naturally taken seriously in the West, one can hardly blame Westerners alone for creating a grandiosely false image of Tagore.

THE MAN HIMSELF

An author who has made bold to claim that the Western image of Tagore is ersatz will perhaps be expected to set forth an account of his true identity, undistorted and unaberrated. The fact of the matter, unfortunately, is that Tagore's temperament was essentially unsuited to an active public or political life; he was fundamentally a loner whose creative energies found their ideal expression in solitude. Though he was aggressively litigious-he had been engaged in furious lawsuits over property with several of his siblings (inclusive of his once-beloved Jyotirindranath) and even when on his deathbed in 1941, was involved in a legal battle with his only surviving sibling Barnakumari (who was at that time about 90)-he was not emotionally equipped to withstand the wear and tear of public censure and ridicule to which every politician and active public person is inevitably subject; poets seldom are.

Here I must let the man speak for himself. When he was thirty-one, he wrote: "Intimacy with men is absolutley intolerable to me. Unless I have plenty of room around myself I cannot stretch my limbs, settle down and unpack my mind. I pray that mankind may prosper, but they should not jostle me... " Again, when he was thirty-two he wrote, speaking of his mind: "It is only when it gets a little solitude that it can muse to its heart's content, look round itself, and express its feelings in all their meanderings exactly as it pleases."

Chaudhuri rightly states, "It is from this Tagore that his greatest literary achievement came out. He is at his greatest as a writer when he is speaking as a lone soul with a lone voice to lone souls."

As for romantic love, the exultant eroticism of ancient and medieval Sanskrit literature provided him with imageries, but the mood of his songs of love are often, if not always, of sorrow and despair. Throughout his life he yearned in vain for an idealised form of romantic love, and this failure caused him intense anguish till his last days. His songs express it in a delicate manner with which many Bengalis, similarly deprived, can identify their feelings.

Out of a plethora of songs as examples, I choose only one:

"You are indeed my heart's desire,
I have nothing and no one in this world except you.
I shall lose myself in my separation from you, and thereby live in you
Through long days, long nights, long months, and long years.
If you love someone else, and never come back,
May you get all that you seek,
And I bear all the sorrow that there may be."

But it was his profound love of nature that enabled him to save his soul. Once again, we must let the man speak for himself: "I feel that once upon a time I was at one with the rest of the earth, that grass grew green upon me, that the autumn sun fell on me and under its rays the warm scent of youth wafted from every pore of my far-flung evergreen body. As my waters and mountains lay spread out through every land, dumbly soaking up the radiance of a cloudless sky, an elixir of life and joy was inarticulately secreted from the immensity of my being. So it is that my feelings seem to be those of our ancient planet, ever germinant and efflorescent, shuddering with sun-kissed delight. The current of my consciousness streams through each blade of grass, each sucking root, each sappy vein, and breaks out in the waving fields of corn and in the rustling leaves of the palms."

One man, his solitude, his yearnings for love, and his love of nature — all experienced and expressed through a highly sensuous musical and poetic intuition : this is the essential Tagore.

MAHATMA GANDHI

Mohandas Gandhi was born on October 2,1869, at Porbandar, on the western coast of India. His grandfather Uttamchand Gandhi and father Karamchand Gandhi occupied the high office of the diwan (Chief Minister) of Porbandar. To be Diwan of one of the princely states was on sinecure. Porbandar was one of some three hundred 'native' states in western India which were ruled by princes whom the accident of birth and the support of the British kept on the throne. To steer one's course safely between wayward Indian princes, the overbearing British 'Political Agent' of the suzerain power and the long-suffering subjects required a high degree of patience, diplomatic skill and commonsense. Both Uttamchand and Karamchand were good administrators. But they were also upright and honourable men. Loyal to their masters, they did not flinch from offering unpalatable advice. They paid the price for the courage of their convictions. Uttamchand Gandhi had his hose besieged and shelled by the ruler's troops and had to flee the State; his son Karamchand also preferred to leave Porbandar, rather than compromise with his principles.

Karamchand Gandhi was, in the words of his son, "a lover of his clan, truthful, brave, generous." The strongest formative influence on young Mohandas, however, was that of his mother Putlibai. She was a capable woman who made herself felt in court circles through her friendship with the ladies of the palace, but her chief interest was in the home. When there was sickness in the family, she wore herself out in days and nights of nursing. She had little of the weaknesses, common to women of her age and class, for finery or jewellery. Her life was an endless chain of fasts and vows through which her frame seemed to be borne only by the strength of her faith.

The children clung to her as she divided her day between the home and the temple. Her fasts and vows puzzled and fascinated them. She was not versed in the scriptures; indeed except for a smattering of Gujarati, she was practically unlettered. But her abounding lover, her endless austerities and her iron will, left a permanent impression upon Mohandas, her youngest son. The image of woman he imbibed from his mother was one of love and sacrifice. Something of her maternal love he came to possess himself, and as he grew, it flowed out in an ever-increasing measure, bursting the bonds of family and community, until it embraced the whole of humanity. To his mother, he owed not only a passion for nursing which later made him wash leper's sores in his ashram, but also an inspiration for his techniques of appealing to the heart through self-suffering-a technique which wives and mothers have practised from time immemorial.

Young Mohandas' school career was undistinguished. He did not shine in the classroom or in the playground. Quiet, shy and retiring, he was tongue-tied in company. He did not mind being rated as a mediocre student, but he was exceedingly jealous of his reputation. He was proud of the fact that he had never told a lie to his teachers or classmates; the slightest aspersion on his character drew his tears. Like most growing children he passed through a rebellious phase, but contrary to the impression fostered by his autobiography, Gandhi's adolescence was no stormier than that of many of his contemporaries. Adventures into the forbidden land of meat-eating and smoking and petty pilfering were, and are not uncommon among boys of his age. What was extraordinary was the way his adventures ended. In every case when he had gone astray, he posed for himself a problem for which he sought a solution by framing a proposition in moral algebra. 'Never again' was his promise to himself after each escapade. And he kept the promise.

A NEW DEAL FOR THE VILLAGE

Ever since Gandhi had entered Indian public life in 1915, he had been pleading for a new deal for the village. The acute pressure on land and the absence of supplementary industries had caused chronic unemployment and underemployment among the peasants whose appalling poverty never ceased to weigh upon Gandhi's mind. His advocacy of the spinning wheel really derived from its immediate value as a palliative. Since eighty-five per cent of the population of India lived in villages, their economic and social resuscitation seemed to Gandhi to be a sine qua non for freedom from foreign rule. The growing gap in economic standards and social amenities between the village and the town had to be bridged. This could best be done by volunteers from the towns who spread themselves in the countryside to help revive dead or dying village industries, and to improve standards of nutrition, education and sanitation.

It was not Gandhi's habit to preach what he did not practise; he decided to settle in a village. His choice fell upon Segaon which was situated near Wardha. It had a population of six hundred, and lacked such bare amenities as a pucca road, a shop and a post office. Here, on land owned by his friend and disciple Jamnalal Bajaj, Gandhi occupied a one-room hut. Those who came to see him during the rains had to wade through ankle-deep mud. The climate was inhospitable; there was not an inhabitant of this village who had not suffered from dysentery or malaria. Gandhi himself fell sick but was resolved not to leave Segaon. He hoped he would draw his team for village uplift from Segaon itself, but could not prevent his disciples, old and new, from collecting around him. When Dr. John Mott interviewed him in 1937, Gandhi's was the solitary hut; before long a colony of mud and bamboo grew up. Among its residents were Prof. Bhansali, who had roamed in forests naked and with sealed lips, subsisting on neem leaves; Maurice Frydman, a Pole, who became a convert to the Gandhian of a handicraft civilization based on nonviolence; a Sanskrit scholar who was a leper and was housed next to Gandhi's hut so that he could tend him; a Japanese monk who (in the words of Mahadev Desai, Gandhi's Secretary) worked like a horse and lived like a hermit.

Sevagram (as Segaon came to be known) was not planned as an ashram. Gandhi never conceived it as such and did not impose any formal discipline upon it. It became a centre of the Gandhian scheme of village welfare. A number of institutions grew up in and around it to take up he various strands of economic and social uplift. The All India Village Industries Association supported and developed such industries as could easily be fostered, required little capital and did not need help from outside the village. The Association set up a school for training village workers and published its own periodical, the Gram Udyog Patrika. There were other organizations such as the Goseva Sangh, which sought to improve the condition and breed of the Hindustani Talimi Sangh, which experimented in Gandhi's ideas on education. The educational system in India had always struck Gandhi as inadequate and wasteful. The vast majority of the population could not get the rudiments of education, but even those who went to village primary schools soon unlearnt what was taught to them because it had little to do with their daily lives and environment. Gandhi suggested that elementary education suited to the Indian village could best be imparted through handicrafts so as to substitute a coordinated training in the use of the hand and the eye for a notoriously bookish and volatile learning. His ideas found an expression in the scheme of "Basic Education" which stirred the stagnant pools of the Indian educational system and stimulated administrators and educationists along new lines.

Work in the village was an arduous and slow affair; it was plodder's work, as Gandhi once put it. It did not earn banner headlines in the press and did not seem to embarrass the Government. Many of Gandhi's colleagues did not see how this innocuous activity could help India in advancing to the real goal-that of political freedom. On the other hand, the first official reaction to Gandhi's village uplift work was to consider it a well-laid plan to spread sedition among the rural masses; the government of India warned the provincial governments to be on their guard and to start counter-propaganda in the villages.

THE NEW CONSTITUTION

Indian politics were in the doldrums during the years 1934-35, but as the time came for elections to the provincial legislatures in accordance with the Act of 1935, political excitement rose to a high pitch. From the point of view of the Indian National Congress, the new Constitution was the inadequate and unsatisfactory. The scheme of the Indian Federation gave a sizeable representation to the princely states, and since their representatives, because of the absence of elective bodies, were likely to be the nominees of the princes, (who in turn were dependant for their very existence on the British Government) Indian nationalists viewed the new Constitution with a feeling bordering on dismay. In the provinces a wider field was permitted to Ministers responsible to elected legislatures, but even here the Governors had been invested with over-riding and preventive authority.

Because of these limitations, there was a large and vocal section in the Congress led by Jawaharlal Nehru which did not want to have anything to do with the new Constitution. Nevertheless, the Congress decided to contest the elections, which were held early in 1937. It acquitted itself very well indeed, and was in a position to form ministries in six out of eleven provinces. A section of the Congress even favoured acceptance of office and its hands were strengthened by the moral support it received from Gandhi. The Mahatma felt that with all its deficiencies, the new Constitution could promote the programme of village uplift. He saw no reason why Congress ministries in the provinces could not encourage village industries, introduce prohibition, reduce the burden on the peasantry, promote the use of hand-spun cloth, extend education and combat untouchability.

The acceptance of office by the Congress party was facilitated by a statement issued by the Viceroy, Lord Linlithgow, which did not change the legal position or the powers of the Governors, but breathed a spirit of conciliation to which the Congress responded by deciding to form ministries.

For a political party which had remained so long in opposition, to get into the seat of power was a novel, and even a hazardous experience. The left wing in the Congress, which opposed formation of ministries, had in fact stressed the possibilities of internal dissensions and scramble for loaves and fishes among Congressmen. Gandhi found himself inundated with requests for jobs and minister ships; he expressed his surprise and distress at this trend, because to him the legislatures and ministerships were only one and a limited medium of serving the country.

He felt that for the majority of Congressmen the work lay in the villages in the constructive fields of social and economic reform. The caucus system, the struggle for power and pressure politics, which are accepted as part of political democracy, were repellent to Gandhi. As an 'experienced servant and general', he deprecated the struggle for "the spoils of office", and the dissipation of energy in factional rivalries.

HINDU-MUSLIM ANTAGONISM

During these years Gandhi was also much distressed by the rise in communal tension. To some extent this increased tension was attributable to the elections to the legislatures. The religious minorities were allowed to elect their representatives only from a purely communal electorate, from which adherents of all other religions were excluded. It was only natural that Muslim candidates should raise religious issues which could make the widest and easiest appeal to a largely illiterate electorate. It so happened that from 1937 onwards it suited the All India Muslim League, under the leadership of M.A. Jinnah, to whip up religious feeling. The League had done badly in the elections, but it sought to retrieve its position by launching a tirade against the Congress and Gandhi. Gandhi was alleged to be 'Enemy Number One' of the Muslim community and the British Governors were accused of conniving at a systematic oppression of the Muslim minority by the Hindus. Vague and exaggerated accusations were made about "atrocities" on the Muslims.

The Muslim League's antagonism to the Congress acquired a progressively sharper edge. Jinnah began even to question the suitability of a democratic system of government for India, in 1940 came out with the theory that Hindus and Muslims were two separate nations and the Muslim nation needed a 'homeland' of its own in the northwest and northeast of the sub-continent.

Gandhi's reaction to the two-nation theory and the demand for Pakistan was one of bewilderment, almost of incredulity. Was it the function of religion to separate men or to unite them? He described the two-nation theory as an "untruth"; in his dictionary there was no stronger word. He discussed the attributes of nationality. A change of religion did not change nationality; the religious divisions did not coincide with cultural differences. A Bengali Muslim, He wrote, "speaks the same tongue that a Bengali Hindu does, cats the same food, has the same amusements as his Hindu neighbour. They dress alike. His (Jinnah's) name could be that of any Hindu. When I first met him, I did not know he was a Muslim."

To divide India was to undo the centuries of work done by Hindus and Muslims. Gandhi's soul rebelled against the idea that Hinduism and Islam represented antagonistic cultures and doctrines, and that eighty million of Muslims had really nothing in common with their Hindu neighbours. And even if there were religious and cultural differences, what clash of interests could there be on such matters as revenue, industry, sanitation or justice? The differences could only be in religious usage and observances with which a secular state should have no concern.

NONVIOLENCE IN VIOLENT WORLD

The separatist ideology was to receive a fillip from the outbreak of the Second by Nehru in international affairs, Gandhi sympathized with the victims of Fascist and Nazi aggression. Gandhi's own life had been one long struggle against the forces of violence. For more then thirty years he had been experimenting with technique-Satyagraha-which, while eschewing violence, was designed to resolve conflicts.

Gandhi's ideas on nonviolence had matured over many years. In the Boer War and the Fist World War he had raised ambulance units and enlisted soldiers for the British Empire. The fact that he not handled a gun himself did not, in his opinion, make a material difference. As he confessed later: "There is no defence for my conduct only in the scales of nonviolence (ahimsa). I draw no distinction between those who wield weapons of destruction and those who do Red Cross work. Both participate in war and advance its cause. Both are guilty of the crime of war. But even after introspection during all these years, I feel that in the circumstances in which I found myself I was bound to adopt the course I did."

The Indians whom Gandhi led in the battle fronts of the Boer War or exhorted to join the British Indian army in 1914-18 did not believe in nonviolence; it was not repugnance to violence, but indifference or cowardice which had kept them from bearing arms. Believing as he did in those days in the British Empire, as a benign institution, Gandhi also thought that as citizens of the Empire, Indians had duties as well as rights; one of these duties was to participate in the defence of the Empire.

In the twenty years which spanned the First and Second World Wars, Gandhi's faith in the British Empire had been irrevocably shaken. At the same time his own belief in the power of nonviolence had grown. As the threat of war grew and the forces of violence gathered momentum in the late thirties, he felt more strongly than ever that at that moment of crisis in world history, he had a message for India and India had a message for the bewildered humanity. Through the pages of Harijan, his weekly paper, he expounded the nonviolent approach to military aggression and political tyranny He advised the weaker nations to defend themselves not by seeking protection from better armed states, but by nonviolent resistance to the aggressor. A nonviolent Abyssinia, he explained, needed no arms and succour from the League of Nations; if every Abyssinian man, woman and child refused cooperation, willing or forced, with the Italians, the aggressor would have to walk over the dead bodies of their victims and to occupy the country without the people.

It may be argued that Gandhi was making a heavy overdraft upon human endurance. It required supreme courage for a whole people to die to the last man, woman and child, rather than surrender to the enemy. Gandhi's nonviolent resistance was thus not a soft doctrine-a convenient refuge from a dangerous situation. Nor was it an offer on a silver platter to the dictators of what they plotted to wrest by force. Those who offered nonviolent resistance had to be prepared for the extreme sacrifice.

EDUCATION AS PER MAHATMA GANDHI

Medium of Education

I find daily proof of the increasing & continuing wrong being done to the millions by our false de-Indianizing education.

We seem to have come to think that no one can hope to be like a Bose unless he knows English. I cannot conceive a grosser superstition than this. No Japanese feels so helpless as we seem to do....

The medium of instruction should be alerted at once, and at any cost, the provincial languages being given their rightful place. I would prefer temporary chaos in higher education to the criminal waste that is daily accumulating.

Education through a foreign Language entails a certain degree of strain, and our boys have to pay dearly for it. To a large extent, they lose the capacity of shouldering any other burden afterwards., for they become a useless lot who are weak of body, without any zest for work and imitators of the West. They have little interest in original research or deep thinking, and the qualities of courage, perseverance. bravery and fearlessness are lacking. That is why we are unable to make new plans or carry our projects to meet our problems. In case we make them to fail to implement them. A few who do show promise usually die young.......

We, the English educated people alone are unable to assess the great loss that this factor has caused. Some idea of its immensity would be had if we could estimate how little we have influenced the general mass of our people.

The school must be an extension of home there must be concordance between the impressions which a child gathers at home and at school, if the best results are to be obtained. Education through the medium of strange tongue breaks the concordance which should exist. Those who breaks this relationship are enemies of the people even though their motives may be honest. To be a voluntary victim of this system of education is as good as the betrayal of our duty towards our mothers. The harm done by this alien type of education does not stop here; it goes much further. It has produced a gulf between the educated classes and the masses. The people look on us as beings apart from them.

It is my considered opinion that English education in the manner it has been given has emasculated the English educated Indian, it has put a severe strain upon the Indian students' nervous energy and has made of us imitators. The process of displacing the vernaculars has been one of the saddest chapters in the British connection. Ram Mohan Rai would have been a greater reformer, and Lokmanya Tilak would have been a greater scholar, if they had not to start with the handicap of having to think in English and transmit their thoughts chiefly in English. Their effect on their own people, marvellous as it was, would have been greater if they would have been brought under a less unnatural system. No dought they both gained from their knowledge of the rich treasures of English literature. But these should have been accessible to them through their own vernaculars. No country can become a nation by producing a race of imitators.

English is today studied because of its commercial and so called political value. Our boys think and rightly in the present circumstances, that without English they cannot get Government service. Girls are taught English as a passport to marriage. I know several instances of women wanting to learn

English so that they may be able to talk in English. I know families in which English is made a mother tongue. Hundreds of youth believe that without the Knowledge of English, freedom of India is practically impossible.

The canker has so eaten into the society that in many cases the only meaning of education is Knowledge of English. All these are for me signs of our slavery and degradation. It is unbearable to me that the vernaculars should be crushed and starved as they have been. I cannot tolerate the idea of parents writing to their children, or husbands writing to their wives, not in their own vernaculars but in English.

The foreign medium has caused brains fag, put an undue strain upon the nerves of our children, made them crammers and imitators, unfitted them for original work and thought, and disabled them for filtrating their learning to the family or the masses. The foreign medium has made our children practically foreigners in their own lands. It is the greatest tragedy of the existing system. The foreign medium has prevented the growth of our vernaculars. If I had the powers of a despot, I would today stop the tuitions of our boys and girls through a foreign medium and require all the teachers and professors on pain of dismissal to introduce the change forthwith. I would not wait for the preparation of Text books. They will follow the change. It is an evil that need a summary remedy.

Among the many evils of foreign rule, this blighting imposition of a foreign medium upon the youth of the country will be counted by history as one of the greatest. It has sapped the energy of the nation, it has estranged them for the masses, it has made education unnecessarily expensive. If this process is still persisted in, it bids fair to rob the nation of its soul. The sooner, therefore educated India shakes itself free from the hypnotic spell of the foreign medium, the better it would be for them and the people

Buniyadi Shiksha (Basic Education)

The ancient aphorism "Education is that which liberates", is as true as it was before. Education here does not mean mere spiritual knowledge, nor does liberation signify spiritual liberation after death. Knowledge includes all training that is useful for the service of mankind and liberation means freedom of all manner of servitude is of two kinds: slavery to domination from outside and to one's own artificial needs. The knowledge acquired in the pursuit of this ideal alone contributed true study.

Persistent questioning and healthy inquisitiveness are the first requisite for acquiring learning of any kind. Inquisitiveness should be tempered by humility and respectful regard for the teacher. It must not degenerate into impudence. The latter is the enemy of the receptivity of mind. There can be no knowledge without humility and the will to learn education must be of a new type for the sake of the creation of the new world. Everyone of us has good inherent in the soul it needs to be drawn out by the teachers, and only those teachers can perform this sacred function whose own character is unsullied, who are always ready to learn and to grow from perfection to perfection.

Useful manual labour, intelligently performed is the means par excellence for developing the intellect......

A balance intellect presupposes a harmonious growth of body mind & soul..... An intellect that is developed through the medium of socially useful labour will be an instrument for service and will not easily be led astray or fall into devious paths.

Craft, Art, Health and education should all be integrated into one scheme. Nai Taleem is a beautiful blend of all the four and covers the whole education of the individual from the time of conception to the moment of death...... Instead of regarding craft & industry as different from education. I will regard the former as the medium for the latter.

Our system of education leads to the development of the mind, body and soul. The ordinary system cares only for the mind.

The teachers earn what they take. It stands for the art of living. Therefore, both the teacher and the learning. It enriches life from the commencement. It makes the nation independent of the search for employment.

It is popularly and correctly described as education through handicrafts. This is part of the truth. The root of this new education goes much deeper. It lies in the application of the truth and love in every variety of human activity, weather in individual life or a corporate one. The notion of education through handicrafts rises from the contemplation of truth and love permeating life's activities. Love requires that true education should be easily accessible to all, and should be of use to every villager in his daily life, such education is not derived from nor does it depend upon books. It has no relation to sectional religion. If it can be called religious, it is universal religion from which all select religions are derived. Therefore it is learned from the book of life which costs nothing and which cannot be taken away from one by any force on earth.

I hold that the largest time is devoted of our time is devoted to labour for earning our bread, our children must from their infancy be taught the dignity of such labour. Our children should not be taught as to despise labour. There is no reason why a peasants son after having gone to school should become useless as he does become, as an agricultural labourer.

Gandhi's Views on Education

Character cannot be built with mortar and stone. It cannot be built by hands other than your own.

An education which does not teach us to discriminate between good and bad, to assimilate the one and eschew the other, is a misnomer.

Education should be so revolutionized as to answer the wants of the poorest villager, instead of answering those of an imperial exploiter.

Education in the understanding of citizenship is a short-term affair if we are honest and earnest.

Basic education links the children, whether of cities or the villages, to all that is best and lasting in India.

Is not education the art of drawing out full manhood of the children under training?

Literacy in itself is no education.

Literacy is not the end of education nor even the beginning.

Literacy education should follow the education of the hand-the one gift that visibly distinguishes man from beast.

Real education has to draw out the best from the boys and girls to be educated.

True education must correspond to the surrounding circumstances or it is not a healthy growth.

What is really needed to make democracy function is not knowledge of facts, but right education.

National education to be truly national must reflect the national condition for the time being.

The function of Nayee-Taleem is not to teach an occupation, but through it to develop the whole man.

I believe that religious education must be the sole concern of religious associations.

By education I mean an all-round drawing out of the best in the child and man-body, mind and spirit.

By spiritual training I mean education of the heart.

Experience gained in two schools under my control has taught me that punishment does not purify, if anything, it hardens children.

I consider writing as a fine art. We kill it by imposing the alphabet on little children and making it the beginning of learning.

I do regard spinning and weaving as the necessary part of any national system of education.

The aim of university education should be to turn out true servants of the people who will live and die for the country's freedom.

A balanced intellect presupposes a harmonious growth of body, mind and soul.

Love requires that true education should be easily accessible to all and should be of use to every villager in this daily life.

The notion of education through handicrafts rises from the contemplation of truth and love permeating life's activities.

The fees that you pay do not cover even a fraction of the amount that is spent on your education from the public exchanger.

Persistent questioning and healthy inquisitiveness are the first requisite for acquiring learning of any kind.

If we want to impart education best suited to the needs of the villagers, we should take the Vidyapith to the villages.

In a democratic scheme, money invested in the promotion of learning gives a tenfold return to the people even as a seed sown in good soil returns a luxuriant crop.

All education in a country has got to be demonstrably in promotion of the progress of the country in which it is given.

The schools and colleges are really a factory for turning out clerks for Government.

The canker has so eaten into the society that in many cases the only meaning of education is a knowledge of English.

The emphasis laid on the principle of spending every minute of one's life usefully is the best education for citizenship

To Students

Character cannot be built with mortar and stone. It cannot be built by hands other than your own. The Principal and the professor cannot give you character from the pages of the books. Character building comes from their very lives and really speaking, it must come within yourselves.

Put all tour knowledge, learning & scholarship in one scale and truth and purity in the other and the latter will far outweigh the other. The miasma of moral impurity has today spread among our school going children and like a hidden epidemic is working havoc among them. All your scholarship, all your study of the scriptures will be in vain if you fail to translate their teachings into your daily life.....

If teachers impart all the knowledge in the world to their students but inculcate not truth and purity among them., they will have betrayed them and instead of raising them set them on the downward road to perdition. Knowledge without character is a power for evil only, as seen in the instances of so many talented thieves and gentlemen rascals in the world.

As to use of the vacation by students, if will they approach the work with zeal, they can undoubtedly do many things. I enumerate a few of them:

1. Conduct night & day schools with just a short course, well conceived, to last the period of the vacation.
2. Visit Harijan quarters and clean them, taking the assistance of Harijan if they would give it.

3. Taking Harijan children for excursions, showing them sights near the villages and teaching them how to study nature, and generally interesting them in their surroundings giving them by the way a working knowledge of geography & history.
4. Reading to them simple stories from the Ramayana and the Mahabharata.
5. Teaching them simple Bhajans.
6. Cleaning the Harijan boys of all the dirt that they would find about their persons and giving both the grown ups and the children simple lessons in hygiene.
7. Taking a detailed census in selected areas of the conditions of the Harijans.
8. Taking medical aid to the ailing Harijans. This is but a sample of what is possible to do among the Harijans. It is a list hurriedly made, but a thoughtful student will, I have no doubt, add many other items.

You are at the hope of the future. You will be called upon, when you are discharged from your colleges and schools, to enter upon public life to lead the poor people of this country. I would, therefore like you students to have a sense of your responsibility and show it in a much tangible manner. It is a remarkable fact, and a regrettable fact, that in the case of the vast majority of the students, whilst they entertain noble impulses during their student days, these disappear when they finish their studies. The vast majority of them look out for loaves and fishes. Surely there is something wrong in this. There is one reason which is obvious. Every educational system is faulty. It dos not respond to the requirements of the country, certainly not to the requirements of pauper India. There is no correspondence between the education that is given and the home life and the village life.

These are not necessities of life. There are some who manage to take ten cups of coffee a day.. Is it necessary for their healthy development and for keeping them awake, let them not drink coffee or tea but go to sleep. We must not become slaves to these things. But the majority of the people who drink coffee or tea are slaves to them. Cigars and Cigarettes, wealth foreign or indigenous must be avoided.

Cigarette smoking is like an opiate and the cigars that you smoke have a touch of opium about them. They get to your nerves and you cannot leave them afterwards. How can a single student foul his mouth in converting it into a chimney.? If you give up these habits of smoking cigars and cigarettes and drinking coffee and tea you will find out for yourselves how much you are able to save.

A drunkard in Tolstoy's story is hesitating to execute his design of murder so long as he has not smoked his cigar. But he puffs it, and then gets up smiling and saying, "What a coward am I!" takes the dagger and does the deed. Tolstoy spoke from experience of it. And he is much more against cigars and cigarettes than against drinks. But do not make the mistake that between drink and tobacco, drink is a lesser evil. No. If cigarette is Beelzebub than drink is Satan. The students should be above all humble, and correct..... The greatest to remain great has to be the lowliest by choice. If I can speak from my knowledge of Hindu belief, the life of the student is to correspond to the life of the sanyasi up to the time his studies end. He is to be under the strictest discipline. He cannot marry, nor indulge in dissipation. He cannot indulge in drinks and the like. His behaviour is to be a pattern of exemplary self-resistant.

WESTERN VERSUS EASTERN CULTURE

Of myself, whilst I have freely acknowledged my debt to Western culture, I can say that whatever service I have been able to render to the nation has been due *entirely* to the retention by me of Eastern culture to the extent it has been possible. I should have been thoroughly useless to the masses as an anglicized, denationalized being, knowing little of, caring less for and perhaps even despising their ways, habits, thoughts and aspirations. European civilization is no doubt suited for the Europeans, but it will mean ruin for India if we endeavour to copy it. This is not to say that we may not adopt and assimilate whatever may be good and capable of assimilation by us, as it does not also mean that even the European will not have to part with whatever evil might have crept into it.

The incessant search for material comforts and their multiplication is such an evil; and I make bold to say that the Europeans themselves will have to remodel their outlook if they are not to perish under the weight of the comforts to which they are becoming slaves. It may be that my reading is wrong, but I know that for India to run after the Golden Fleece is to court certain death. Let us engrave on our hearts the motto of a Western philosopher, 'Plain living and high thinking'. Today it is certain that the millions cannot have high living and we the few who profess to do the thinking for the masses run the risk, in a vain search after higher living, of missing high thinking.

Village Movement

The village movement is as much an education of the city people as of the villagers. Workers drawn from cities have to develop village mentality and learn the art of living after the manner of villagers. This does not mean that they have to starve like the villagers. But it does mean that there must be a radical change in the old style of life. In [my picture of independence], the unit is the village community. The superstructure of independence is not to be built at the village unit, so that the top weighs down on and crushes the forty cores of people who constitute the base.... A village unit as conceived by me is as strong as the strongest. My imaginary village consists of 1,000 souls. Such a unit can give a good account of itself if it is well organized on a basis of self-sufficiency.

We stand today in danger of forgetting how to use our hands. To forget how to dig the earth and tend the soil is to forget ourselves. To think that your occupation of the Ministerial chair will be vindicated if you serve the cities only would be to for get that India really resides in her 7,00,000 village units. What would it profit a man if he gained the world but lost his soul into the bargain.

All-Round Village Service

The real India lies in the 7,00,000 villages. If Indian civilization is to make its full contribution to the building up of a stable world order, it is this vast mass of humanity that has....to be made to live again. We have to tackle the triple malady which holds our villages fast in its grip : (i) want of corporate sanitation; (ii) deficient diet; (iii) inertia... They [villagers] are not interested in their own welfare. They don't appreciate modern sanitary methods. They don't want to exert themselves beyond scratching their farms or doing such labour as they are used to. These difficulties are real and serious. But they must not baffle us...

We must have an unquenchable faith in our mission. We must be patient with the people. We are ourselves novices in village work. We have to deal with a chronic disease. Patience and perseverance, if we have them, overcome mountains of difficulties. We are like nurses who may not leave their patients because they are reported to have an incurable disease. Villages have suffered long from neglect by those who have had the benefit of education. They have chosen the city life. The village movement is an attempt to establish healthy contact with the villages by inducing those who are fired with the spirit of service to settle in them and find self-expression in the service of villagers.... Those who have settled in villages in the spirit of service are not dismayed by the difficulties facing them. They knew before they went that they would have to contend against many difficulties, including even sullenness on the part of villagers. Only those, therefore, who have faith in themselves and in their mission will serve the villagers and influence their lives.

Village Republics

India has had experience of..... village republics, as they were called by Mayne. I fancy that they were unconsciously governed by nonviolence...... An effort has now to be made to revive them under a deliberate nonviolent plan. The best, quickest and most efficient way is to build up from the bottom..... Every village has to become a self-sufficient republic. This does not require brave resolutions. It requires brave, corporate, intelligent work.....

Independence must begin at the bottom. Thus, every village will be a republic or Panchayat having full powers. It follows, therefore, that every village has to be self-sustained and capable of managing its affairs even to the extent of defending itself against the whole world. It will be trained and prepared to perish in the attempt to defend itself against any onslaught from without. Thus, ultimately, it is the individual who is the unit. This does not exclude dependence on and willing help from neighbours or from the world. It will be free and voluntary play of mutual forces. Such a society is necessarily highly cultured in which every man and woman knows what he or she wants and, what is more, knows that no one should want anything that others cannot have with equal labour.

This society must naturally be based on truth and nonviolence which, in my opinion, are not possible without a living belief in God, meaning a self-existent, All-knowing living Force which inheres every other force known to the world and which depends on none and which will live when all other forces may conceivably perish or cease to act. I am unable to account for my life without belief in this all-embracing living light.

AMBEDKAR AS A RADICAL THINKER

Dr. B.R. Ambedkar is viewed as messiah of dalits and downtrodden in India. He was the chairman of the drafting committee that was constituted by the Constituent Assembly in 1947 to draft a constitution for the independent India. He played a seminal role in the framing of the constitution. Bhimrao Ambedkar was also the first Law Minister of India. For his yeoman service to the nation, B.R. Ambedkar was bestowed with Bharat Ratna in 1990. Dr. Bhimrao Ambedkar was born on April 14, 1891 in Mhow (presently in Madhya Pradesh). He was the fourteenth child of Ramji and Bhimabai Sakpal Ambedkar. B.R. Ambedkar belonged to the "untouchable" Mahar Caste. His father and grandfather served in the British Army. In those days, the government ensured that all the army personnel and their children were educated and ran special schools for this purpose. This ensured good education for Bhimrao Ambedkar, which would have otherwise been denied to him by the virtue of his caste.

Bhimrao Ambedkar experienced caste discrimination right from the childhood. After his retirement, Bhimrao's father settled in Satara Maharashtra. Bhimrao was enrolled in the local school. Here, he had to sit on the floor in one corner in the classroom and teachers would not touch his notebooks. In spite of these hardships, Bhimrao continued his studies and passed his Matriculation examination from Bombay University with flying colours in 1908. Bhimrao Ambedkar joined the

Elphinstone College for further education. In 1912, he graduated in Political Science and Economics from Bombay University and got a job in Baroda. In 1913, Bhimrao Ambedkar lost his father. In the same year Maharaja of Baroda awarded scholarship to Bhimrao Ambedkar and sent him to America for further studies. Bhimrao reached New York in July 1913. For the first time in his life, Bhimrao was not demeaned for being a Mahar. He immersed himself in the studies and attained a degree in Master of Arts and a Doctorate in Philosophy from Columbia University in 1916 for his thesis "National Dividend for India: A Historical and Analytical Study." From America, Dr. Ambedkar proceeded to London to study economics and political science. But the Baroda government terminated his scholarship and recalled him back.

The Maharaja of Baroda appointed Dr. Ambedkar as his political secretary. But no one would take orders from him because he was a Mahar. Bhimrao Ambedkar returned to Bombay in November 1917. With the help of Shahu Maharaj of Kolhapur, a sympathiser of the cause for the upliftment of the depressed classes, he started a fortnightly newspaper, the "Mooknayak" (Dumb Hero) on January 31, 1920. The Maharaja also convened many meetings and conferences of the "untouchables" which Bhimrao addressed. In September 1920, after accumulating sufficient funds, Ambedkar went back to London to complete his studies. He became a barrister and got a Doctorate in science.

After completing his studies in London, Ambedkar returned to India. In July 1924, he founded the Bahishkrit Hitkarini Sabha (Outcastes Welfare Association). The aim of the Sabha was to uplift the downtrodden socially and politically and bring them to the level of the others in the Indian society. In 1927, he led the Mahad March at the Chowdar Tank at Colaba, near Bombay, to give the untouchables the right to draw water from the public tank where he burnt copies of the 'Manusmriti' publicly. In 1929, Ambedkar made the controversial decision to cooperate with the all-British Simon Commission which was to look into setting up a responsible Indian Government in India. The Congress decided to boycott the Commission and drafted its own version of a constitution for free India. The Congress version had no provisions for the depressed classes.

Ambedkar became more skeptical of the Congress's commitment to safeguard the rights of the depressed classes.

When a separate electorate was announced for the depressed classes under Ramsay McDonald 'Communal Award', Gandhiji went on a fast unto death against this decision. Leaders rushed to Dr. Ambedkar to drop his demand. On September 24, 1932, Dr. Ambedkar and Gandhiji reached an understanding, which became the famous Poona Pact. According to the pact the separate electorate demand was replaced with special concessions like reserved seats in the regional legislative assemblies and Central Council of States. Dr. Ambedkar attended all the three Round Table Conferences in London and forcefully argued for the welfare of the "untouchables". Meanwhile, British Government decided to hold provincial elections in 1937. Dr. B.R. Ambedkar set up the "Independent Labour Party" in August 1936 to contest the elections in the Bombay province. He and many candidates of his party were elected to the Bombay Legislative Assembly.

In 1937, Dr. Ambedkar introduced a Bill to abolish the "khoti" system of land tenure in the Konkan region, the serfdom of agricultural tenants and the Mahar "watan" system of working for the Government as slaves. A clause of an agrarian bill referred to the depressed classes as "Harijans," or people of God. Bhimrao was strongly opposed to this title for the untouchables. He argued that if the "untouchables" were people of God then all others would be people of monsters. He was against any such reference. But the Indian National Congress succeeded in introducing the term Harijan. Ambedkar felt bitter that they could not have any say in what they were called. In 1947, when India became independent, the first Prime Minister Pt. Jawaharlal Nehru, invited Dr. Bhimrao Ambedkar, who had been elected as a Member of the Constituent Assembly from Bengal, to join his Cabinet as a Law Minister. The Constituent Assembly entrusted the job of drafting the Constitution to a committee and Dr. Ambedkar was elected as Chairman of this Drafting Committee. In February 1948, Dr. Ambedkar presented the Draft Constitution before the people of India; it was adopted on November 26, 1949.

In October 1948, Dr. Ambedkar submitted the Hindu Code Bill to the Constituent Assembly in an attempt to codify the

Hindu law. The Bill caused great divisions even in the Congress party. Consideration for the bill was postponed to September 1951. When the Bill was taken up it was truncated. A dejected Ambedkar relinquished his position as Law Minister. On May 24, 1956, on the occasion of Buddha Jayanti, he declared in Bombay, that he would adopt Buddhism in October. On October 14, 1956 he embraced Buddhism along with many of his followers. On December 6, 1956, Baba Saheb Dr. B.R. Ambedkar died peacefully in his sleep. Overcoming numerous social and financial obstacles, Ambedkar became one of the first untouchables to obtain college education in India. He went on to pursue higher studies in the United States and England, where he earned law degrees and multiple doctorates for his studies and works in law, economics and political science. A famous scholar, Ambedkar practised law for a few years before he began publishing journals advocating political rights and social freedom for India's untouchables. Leading numerous public agitations, he would become a fierce critic of Mahatma Gandhi and the Indian National Congress.

Ambedkar organised untouchable political parties and social organisations, and served in the legislative councils of British India. He would intensify his criticism of orthodox Hindu society and would oppose nationalist rebellions. Despite this, his reputation as a scholar led to his appointment as free India's first law minister, and chairman of the committee responsible to draft a constitution. Ambedkar's work would guarantee political, economic and social freedoms for untouchables and other ethnic, social and religious communities of India. His polemical condemnation of Hinduism and attacks on Islam would make him unpopular and controversial, although his conversion to Buddhism sparked a revival in interest of Buddhist philosophy in India.

Bhimrao Ramji Ambedkar was born in the British-founded town and military cantonment of Mhow in the Central Provinces (now in Madhya Pradesh). He was the 14th and last child of Ramji Maloji Sakpal and Bhimabai Murbadkar. His family was of Marathi background from the town of Ambavade in the Ratnagiri district of modern-day Maharashtra. They belonged to the Hindu Mahar caste, who were treated as untouchables and subjected to intense socioeconomic discrimination.

Ambedkar's ancestors had for long been in the employ of the army of the British East India Company, and his father served in the Indian Army at the Mhow cantonment, rising to the rank of Subedar. He had received a degree of formal education in Marathi and English, and encouraged his children to learn and work hard at school. Belonging to Kabir Panth, Ramji Sakpal encouraged his children to read the Hindu classics, especially the Mahabharata and the Ramayana. He used his position in the army to lobby for his children to study at the government school, as they faced resistance owing to their caste. Although able to attend school, Ambedkar and other Untouchable children were segregated and given no attention or assistance from the teachers. Ramji Sakpal retired in 1894 and the family moved to Satara two years later. Shortly after their move, Ambedkar's mother died. The children were cared for by their paternal aunt, and lived in difficult circumstances. Only three sons—Balaram, Anandrao and Bhimrao—and two daughters—Manjula and Tulasa—of the Ambedkars would go on to survive them. Of his brothers and sisters, only Ambedkar succeeded in passing his examinations and graduate to a bigger school. His native village name was "Ambavade" in Ratnagiri District so he changed his name from "Sakpal" to "Ambedkar" with the recommendation and faith of a Brahmin teacher that believed in Bhimrao.

Ramji Sakpal remarried in 1898, and the family moved to Mumbai (then Bombay), where Ambedkar became the first untouchable student at the Government High School near Elphinstone Road. Although excelling in his studies, Ambedkar was increasingly disturbed by his segregation and discrimination. In 1907, he passed his matriculation examination and entered the University of Mumbai, becoming one of the first persons of untouchable origin to enter college in India. This success provoked celebrations amongst his community, and after a public ceremony, he was given a biography of the Buddha by his teacher Krishnaji Arjun Keluskar also known as Dada Keluskar a Maratha caste scholar. Ambedkar's marriage had been arranged the previous year as per Hindu custom, to Ramabai, a nine-year old girl from Dapoli. In 1908, he entered the Elphinstone College and obtained a scholarship of Rs. 25 a month from the Gaikwad ruler of Baroda, Sahyaji

Rao III for higher studies in USA. By 1912, he obtained his degree in economics and political science, and prepared to take up employment with the Baroda state government. His wife gave birth to his first son, Yashwant in the same year. Ambedkar had just moved his young family and started work, when he dashed back to Mumbai to see his ailing father, who died on February 2, 1913.

A few months later, Ambedkar was selected by the Gaikwad ruler to travel to the United States and enrol at Columbia University, with a scholarship of $11.5 pounds per month. Arriving in New York City, Ambedkar was admitted for graduate studies at the political science department. After a brief stay at the dormitory, he moved to a housing club run by Indian students and took up rooms with a Parsi friend, Naval Bhathena. In 1916, he was awarded a Ph.D. for a thesis which he eventually published in book form as The Evolution of Provincial Finance in British India. His first published work, however, was a paper on Castes in India: Their Mechanism, Genesis and Development. Winning his degree and doctorate, he travelled to London and enrolled at Gray's Inn and the London School of Economics, studying law and preparing a doctoral thesis in economics. The expiration of his scholarship the following year forced him to temporarily abandon his studies and return to India amidst World War I. Ambedkar wrote very learned and theories obtained his M.A and Ph.D. degrees. He returned to India on the 21st of August 1917. There is one thing to note in the years of Ambedkar's education. He studied English and Persian languages in India. In America he studied Political Science, Ethics, Anthropology, Social Science and Economics. In this way he studied many subjects. He obtained his doctorate. Even at that time Ambedkar had a revolutionary mind. He had made an unshakable resolution to wipe out the injustice done to the people of the low cast; in this way he wanted to bring about a revolution in the Hindu Society. But–and this is important before becoming a revolutionary he increased his knowledge. Because of this his thoughts were not mere froth. They had a solid foundation of information. This enabled him to pay a very effective part in framing the Constitution of India.

Returning to work as military secretary for Baroda state, Ambedkar was distressed by the sudden reappearance of discrimination in his life, and left his job to work as a private tutor and accountant, even starting his own consultancy business that failed owing to his social status. With the help of an English acquaintance, the former Bombay Governor Lord Syndenham, he won a post as professor of political economy at the Syndenham College of Commerce and Economics in Mumbai. He was able to return to England in 1920 with the support of the Maharaja of Kolhapur, his Parsi friend and his own savings. By 1923 he completed a thesis on The Problem of the Rupee. He was awarded a D.Sc. by the University of London, and finishing his law studies, he was simultaneously admitted to British Bar as a barrister. On his way back to India, Ambedkar spent three months in Germany, where he conducted further studies in economics at the University of Bonn. He would be formally awarded a Ph.D. by the Columbia University on June 8, 1927.

In 1926, he became a nominated member of the Bombay Legislative Council, and led a satyagraha — nonviolent protest and civil disobedience as pioneered by Mahatma Gandhi — Mahad to fight for the right of the untouchable community to draw water from the main water tank of the town. On January 1, 1927 Ambedkar organised a ceremony at the Koregaon Victory Memorial near Pune, which commemorated the Indian soldiers who died during World War I. Here he inscripted the names of the soldiers from his Mahar community on a marble tablet. In a Depressed Classes Conference on December 24, he condemned the ancient Hindu classical text, the Manusmriti (Laws of Manu). Condemning it for justifying the system of caste discrimination and untouchability, Ambedkar and his supporters burned copies of the texts. In 1927, he would begin his second journal, the Bahiskrit Bharat (Excluded India), later rechristened as Janata (The People). He would be appointed to the Bombay Presidency Committee to work with the all-European Simon Commission in 1928. This commission had sparked great protests across India, and while its report was ignored by most Indians, Ambedkar himself wrote a separate set of recommendations for future constitutional reforms. He was injured in an accident that occurred during a visit to Chalisgaon on October 23, 1929. Hoping to help the untouchable community, which was facing a social boycott from orthodox

Hindus, he was confined in bed there till the end of the year. In this speech, Ambedkar criticized the Salt Satyagraha launched by Gandhi and the Congress. Ambedkar's criticisms and political work had made him very unpopular with orthodox Hindus, as well as many Congress politicians who had condemned untouchability and worked against discrimination across India.

His prominence and popular support amongst the untouchable community had increased, and he was invited to attend the Second Round Table Conference in London in 1931. Here he sparred verbally with Gandhi on the question of awarding separate electorates to untouchables. A fierce opponent of separate electorates on religious and sectarian lines, Gandhi feared that separate electorates for untouchables would divide Hindu society for future generations.

When the British agreed with Ambedkar and announced the awarding of separate electorates, Gandhi began a fast-unto-death while imprisoned in the Yeravada Central Jail of Pune in 1932. Exhorting orthodox Hindu society to eliminate discrimination and untouchability, Gandhi asked for the political and social unity of Hindus. Gandhi's fast provoked great public support across India, and orthodox Hindu leaders, Congress politicians and activists such as Madan Mohan Malaviya and Pawlankar Baloo organized joint meetings with Ambedkar and his supporters at Yeravada. Fearing a communal reprisal and killings of untouchables, had Gandhi died, Ambedkar agreed to drop the demand for separate electorates, under massive coercion from the supporters of Gandhi, and settled for a reservation of seats. Ambedkar was to criticise the fast of Gandhi as a gimmick to deny political rights to the untouchables and the coercion he faced to give up the demand of separate electorates, in all his writings later.

His Birth and Greatness Foretold : On April 14th, 1891 a son was born to Bhimabai and Ramji Ambedkar. His father Ramji was an army officer stationed at Mhow in Madhya Pradesh—he had risen to the highest rank an Indian was allowed to hold at that time under British rule. His mother decided to call her son Bhim. Before the birth, Ramji's uncle, who was a man living the religious life of a sanyasi, foretold that this son would achieve worldwide fame. His parents already had many children. Despite that, they resolved to make every effort to give him a good education.

Early Life and First School: Two years later, Ramji retired from the army, and the family moved to Dapoli in the Ratnagiri district of Maharashtra, from where they came originally. Bhim was enrolled at school when he was five years old. The whole family had to struggle to live on the small army pension Ramji received.

Even from his boyhood Ambedkar had a mind of steel. Once it was raining very heavily. The boy Ambedkar said the would go to school. His friends said, "These are empty words, how can you go in this heavy rain?" In the downpour, the boy did go to school and that, too, without an umbrella! When some friends found Ramji a job at Satara, things seemed to be looking up for the family, and they moved again. Soon after, however, tragedy struck. Bhimabhai, who had been ill, died. Bhim's aunt Mira, though she herself was not in good health, took over the care of the children. Ramji read stories from the epics Mahabharata and Ramayana to his children, and sang devotional songs to them. In this way, home life was still happy for Bhim, his brothers and sisters. He never forgot the influence of his father. It taught him about the rich cultural tradition shared by all Indians.

The Shock of Prejudice—Casteism: Bhim began to notice that he and his family were treated differently. At high school he had to sit in the corner of the room on a rough mat, away from the desks of the other pupils. At break-time, he was not allowed to drink water using the cups his fellow school children used. He had to hold his cupped hands out to have water poured into them by the school caretaker. Bhim did not know why he should be treated differently—what was wrong with him? Once, he and his elder brother had to travel to Goregaon, where their father worked as a cashier, to spend their summer holidays. They got off the train and waited for a long time at the station, but Ramji did not arrive to meet them. The station master seemed kind, and asked them who they were and where they were going. The boys were very well-dressed, clean, and polite. Bhim, without thinking, told him they were Mahars (a group classed as 'untouchables'). The station master was stunned—his face changed its kindly expression and he went away.

Bhim decided to hire a bullock-cart to take them to their father—this was before motor cars were used as taxis—but the cart-men had heard that the boys were 'untouchables', and wanted nothing to do with them. Finally, they had to agree to pay double the usual cost of the journey, plus they had to drive the cart themselves, while the driver walked beside it. He was afraid of being polluted by the boys, because they were 'untouchables'. However, the extra money persuaded him that he could have his cart 'purified' later! Throughout the journey, Bhim thought constantly about what had happened—yet he could not understand the reason for it. He and his brother were clean and neatly dressed. Yet they were supposed to pollute and make unclean everything they touched and all that touched them. How could that be possible?

Bhim never forgot this incident. As he grew up, such senseless insults made him realise that what Hindu society called 'untouchability' was stupid, cruel, and unreasonable. His sister had to cut his hair at home because the village barbers were afraid of being polluted by an 'untouchable'. If he asked her why they were 'untouchables', she could only answer—that is the way it has always been." Bhim could not be satisfied with this answer. He knew that—it has always been that way" does not mean that there is a just reason for it—or that it had to stay that way forever. It could be changed.

An Outstanding Scholar: While in school, Bhim's teacher Ambedkar, entered his last name into the school records as Ambedkar. Teacher Ambedkar and Pendse, were the only ones in the entire school who were kind and affectionate to young him. They made the few fond memories Dr. B.R. Ambedkar had of his school days. At this time in his young life, with his mother dead, and father working away from the village where Bhim went to school, he had some good fortune. His teacher, though from a 'high' caste, liked him a lot. He praised Bhim's good work and encouraged him, seeing what a bright pupil he was. He even invited Bhim to eat lunch with him—something that would have horrified most high caste Hindus. The teacher also changed Bhim's last name to Ambedkar—his own name.

When his father decided to remarry, Bhim was very upset—he still missed his mother so much. Wanting to run away to Bombay, he tried to steal his aunt's purse. When at last he managed to get hold of it, he found only one very small coin. Bhim felt so ashamed. He put the coin back and made a vow to himself to study very hard and to become independent.

Soon he was winning the highest praise and admiration from all his teachers. They urged Ramji to get the best education for his son Bhim. So Ramji moved with his family to Bombay. They all had to live in just one room, in an area where the poorest of the poor lived, but Bhim was able to go to Elphinstone High School—one of the best schools in all of India. In their one room everyone and everything was crowed together and the streets outside were very noisy. Bhim went to sleep when he got home from school. Then his father would wake him up at two o'clock in the morning! Everything was quiet then—so he could do his homework and study in peace. In the big city, where life was more modern than in the villages, Bhim found that he was still called an 'untouchable' and treated as if something made him different and bad—even at his famous school.

One day, the teacher called him up to the blackboard to do a sum. All the other boys jumped up and made a big fuss. Their lunch boxes were stacked behind the blackboard—they believed that Bhim would pollute the food! When he wanted to learn Sanskrit, the language of the Hindu holy scriptures, he was told that it was forbidden for 'untouchables' to do so. He had to study Persian instead—but he taught himself Sanskrit later in life.

Matriculation and Marriage: In due course, Bhim passed his Matriculation Exam. He had already come to the attention of some people interested in improving society. So when he passed the exam, a meeting was arranged to congratulate him—he was the first 'untouchable' from his community to pass it. Bhim was then 17 years old. Early marriage was common in those days, so he was married to Ramabai the same year. He continued to study hard and passed the next Intermediate examination with distinction. However, Ramji found himself unable to keep paying the school fees. Through someone interested in his progress, Bhim was recommended to the Maharaja Gaikwad of Baroda. The Maharaja granted him a monthly scholarship. With the help of this, Bhimrao ('rao' is added to names in Maharashtra as a sign of respect) passed his B.A. in 1912. Then he was given a job in the civil service—but only two weeks after starting, he had to rush home to Bombay. Ramji was very ill, and died soon afterwards. He had done all he could for his son, laying the foundations for Bhimrao's later achievements.

Studies in the USA and the UK: The Maharaja of Baroda had a scheme to send a few outstanding scholars abroad for further studies. Of course, Bhimrao was selected—but he had to sign an agreement to serve Baroda state for ten years on finishing his studies. In 1913, he went to the USA where he studied at the world-famous Columbia University, New York. The freedom and equality he experienced in America made a very strong impression on Bhimrao. It was so refreshing for him to be able to live a normal life, free from the caste prejudice of India. He could do anything he pleased—but devoted his time to studying. He studied eighteen hours a day. Visits to bookshops were his favourite entertainment!

His main subjects were Economics and Sociology. In just two years he had been awarded an M.A.—the following year he completed his Ph.D. thesis. Then he left Columbia and went to England, where he joined the London School of Economics. However, he had to leave London before completing his course because the scholarship granted by the State of Baroda expired. Bhimrao had to wait three years before he could return to London to complete his studies. The British Museum in London has a very good library. It used to open at eight in the morning, and every day Ambedkar would be there by eight. He read till five o'clock. In London he came to know a student called Asnodkar. He belonged to a rich family. He was not interested in study. Ambedkar said to him, "Your people may have made plenty of money. But think, you have born a man, what are you going to achieve? The Goddess of Learning will not come to you whenever you want. We must get her blessings when she comes." In 1922 Ambedkar became a barrister and the nest year he came back to India.

Return to India—Nightmare in Baroda: So he was called back to India to take up a post in Baroda as agreed. He was given an excellent job in the Baroda Civil Service. Bhimrao now held a doctorate, and was being trained for a top job. Yet, he again ran into the worst features of the Hindu caste system. This was all the more painful, because for the past four years he had been abroad, living free from the label of 'untouchable.'

No one at the office where he worked would hand over files and papers to him—the servant threw them onto his desk. Nor would they give him water to drink. No respect was given to him, merely because of his caste. He had to go from hotel to hotel looking for a room, but none of them would take him in. At last he had found a place to live in a Parsi guest house, but only because he had finally decided to keep his caste secret. He lived there in very uncomfortable conditions, in a small bedroom with a tiny cold-water bathroom attached. He was totally alone there with no one to talk to. There were no electric lights or even oil lamps—so the place was completely dark at night. Bhimrao was hoping to find somewhere else to live through his civil service job, but before he could, one morning as he was leaving for work a gang of angry men carrying sticks arrived outside his room. They accused him of polluting the hotel and told him to get out by evening—or else! What could he do? He could not stay with either of the two acquaintances he had in Baroda for the same reason—his low caste. Bhimrao felt totally miserable and rejected.

Bombay—Beginning Social Activity: He had no choice. After only eleven days in his new job, he had to return to Bombay. He tried to start a small business there, advising people about investments—but it too failed once customers learned of his caste. In 1918, he became a lecturer at Sydenham College in Bombay. There, his students recognised him as a brilliant teacher and scholar. At this time he also helped to found a Marathi newspaper 'Mook Nayak' (Leader of the Dumb) to champion the cause of the 'untouchables'. He also began to organise and attend conferences, knowing that he had to begin to proclaim and publicise the humiliations suffered by the Dalits—'the oppressed'—and fight for equal rights. His own life had taught him the necessity of the struggle for emancipation.

Completion of Education—Leader of India's Untouchables: In 1920, with the help of friends, he was able to return to London to complete his studies in Economics at

LSE. He also enrolled to study as a Barrister at Gray's Inn. In 1923, Bhimrao returned to India with a Doctorate in Economics from the LSE—he was perhaps the first Indian to have a Doctorate from this world-famous institution. He had also qualified as a Barrister-at-Law. Back in India, he knew that nothing had changed. His qualifications meant nothing as far as the practice of Untouchability was concerned—it was still an obstacle to his career. However, he had received the best education anyone in the world could get, and was well equipped to be a leader of the Dalit community. He could argue with and persuade the best minds of his time on equal terms. He was an expert on the law, and could give convincing evidence before British commissions as an eloquent and gifted speaker. Bhimrao dedicated the rest of his life to his task.

He became known by his increasing number of followers—those 'untouchables' he urged to awake—as Baba Saheb. Knowing the great value and importance of education, in 1924 he founded an association called Bahiskrit Hitakarini Sabha. This set up hostels, schools, and free libraries. To improve the lives of Dalits, education had to reach everyone. Opportunities had to be provided at grass roots level—because knowledge is power.

Leading Peaceful Agitation: In 1927 Baba Saheb presided over a conference at Mahad in Kolaba District. There he said:— It is time we rooted out of our minds the ideas of high and low. We can attain self-elevation only if we learn self-help and regain our self-respect."

Because of nis experience of the humiliation and injustice of untouchability, he knew that justice would not be granted by others. Those who suffer injustice must secure justice for themselves. The Bombay Legislature had already passed a Bill allowing everyone to use public water tanks and wells. Mahad Municipality had thrown open the local water tank four years earlier, but so far not one 'untouchable' had dared to drink or draw water from it. Baba Saheb led a procession from the Conference on a peaceful demonstration to the Chowdar Tank. He knelt and drank water from it. After he set this example, thousands of others felt courageous enough to follow him. They drank water from the tank and made history. For many hundreds of years, 'untouchables' had been forbidden to drink public water. When some caste Hindus saw them drinking water, they believed the tank had been polluted and violently attacked the Conference, but Baba Saheb insisted violence would not help—he had given his word that they would agitate peacefully. Baba Saheb started a Marathi journal Bahishkrit Bharat ('The Excluded of India'). In it, he urged his people to hold a satyagraha (nonviolent agitation) to secure the right of entry to the Kala Ram Temple at Nasik, 'untouchables' had always been forbidden to enter Hindu temples. The demonstration lasted for a month. Then they were told they would be able to take part in the annual temple festival. However, at the festival they had stones thrown at them—and were not allowed to take part. Courageously, they resumed their peaceful agitation. The temple had to remain closed for about a year, as they blocked its entrance.

Round Table Conferences—Gandhi: Meanwhile, the Indian Freedom Movement had gained momentum under the leadership of Mahatma Gandhi. In 1930, a Round Table Conference was held by the British Government in London to decide the future of India. Baba Saheb represented the 'untouchables'. He said there:—The Depressed Classes of India also join in the demand for replacing the British Government by a Government of the people and by the people... Our wrongs have remained as open sores and have not been righted although 150 years of British rule have rolled away. Of what good is such a Government to anybody?"

The British had done nothing to alleviate the status of the depressed classes. He declared that India must have a minimum of Dominion Status. He pressed for a separate electorate for the depressed classes. Soon a second conference was held, which Mahatma Gandhi attended representing the Congress Party. Baba Saheb met Gandhi in Bombay before they went to London. Gandhi told him that he had read what Baba Saheb said at the first conference. Gandhi told Baba Saheb he knew him to be a real Indian patriot.

At the Second Conference, Baba Saheb asked for a separate electorate for the Depressed Classes—Hinduism, "he said—has given us only insults, misery, and humiliation." A separate electorate would mean that the 'untouchables' would vote for their own candidates and be allotted their votes separate from the Hindu majority. Baba Saheb was made a hero by thousands of his followers on his return from Bombay—even though he always said that people should not idolise him. News came that separate electorates had been granted. Gandhi felt that separate electorates would separate the Harijans from the Hindus. The thought that the Hindus would be divided pained him grievously. He started a fast, saying that he would fast unto death.

The Mahatma's Fast: Gandhiji felt that separate electrorates would only separate the Harijans from the Hindus. The very thought that the Hindu would be divided pained him much. He started a fast against separate electorates. He said he would fast unto death in necessary. There was anxiety in the country because of Gandhiji's fast.

Many Congress leaders went to Ambedkar to save Gandhiji. "Muslims, Christians and Sikhs have obtained the right of separate electorates. Gandhiji did not fast to oppose them. Why should Gandhiji fast to oppose Harijans getting separate electorates?" questioned Ambedkar. "If you are unwilling to give the 'untouchables' separate electorates, what other solution is there? It is essential to save Gandhiji. But just to save him I am not prepared to give up the interests of the backward classes," he declared. He said, reserve a larger number of seats for the untouchables' than the British have given; then I will give up the claim for separate electorates."

Only Baba Saheb could save Gandhi's life—by withdrawing the demand for separate electorates. At first he refused, saying it was his duty to do the best he could for his people—no matter what. Later he visited Gandhi, who was at that time in Yeravda jail. Gandhi persuaded Baba Saheb that Hinduism would change and leave its bad practices behind. Finally Baba Saheb agreed to sign the Poona Pact with Gandhi in 1932. Instead of separate electorates, more representation was to be given to the Depressed Classes. However, it later became obvious that this did not amount to anything concrete.

In the Prime of His Life: Baba Saheb had by this time collected a library of over 50,000 books, and had a house named Rajgriha built at Dadar in north Bombay to hold it. In 1935 his beloved wife Ramabai died. The same year he was made Principal of the Government Law College, Bombay. Also in 1935 a conference of Dalits was held at Yeola. Baba Saheb told the conference:—We have not been able to secure the barest of human rights... I am born a Hindu. I couldn't help it, but I solemnly assure you that I will not die a Hindu." This was the first time that Baba Saheb stressed the importance of conversion from Hinduism for his people—for they were only known as 'untouchables' within the fold of Hinduism.

During the Second World War, Baba Saheb was appointed Labour Minister by the Viceroy. Yet he never lost contact with his roots—he never became corrupt or crooked. He said that he had been born of the poor and had lived the life of the poor, he would remain absolutely unchanged in his attitudes to his friends and to the rest of the world. The All-India Scheduled Castes Federation was formed in 1942 to gather all 'untouchables' into a united political party.

Architect of the Constitution: After the war Baba Saheb was elected to the Constituent Assembly to decide the way that India—a country of millions of people—should be ruled. How should elections take place? What are the rights of the people? How are laws to be made? Such important matters had to be decided and laws had to be made. The Constitution answers all such questions and lays down rules.

When India became independent in August 1947, Baba Saheb Ambedkar became First Law Minister of Independent India. The Constituent Assembly made him chairman of the committee appointed to draft the constitution for the world's largest democracy.

All his study of law, economics, and politics made him the best qualified person for this task. A study of the Constitutions of many countries, a deep knowledge of law, a knowledge of the history of India and of Indian Society—all these were essential. In fact, he carried the whole burden alone. He alone could complete this huge task.

On July 15, 1947, the British Parliament passed the act of Indian Independence and on August 15, 1947, India became free. The Constituent Assemble of Independent India appointed a Drafting Committee with Dr. Ambedkar as its Chairman to draft the Constitution of India. Dr. Ambedkar was also invited to join the Cabinet as the Minister of Law. Ambedkar toiled over the Constitution while he took care of his ministry. In-

February 1948, Dr. Ambedkar presented the Draft Constitution before the people of India.

After completing the Draft Constitution, Baba Saheb fell ill. At a nursing home in Bombay he met Dr. Sharda Kabir and married her in April 1948. On November 4, 1948 he presented the Draft Constitution to the Constituent Assembly, and on November 26, 1949 it was adopted in the name of the people of India. On that date he said: I appeal to all Indians to be a nation by discarding castes, which have brought separation in social life and created jealousy and hatred."

Later Life—Buddhist Conversion: In 1950, he went to a Buddhist conference in Sri Lanka. On his return he spoke in Bombay at the Buddhist Temple. In order to end their hardships, people should embrace Buddhism. I am going to devote the rest of my life to the revival and spread of Buddhism in India."

Why did he choose Buddhism?: Ambedkar told his friend Dattopant Thengadi: "I am in the evening of my life. There is an onslaught of ideas on our people from different countries from the four corners of the world. In this flood our people may be confused. There are strong attempts to separate the people struggling hard, from the main life-stream of this country and to attract them towards other countries. This tendency is fast growing. Even some of my colleagues who are disgusted with 'untouchability', poverty and inequality are ready to be washed away by this flood. What about the others? They should not move away from the main stream of the nation's life; and I must show them the way. At the same time, we have to make some changes in the economic and political life. That is way I have decided to follow Buddhism." There is a way of life which has come down as a steady stream in India for thousand of years. Buddhism is not opposed to it. The backward people must rebel against the injustice done to them; they must wipe it out. But 'untouchability' is a problem of the Hindu Society. To solve this, a path which does not harm the culture and the history of Bharat must be followed. This is the basis of his resolution.

He did not believe in the theory that Aryans came from a different land and that they defeated the Dasyus' (the Dravidians) of this country. There is no foundation for this in the Vedas. The word 'Arya' appears some 33 or 34 times in the Vedas. The word has been used as an adjective meaning 'the noble' or 'the elder'. It is said in the Mahabharata that 'Dasyus' can be found in all 'varnas' (castes) and 'ashramas' (stage of life). In this way Ambedkar used to support this view.

On 14th October 1956 at a big function in Nagpur, Ambedkar, with his wife, embraced Buddhism. In May 1956, on Buddha's Anniversary, Dr. Ambedkar announced that on October 14 he would embrace Buddhism. With him his wife and some three lakh followers also converted to the faith. When asked why, Dr. Ambedkar replied, "Why can't you ask this question to yourself and... your forefathers...?"

For the next five years Baba Saheb carried on a relentless fight against social evils and superstitions. On October 14, 1956 at Nagpur he embraced Buddhism. He led a huge gathering in a ceremony converting over half a million people to Buddhism. He knew that Buddhism was a true part of Indian history and that to revive it was to continue India's best tradition. 'Untouchability' is a product only of Hinduism.

Bhim was an average student. He became fond of gardening and, whenever he could, he bought saplings and with great devotion nurtured them to full growth. While studying in Satara, many of his classmates left for good jobs in Bombay. He too wanted to go to Bombay and get a job and become independent. He realized that if he ever were to be successful, he would have to concentrate more on his studies. He became interested in reading. He read not just the prescribed books in school but any book in general. His father was too pleased when he digressed from school books but he never said "no" when Bhim wanted a book.

Fight against Untouchability: As a leading Dalit scholar, Ambedkar had been invited to testify before the Southborough Committee, which was preparing the Government of India Act 1919. At this hearing, Ambedkar argued for creating separate electorates and reservations for Dalits and different religious communities. In 1920, he began the publication of the weekly *Mooknayak* (*Leader of the Dumb*) in Mumbai. Attaining popularity, Ambedkar used this journal to criticize orthodox Hindu politicians and a perceived reticence in the Indian political community to fight caste discrimination. His speech at a

Depressed Classes Conference in Kolhapur impressed the local state ruler Shahu IV, who shocked orthodox society by dining with Ambedkar and his untouchable colleagues. Ambedkar exhorted his Mahar community to abandon the idea of sub-castes, and held a joint communal dinner in which the principle of segregation was abandoned. Upon his return from Europe, Ambedkar established a successful legal practise, and also organised the Bahishkrit Hitakarini Sabha (*Group for the Wellbeing of the Excluded*) to promote education and socioeconomic upliftment of the depressed classes.

In the same vein, he was highly critical of the practice of untouchability in Indian Muslim Society, lending credence to the view that he was not exclusively against Hindus or Hinduism, but was speaking of reforming social evils. In his illustrious publication "Pakistan and the Partition of India", he writes that, while Islam speaks of "brotherhood", the practice of slavery and caste discrimination were rampant in Muslim society in South Asia, such as the Ashraf/Ajlaf caste divide and the severe discrimination against the *Arzal* castes or Dalit Muslim untouchables. With the help of Shahu Maharaj of Kolhapur, a sympathizer of the cause for the upliftment of the depressed classes, Bhimrao started a fortnightly newspaper, the Mooknayak (Leader of the Dumb) on January 31, 1920. The Maharaj also convened many meeting and conferences of the "untouchables" which Bhimrao addressed. Impressed by Ambedkar, the Maharaj declared at a meeting, "You have found your saviour in Ambedkar. I am confident he will break your shackles."

In July 1924, Ambedkar founded the Bahishkrut Hitkarini Sabha. The aim of the Sabha was to uplift the downtrodden socially and politically and bring them to the level of the others in the Indian society. The Sabha aimed at scrapping the caste system from the Hindu religion. The Sabha started free school for the young and the old and ran reading rooms and libraries. Dr. Ambedkar took the grievances of the "untouchables" to court and gave them justice. Soon he became a father-figure to the poor and downtrodden and was respectfully called "Baba Saheb."

On March 19-20, 1927 a conference of the depressed classes was held at Mahad. Ten thousand delegates attended, workers and leaders attended. Baba Saheb condemned the British for banning the recruitment of "untouchables" into the military. He declared:

"No lasting progress can achieved unless we put ourselves through a threefold process of purification. We must improve the general tone of our demeanour, re-tone our pronunciation and revitalize our thoughts. I, therefore, ask you now to take a vow to renounce eating carrion, the... flesh of... animals, from this moment....Make an unflinching resolve not to eat the thrown away crumbs. We will attain self-elevation only if we learn self-help, regain our self respect and gain self-knowledge."

On December 25 of the same year, thousands responded to Ambedkar's call. Speaker after speaker spoke, passions rose and the vast gathering waited for the satyagraha to begin with intense anticipation. The satyagraha was deferred when the matter was referred to the court. At the end of conference, a copy of the Manusmruti, the age-old code of the Hindus that gave rise to the caste system, was ceremoniously burnt. In a thundering voice, Ambedkar demanded in its place a new smruti, devoid of all social stratification.

This act sent shockwaves through the nation. On October 13, 1935, at a conference at Nasik, Dr. Ambedkar reviewed the progress made on the condition of the "untouchables" in the decade since Ambedkar started his agitation. Ambedkar declared that their efforts had not borne the kind of results he had expected. He then made a fantastic appeal to the "untouchables." He encouraged them to forsake the Hindu religion and convert to a religion where they would be treated with equality. The nation was shocked.

The British Government agreed to hold elections on the provincial level in 1937. The Congress, Muslim League and Hindu Mahasabha started gearing up for the elections. Dr. Ambedkar set up the Independent Labour Party in August 1936 to contest the elections in the Bombay province. On February 17, 1937, Ambedkar and many of his candidates won this a thumping majority. Around the same time, the Chavdar Taley water dispute which was referred to the Bombay High Court in 1927 finally handed down its verdict in favour of the depressed classes. The Constituent Assemble adopted the Draft

Constitution as the Constitution of India on November 26, 1949 with all its 356 Articles and eight Schedules and Article 11 which abolished untouchability in all forms.

A Legacy Marking Indian Sociopolitical History: Ambedkar's legacy, as a sociopolitical reformer, has been long-lasting on modern India. In post independence India his sociopolitical thought has acquired respect across political spectrum and influenced various spheres of life like socioeconomic, education and Government policies of affirmative action by socioeconomic and legal incentives.

Ambedkar organized untouchable political parties and social organizations, and served in the legislative councils of British India. He would intensify his criticism of orthodox Hindu society, as well as his criticism of slavery and exclusivism in Islam. Despite this, his reputation as a scholar led to his appointment as free India's first law minister, and chairman of the committee responsible to draft a constitution. Ambedkar's work would guarantee political, economic and social freedoms for untouchables and other ethnic, social and religious communities of India. His polemical condemnation of Hinduism and attacks on Islam would make him unpopular and controversial, although his conversion to Buddhism sparked a revival in interest of Buddhist philosophy in India. In 1926, he became a nominated member of the Bombay Legislative Council. By 1927 Dr. Ambedkar decided to launch active movements against untouchability. He did begin with public movements and marches to open up & share public drinking water resources to which until then untouchable communities had no access; also he put up a struggle for entry in Hindu Temples which was not allowed by upper caste communities.

Poona Pact: Ambedkar had become one of the most prominent untouchable political figures of the time. He had grown increasingly critical of mainstream Indian political parties for their perceived lack of emphasis for the elimination of the caste system. Ambedkar criticized the Indian National Congress and its leader Mahatma Gandhi, whom he accused of reducing the untouchable community to a figure of pathos. Ambedkar was also dissatisfied with the failures of British rule, and advocated a political identity for untouchables separate from both the Congress and the British. At a Depressed Classes

Conference on August 8, 1930 Ambedkar outlined his political vision:

> *"...Safety of the Depressed Classes hinged on their being independent of the Government and the Congress" both: "We must shape our course ourselves and by ourselves... Political power cannot be a panacea for the ills of the Depressed Classes. Their salvation lies in their social elevation. They must cleanse their evil habits. They must improve their bad ways of living.... They must be educated.... There is a great necessity to disturb their pathetic contentment and to instill into them that divine discontent which is the spring of all elevation."*

Born in a class considered low and outcast. Dr. Ambedkar fought untiringly for the downtrodden. The boy who suffered bitter humiliation became the first Minister for Law in free India, and shaped the country's Constitution. A determined fighter, a deep scholar, human to the tips of his fingers.

We Need Dharma—But Casteism Should Go: 'Undouchablity' is a branch of casteism; until casteism is wiped out 'untouchability' will not go – this was Ambedkar's firm belief. He argued that to wipe out casteism, political power was very necessary. He believed that Dharma was essential for men. But he revolted against those who, in the name of Dharma, treated some of their fellowmen like animals. Many people criticised him. Some newspapers also wrote against him. There were many occasions when his life was in danger. Also, Ambedkar knew from his own experience that even a bright man could not come up in life vacuse of casteism. People give his cast importance and make him powerless. Ambedkar fought casteism. He was disgusted to find how difficult it was to secure justice and to find how many men were still narrow-minded. He even said that it would be better to give up the Hindu Dharma itself. Muslim and Christian priest and missionaries learnt about this declaration; they tried very hard to attract Ambedkar. They met and assured him that the 'untouchables' who changed their religion would be given equal status in their society.

SWAMI VIVEKANANDA

Swami Vivekananda, the great soul loved and revered in East and West alike as the rejuvenator of Hinduism in India and the preacher of its eternal truths abroad, was born at 6:33, a few minutes before sunrise, on Monday, January 12, 1863. It was the day of the great Hindu festival Makarasamkranti, when special worship is offered to the Ganga by millions of devotees. Thus the future Vivekananda first drew breath when the air above the sacred river not far from the house was reverberating with the prayers, worship, and religious music of thousands of Hindu men and women. Before Vivekananda was born, his mother, like many other pious Hindu mothers, had observed religious vows, fasted, and prayed so that she might be blessed with a son who would do honour to the family. She requested a relative who was living in Varanasi to offer special worship to the Vireswara Siva of that holy place and seek His blessings; for Siva, the great god of renunciation, dominated her thought. One night she dreamt that this supreme Deity aroused Himself from His meditation and agreed to be born as her son. When she woke she was filled with joy.

The mother, Bhuvaneswari Devi, accepted the child as a boon from Vireswara Siva and named him Vireswara. The family, however, gave him the name of Narendranath Datta, calling him, for short, Narendra, or more endearingly, Naren. The Datta family of Calcutta, into which Narendranath had been born, was well known for its affluence, philanthropy, scholarship, and independent spirit. The grand father, Durgacharan, after the birth of his first son, had renounced the world in search of God. The father, Viswanath, an attorney-at-law of the High Court of Calcutta, was versed in English and Persian literature and often entertained himself and his friends by reciting from the Bible and the poetry of Hafiz, both of which, he believed, contained truths unmatched by human thinking elsewhere.

He was particularly attracted to the Islamic culture, with which he was familiar because of his close contact with the educated Moslems of North-western India. Moreover, he derived a large income from his law practice and, unlike his father, thoroughly enjoyed the worldly life. An expert in cookery, he prepared rare dishes and liked to share them with his friends. Travel was another of his hobbies. Though agnostic in religion and a mocker of social conventions, he possessed a large heart and often went out of his way to support idle relatives, some of whom were given to drunkenness. Once, when Narendra protested against his lack of judgement, his father said: 'How can you understand the great misery of human life? When you realize the depths of men's suffering, you will sympathize with these unfortunate creatures who try to forget their sorrows, even though only for a short while, in the oblivion created by intoxicants.' Naren's father, however, kept a sharp eye on his children and would not tolerate the slightest deviation from good manners.

Bhuvaneswari Devi, the mother, was cast in a different mould. Regal in appearance and gracious in conduct, she belonged to the old tradition of Hindu womanhood. As mistress of a large household, she devoted her spare time to sewing and singing, being particularly fond of the great Indian epics, the Ramayana and the Mahabharata, large portions of which she had memorized. She became the special refuge of the poor, and commanded universal respect because of her calm resignation to God, her inner tranquillity, and her dignified detachment in the midst of her many arduous duties. Two sons were born to her besides Narendranath, and four daughters, two of whom died at an early age.

Narendra grew up to be a sweet, sunny-tempered, but very restless boy. Two nurses were necessary to keep his exuberant energy under control, and he was a great tease to his sisters. In order to quiet him, the mother often put his head under the cold-water tap, repeating Siva's name, which always produced the desired effect. Naren felt a child's love for birds and animals, and this characteristic reappeared during the last days of his life. Among his boyhood pets were a family cow, a monkey, a goat, a peacock, and several pigeons and guinea-pigs. The coachman of the family, with his turban, whip, and bright-coloured livery, was his boyhood ideal of a magnificent person, and he often expressed the ambition to be like him when he grew up.

Narendra bore a striking resemblance to the grand-father who had renounced the world to lead a monastic life, and many thought that the latter had been reborn in him. The youngster developed a special fancy for wandering monks, whose very sight would greatly excite him. One day when such a monk appeared at the door and asked for alms, Narendra gave him his only possession, the tiny piece of new cloth that was wrapped round his waist. Thereafter, whenever a monk was seen in the neighbourhood, Narendra would be locked in a room. But even then he would throw out of the window whatever he found near at hand as an offering to the holy man. In the meantime, he was receiving his early education from his mother, who taught him the Bengali alphabet and his first English words, as well as stories from the Ramayana and the Mahabharata.

During his childhood Narendra, like many other Hindu children of his age, developed a love for the Hindu deities, of whom he had learnt from his mother. Particularly attracted by the heroic story of Rama and his faithful consort Sita, he procured their images, bedecked them with flowers, and worshipped them in his boyish fashion. But disillusionment came when he heard someone denounce marriage vehemently as a terrible bondage. When he had thought this over he discarded Rama and Sita as unworthy of worship. In their place he installed the image of Siva, the god of renunciation, who was the ideal of the yogis. Nevertheless he retained a fondness for the Ramayana. At this time he daily experienced a strange vision when he was about to fall asleep. Closing his eyes, he would see between his eyebrows a ball of light of changing colours, which would slowly expand and at last burst, bathing his whole body in a white radiance. Watching this light he would gradually fall asleep. Since it was a daily occurrence, he regarded the phenomenon as common to all people, and was surprised when a friend denied ever having seen such a thing. Years later, however, Narendra's spiritual teacher, Sri Ramakrishna, said to him, 'Naren, my boy, do you see a light when you go to sleep?' Ramakrishna knew that such a vision indicated a great spiritual past and an inborn habit of meditation. The vision of light remained with Narendra until the end of his life, though later it lost its regularity and intensity.

While still a child Narendra practised meditation with a friend before the image of Siva. He had heard that the holy men of ancient India would become so absorbed in contemplation of God that their hair would grow and gradually enter into the earth, like the roots of the banyan tree. While meditating, therefore, he would open his eyes, now and then, to see if his own hair had entered into the earth. Even so, during meditation, he often became unconscious of the world. On one occasion he saw in a vision a luminous person of serene countenance who was carrying the staff and water-bowl of a monk. The apparition was about to say something when Naren became frightened and left the room. He thought later that perhaps this had been a vision of Buddha. At the age of six he was sent to a primary school. One day, however, he repeated at home some of the vulgar words that he had learnt from his classmates, whereupon his disgusted parents took him out of the school and appointed a private tutor, who conducted classes for him and some other children of the neighbourhood in the worship hall of the house. Naren soon showed a precocious mind and developed a keen memory. Very easily he learnt by heart the whole of a Sanskrit grammar and long passages from the Ramayana and the Mahabharata. Some of the friendships he made at this age lasted his whole lifetime. At school he was the undisputed leader. When playing his favourite game of 'King and the Court,' he would assume the role of the monarch and assign to his friends the parts of the ministers, commander-in-chief, and other state officials. He was marked from birth to be a leader of men, as his name Narendra (lord of men) signified.

Even at that early age he questioned why one human being should be considered superior to another. In his father's office separate tobacco pipes were provided for clients belonging to the different castes, as orthodox Hindu custom required, and the pipe from which the Moslems smoked was set quite apart. Narendra once smoked tobacco from all the pipes, including the one marked for the Moslems, and when reprimanded, remarked, 'I cannot see what difference it makes.'

During these early years, Narendra's future personality was influenced by his gifted father and his saintly mother, both of whom kept a chastening eye upon him. The father had his own manner of discipline. For example, when, in the course of an argument with his mother, the impetuous boy once uttered a few rude words and the report came to the father, Viswanath did not directly scold his son, but wrote with charcoal on the door of his room: 'Narendra today said to his mother-' and added the words that had been used. He wanted Narendra's friends to know how rudely he had treated his mother.

3

The Founding Fathers of Sociological Though

It was during the unprecedented social upheavals in Europe that the formal study of sociology emerged as a discipline to explain social phenomena. The industrialization of topologies at the time meant that people were migrating from rural to urban areas, and the traditional agents of authority, such as the Church and the landed aristocracy, were losing much of their influence. This period earmarked the birth of organized labour, modern industrial capitalism and many revolutions and reform, and meant that new sources of power were emerging in order to fashion a new social space.

The doctrine of sociology emerged in the nineteenth century from the major discipline of philosophy; and it is primarily accredited to Auguste Comte. Despite Comte's formulation of the terminology, sociology, and its basic tenets, the subject was also fashioned by Herbert Spencer, Emile Durkheim and Max Weber. Many academia and other pundits have accredited those scholars as pioneers, fathers, of this branch of thought. One contemporary sociologist, Dr. Orville Taylor, who is a senior lecturer in sociology at the University of the West Indies, Mona, argued that William Edward DuBois must be credited as one of the pioneers of the discipline (Taylor, 2003). His rational for that perspective lies in the scientific contributions of Dubois, in the field of sociology. In an attempt to justify the science of sociology, like that of the natural sciences, Spencer, Durkheim and Weber, and to a lesser degree Comte, postulated its boundaries, scope and the techniques to which the subject matter can address while utilizing the principles of positivism. According to Inkeles, Weber on the other hand, forwarded the perspective that positivism is not the only tool that allows a discipline to attain the status of science when he formulated the principle of verstehen, a method of understanding "and... discussing the vicissitudes of maintaining objectivity and neutrality of value judgment in social science". What then constitutes sociology from the perspective of its founding fathers?

HISTORICAL SOCIOLOGY

According to a sociologist, Auguste Comte (1798 – 1857), who gave sociology its name, devoted more energy to expressing hopes for and to staking out the claims of sociology than to defining its subject matter. He felt that social science in his time stood in the same relation to its future as astrology once stood in regard to the science of astronomy and as alchemy stood in relation to chemistry. Only in the distant future, he argued, would the sub-division of the field become practicable and desirable, and for his time he felt it 'impossible... to anticipate what the principle of distribution may be'."

From Inkeles' monograph, Comte categorized the field of study into "social statics" and "social dynamics" which allowed for the science of this subject matter. According to Inkeles (1964), Spencer wrote that: The science of Sociology has to give an account of [how] successive generation of units are produced, reared and fitted for co-operation, the development of the family thus stands first in order... Sociology has next to describe and explain the rise and development of that political organization which in several ways regulates affairs-which combines the actions of individuals... and which restrains them in certain of the dealings with one another... There has to be similarly described the evolution of ecclesiastical structures and functions... The system of restraints whereby the minor actions of citizens are regulated, also has to be dealt with...The stages through which the industrial part passes... have to be studied...[as well] the growth of those regulative structures which the industrial part develops within itself...

Spencer coined the phrase "the science of Sociology" and although he did not depict the techniques that can be used to derive a conclusion as to its similarities to the natural science, he forwarded the perspective that the discipline must be studied as a '...whole society, this is a unit for analysis' which allows for scientific inquiry. Durkheim, on the other hand, used the words 'the science of societies' to describe sociology. Sociology, therefore, is the scientific inquiry of society in which its foci are social facts, social world, functions of society, structures, institutions, social actions, "arrive through a causal explanation of its course and effects". Wallace and Wolf (1999) wrote that

Davis argued that sociology involves (1) examining the role (or function) that an institution or type of behaviour plays in society to other social features and (2) explaining it in essentially social terms.

From Wallace and Wolf's monograph, Davis concurred with other sociologists such as Waller, Weber, Spencer, Durkheim and other pundits that the subject matter of sociology is a social space in which people operate. Davis' theorizing is similar to that forwarded by Comte, and embedded within his perspective is scientific inquiry in which human roles are examined within society.

The subject matter of sociology "begins with the idea that humans are to be understood in the context of their social life, [and] that we are social animals influenced by interaction, social patterns, and socialization". Waller's monograph highlights the 'social' aspect of man, and accounts for he/she being in a social space. The fact that man operates as a social being; he/she is separated from the other animals because of the socialization process.

Sociology, as a science, studies man as unit and collectively in his/her social world, in an attempt to explaining the behavioural patterns of that individual from a micro as well as a macrocosm perspective. In sociology, we study man's culture, social institutions, and the social events to which he/she subscribes. One of the primary reasons for the discourse as to whether sociology is or is not a science rests squarely on the continuous changeability of man, and his/her irrationality. Some scientists argued that this militates against the objectivity of the space, as social behaviours are unpredictable even when given the same set of conditions and the process is repeated within known conditions.

CONTEMPORARY PERSPECTIVE OF SOCIOLOGY

The discipline of sociology studies social life, social change, and social causes and consequences of human behaviour. The parameters of sociology include an investigation of the structure of groups, organizations, and societies, and how people intermingle within these spaces; thereby generating channels for scientific assessment. Human beings are social animals; and so, they are shaped by social factors. The subject matter of sociology covers from the intimate family to the hostile mob; from organized criminalities to religious denominations; from race, gender and social class to the shared beliefs of a common culture; and from the sociology of work to the sociology of sports. Sociology like anthropology and other areas within the Social Sciences provide plethora perspectives on the world, while generating new ideas and reviewing the old. Despite the subject matter, the field offers a range of research techniques that can be applied to virtually any aspect of social life: street crimes, prostitution, teenage pregnancy, wellbeing of the people, fertility, delinquency, corporate downsizing, how people express emotions, stress, education reform, how families differ and flourish, or issues of peace and war, and how social systems work.

THE NON-COMTE INFLUENCES

From Waller's monograph, Denisoff, Callahan, & Levine (1974) attributed "the fundamental foundations of sociology... [to] ancient Greeks" (Waller, 2005). Taylor (2003) forwarded the perspective that Comte coined the discipline from a Latin word Socios, which means 'group or society, and a Greek word logos which denotes 'the study of' hence "..., we end up with a word which means, 'the study of society". In Waller's (2006) presentation on the creator of sociology, he cited that "even though Plato is not considered the 'father' of sociology –he is probably the first person to systematically study society in a 'sociological' way" to which Taylor equally subscribed in his monograph. Comte as a positivist, borrowed 'statics' and 'dynamics' from Isaac Newton's scientific theories, and applied this to the study of society. To Comte we must accredit the basic tenets of sociology, although he did not categorically state how the subject matter should be studied, the mere fact he postulated that we can apply two fundamental tenets of positivism to social life makes the field of sociology worthwhile studying from a scientific position. "By the middle of the 1800s, Comte had declared what, in his view, should be that task of sociology [and] [t]hen came Emile Durkheim who, influenced by Comte's Positive Philosophy (Comte, 1974), published his ground-breaking The Rules to the Sociological Method (1982) in 1895" (Taylor, 2003). From the works of Waller (2006) and Taylor (2003), sociology owes many of the initial tentacles not only to Comte but in particular to Ibn Khaldun, Plato and to Isaac Newton. Even though Plato was not ascribed as the father of sociology, he argued that there is an order to the universe (or society) and that man is an organism in a social space who must survive, and that he/she does so in groups. It is from the philosophical works of Plato and other scholars that Comte worked to coined the term sociology, which initially was known as social physics. Comte, on the other hand, was the first to use the term sociology in print in 1838 (Waller, 2006) but based on Plato's construct of the world, society is ordered which may have assisted Comte in conceptualizing that societies are governed by some laws, and so can studies using similar techniques as the natural sciences.

AUGUSTE COMTE (1798 - 1857)

Comte was the first to have used sociology in print in 1838 but borrowed 'statics' and 'dynamics' from Isaac Newton as agents that allowed him to foresee the measurability of social man. In using social statics and social dynamics, Comte saw the former as the assessment of the general principles of actions and reaction of the diverse parts of the social system (or society), which he argued cannot be studied separately "as if they had an independent existence" but must be analysed as a whole. With regard to social dynamics, Comte believed that the whole society must be the unit of analysis, and how it develops and how it changes with time is knowable. According to Inkeles (1964), "He [Comte] was convinced that all societies moved through certain fixed stages of development, and that they progressed toward ever increasing perfection", and this explains how comparative study of society was possible for sociological analysis.

HERBERT SPENCER (1820 - 1903)

When Spencer published the three-volume Principles of Sociology in 1877, it was the first comprehensive systematic study devoted to an "exposition of sociological analysis", and in this, he was more precise than Comte was. Spencer used the phrase science of sociology in an attempt to channel the focus of the discipline, while forwarding how the subject matter must be addressed in particular social space. He forwarded areas to which the discipline must study: These were, the family, politics, religion, social control, and industry and work, community, associations, division of labour, social differentiation or stratification, aesthetics, the study of arts, and the sociology of knowledge.

Spencer like Comte believed that the whole society must be studied as a unit of analysis, and that the different parts of a society were ordered as was purported by Plato. This, then, speaks to his theorizing on 'structures' and 'functions' of the society. Which explains Inkeles perspective that "He [Spencer] maintained that the parts of society, although discrete units, were not arranged haphazardly" (Inkeles, 1964). The numerous parts bear some constant interrelationship and these facts make society a meaningful 'entity' fitting for scientific inquiry.

EMILE DURKHEIM (1858 - 1917)

Wallace and Wolf argued that 'science of sociology' as was developed by Durkheim is not possible "until it renounced its initial and overall claim upon the totality of social reality ever more among parts, elements, and different aspects which could serve as subject matter for specific problems" (Wallace & Wolf, p. 380), this is similar to the perspective of the other founding fathers. According to Taylor, Durkheim's sociology is constructed on a set of assumptions of a system having interdependent parts that are held together by a large value system (Taylor, 2003). Durkheim's works emphasized 'consensus' and 'social order' to the exclusion of social change and conflict to which Marx spoke extensively in his monographs. Despite the conservatism nature of Durkheim, "he advanced a discussion of the division of labour in society in which he accounted for the increased specialization, characteristic of modern capitalist society" (Taylor, 2003, p. 14), which would characterize some of his works – for example, religion, capitalism and the 'history of the non-Western world'.

Despite the claim of many sociologists that Durkheim's work on suicide represents the primal piece of social work that substantiates the validity that the discipline can be studied scientifically, Taylor (2003) was somehow sceptical of this laboured 'truth'. From Taylor's work on Re-Appropriating the Stolen Legacy: The African Contribution to the Origin of Sociological Thought, he wrote that...Emile Durkheim who, influenced by Comte's Positive Philosophy (Comte 1974), published his groundbreaking The Rules of the Sociological Method (1982) in 1895. He applied his methodology presented in Rules to suicide, a phenomenon, normally considered psychological. Suicide, published in 1897, though flawed, was important because as Stephen Lukas remarks, 'it represents both a typically bold and clear statement of the aspiration towards a social science that is absolutely objective, specific (to social reality) and autonomous (of non-scientific influences).

Taylor's perspective on Durkheim's theorizing on suicide represents primarily a single piece of critique that insinuates that the positivist techniques used by Durkheim were flawed; however it provides a needed premise upon which the scientific techniques of the natural sciences were used in investigating a social phenomenon. In response to Taylor's viewpoint on the correctness of Durkheim's methodology, what are merits of Taylor's critique in denouncing the validity of Durkheim's monographs on suicide?

MAX WEBER (1864 – 1920)

From Weber's perspective on the study of sociology that may be studied from a non-positivism understanding, Inkeles cited that Weber believed that social action is ordered to arrive at a causal explanation of its course and effect. The method of understanding that he advocated is known as verstehen. This scientific inquiry sees events from a subjective standpoint. Notwithstanding the subjectivity of Weber's theorizing on the subject matter, his method of interpreting social act and social relationship is not non-scientific but presents another channel in the process of garnering information on the actors in their situational, historic, or symbolic contexts.

Unlike Durkheim's work on suicide that embodied the principles of positivism, Weber's work on religion, in which he used a rival paradigm, verstehen methodology, unearth some truths on the substantive issue from the position of the essence of man's actions that sometimes are subtle and irrational. According to Taylor, Weber 'magnum opus' in the Protestant Ethic and the Spirit of Capitalism, cited that "a religious ideology emanating from Calvinism was the driving force behind capitalism" and offered an explanation of the use of the sociology to explain an aspect to man in society by the use of scientific inquiry.

Auguste Comte, the man who is credited for the development and formulation of the doctrines of sociology based the fundamental principles of the subject matter on grounded facts and experiences, which one can reasonably use positivism to analyse various social issues. Within the theorizing, Comte formulated the general framework of the content which allows for the establishment of the claim to a science. This forward thinking of the subject matter allowed Comte to acknowledge how scientific approaches can be applied in the studying structures of and interactions within society. It was Comte's perspective of philosophy that was brought to the study of man in society that leads to Herbert Spencer's work on the discipline.

Inkeles (1964) argued that Spencer unlike Comte explicitly narrowed events in which sociological analysis should be applied. This reality did not contravene the postulations of Comte, but that the specificity of a structure and its functions as depicted by Spencer on societies in different stages can be studied as a unit. Therefore, when Durkheim forwarded a particular construct as to how this field of study can become a science, he obviously approved the idea that sociology can concern itself with a wide array of institutions and social processes. This offers justifications for Durkheim's position of sub-dividing the first sociological journal, L'Annee Sociologiqque, into General Sociology, Sociology of Religion, Sociology of Law and Morals, Sociology of Crime, Economic Sociology and Sociology of Aesthetics. He [Durkeheim] agreed with Spencer by his actions that sociology spans plethora of social actions.

What Weber arrived at in sociology within the era of the dominant paradigm, positivism, in attempting to widen the scope of sociology to study the complete social fact, he developed a different methodology in understanding social action. Verstehen the method of explaining issues within a subjective meaning system was not to lessen the dominance of objectivity and neutrality in social sciences but understanding social man who places certain motives to his/her society, and those actions are not quantifiable as man is irrational, a needed prerequisite for subjectivity and not objectivity as the positivists would want us to belief.

Weber wrote that sociology "is a science which attempts to the interpretive understanding of social action in order thereby to arrive at a causal explanation of its course and effects", and this was not to contradict or militate against the other founding fathers but that he recognized that causality was a critical component of positivism. Offering an alternative methodology in the studying of man in an ordered society allows social scientist to further capture and understand man's social experiences, and so, does not militate against the "scientific ness" of the inquiry purely on the basis that the research did not utilize traditional positivism.

Inkeles (1964) summarized the perspective of the entire piece of this work fittingly, when he said: Although they by no means expressed themselves in precisely the same terms, the four founding fathers we consulted seem in basic agreement about the proper subject matter of sociology.

The use of positivism (a doctrine that is embedded in the utilization of mathematical rigours) in the discipline of sociology shows the similarity between studying a social phenomenon and researching a natural phenomenon. Durkheim's work on suicide, despite the flaws that Taylor purported, adds value to the 'scientific ness' of studying a social space and equally so was DuBois' work on the Philadelphian Negroes. Furthermore the use of positivism in the study of an event adds objectivity of the reality to which alternative paradigms have been used to establish this reality. Despite Comte's recognition of the need to study social phenomenon in a scientific manner (by positivism), the use of interpretivism only adds depth to the understanding of man in his/her social space, and so must be used to enhance the knowledge process.

AUGUSTE COMTE [1798-1857]-THE FOUNDING FATHER OF SOCIOLOGY

Auguste Comte, the French Philosopher, is traditionally considered the "Father of Sociology". Comte who invented the term "Sociology" was the first man to distinguish the subject-matter of sociology from all the other sciences. He worked out in a series of books, a general approach to the study of society. Comte is regarded as the "Father of Sociology" not because of any significant contributions to the science as such, but because of the great influence he had upon it. It would be more appropriate to regard him as a philosopher of science rather than a sociologist. Comte introduced the word "sociology" for the first time in his famous book "Positive Philosophy" at about 1839. The term "Sociology" is derived from the Latin word Socius, meaning companion or associate, and the Greek word logos, meaning study or science. Thus, the etymological meaning of sociology is the science of society. He defined sociology as the science of social phenomena "subject to natural and invariable laws, the discovery of which is the object of investigation".

Comte devoted his main efforts to an inquiry into the nature of human knowledge and tried to classify all knowledge and to analyse the methods of achieving it. He concentrated his efforts to determine the nature of human society and the laws and principles underlying its growth and development. He also laboured to establish the methods to be employed in studying social phenomena. Comte believed that the sciences follow one another in a definite and logical order and that all inquiry goes through certain stages (namely, the theological, the metaphysical and the positive or scientific or empirical). Finally, they arrive at the last or scientific stage or as he called the positive stage. In the positive stage, objective observation is substituted for speculation. Social phenomena like physical phenomena, maintained, can be studied objectively by making use of the positive method. He thought that it was time for inquiries into social problems and social phenomena to enter into this last stage. So, he recommended that the study of society be called the science of society, i. e. 'sociology'. Comte proposed sociology to be studied in two main parts (i) the social statics and (ii) the social dynamics. These two concepts represent a basic division in the subject-matter of sociology. The social statics deals with the major institutions of society such as family, economy or polity. Sociology is conceived of as the study of inter-relations between such institutions. In the words of Comte, "the statical study of sociology consists the investigations of laws of action and reaction of different parts of the social system". He argued that the parts of a society cannot be studied separately, "as if they had independent existence".

If Statics examines how the parts of societies are interrelated, social dynamics focuses on whole societies as the unit of analysis and how they developed and changed through time. "We must remember that the laws of social dynamics are most recognisable when they relate to the largest societies", he said. Comte was convinced that all societies moved through certain fixed stages of development and that progressed towards ever increasing perfection. He felt that the comparative study of societies as "wholes" was major subject for sociological analysis.

COMTE'S POSITIVISM

Comte first described the epistemological perspective of positivism in *The Course in Positive Philosophy*, a series of texts published between 1830 and 1842. These texts were followed by the 1848 work, *A General Viewh of Positivism* (published in English in 1865). The first three volumes of the *Course* dealt chiefly with the physical sciences already in existence (mathematics, astronomy, physics, chemistry, biology), whereas the latter two emphasised the inevitable coming of social science. Observing the circular dependence cf theory and observation in science, and classifying the sciences in this way, Comte may be regarded as the first philosopher of science in the modern sense of the term. For him, the physical sciences had necessarily to arrive first, before humanity could adequately channel its efforts into the most challenging and complex "Queen science" of human society itself. His *View of Positivism* would therefore set-out to define, in more detail, the empirical goals of sociological method. Comte offered an account of social evolution, proposing that society undergoes three phases in its quest for the truth according to a general 'law of three stages'. The idea bears some similarity to Marx's view that human society would progress toward a communist peak. This is perhaps unsurprising as both were profoundly influenced by the early Utopian socialist, Henri de Saint-Simon, who was at one time Comte's teacher and mentor. Both Comte and Marx intended to develop, scientifically, a new secular ideology in the wake of European secularisation.

Comte's stages were (1) the *theological*, (2) the *metaphysical*, and (3) the *positive*. The Theological phase was seen from the perspective of 19th century France as preceding the Enlightenment, in which man's place in society and society's restrictions upon man were referenced to God. Man blindly believed in whatever he was taught by his ancestors. He believed in a supernatural power. Fetishism played a significant role during this time. By the "Metaphysical" phase, he referred not to the Metaphysics of Aristotle or other ancient Greek philosophers. Rather, the idea was rooted in the problems of French society subsequent to the revolution of 1789.

This Metaphysical phase involved the justification of *universal rights* as being on a vauntedly higher plane than the authority of any human ruler to countermand, although said rights were not referenced to the sacred beyond mere metaphor. This stage is known as the stage of investigation, because people started reasoning and questioning although no solid evidence was laid.

The stage of investigation was the beginning of a world that questioned authority and religion. In the Scientific phase, which came into being after the failure of the revolution and of Napoleon, people could find solutions to social problems and bring them into force despite the proclamations of *human rights* or prophecy of *the will of God.* Science started to answer questions in full stretch. In this regard he was similar to Karl Marx and Jeremy Bentham. For its time, this idea of a Scientific phase was considered up-to-date, although from a later standpoint it is too derivative of classical physics and academic history. Comte's law of three stages was one of the first theories of social evolutionism.

The other universal law he called the "encyclopedic law." By combining these laws, Comte developed a systematic and hierarchical classification of all sciences, including inorganic physics (astronomy, earth science and chemistry) and organic physics (biology and, for the first time, *physique sociale,* later renamed *sociologie*). Independently from Emmanuel Joseph Sieyès's introduction of the term in 1780, Comte re-invented "sociologie," and introduced the term as a neologism, in 1838. Comte had earlier used the term "social physics," but that term had been appropriated by others, notably Adolphe Quetelet.

"The most important thing to determine was the natural order in which the sciences stand — not how they can be made to stand, but how they must stand, irrespective of the wishes of any one....This Comte accomplished by taking as the criterion of the position of each the degree of what he called "positivity," which is simply the degree to which the phenomena can be exactly determined. This, as may be readily seen, is also a measure of their relative complexity, since the exactness of a science is in inverse proportion to its complexity. The degree of exactness or positivity is, moreover, that to which it can be subjected to mathematical demonstration, and therefore mathematics, which is not itself a concrete science, is the general gauge by which the position of every science is to be determined. Generalizing thus, Comte found that there were five great groups of phenomena of equal classificatory value but of successively decreasing positivity. To these he gave the names astronomy, physics, chemistry, biology, and sociology." – *Lester F. Ward, The Outlines of Sociology (1898).*

This idea of a special science—not the humanities, not metaphysics—for the social was prominent in the 19th century and not unique to Comte. It has recently been discovered that the term "sociology"-a term considered coined by Comte-had already been introduced in 1780, albeit with a different meaning, by the French essayist Emmanuel Joseph Sieyès(1748–1836). The ambitious—many would say grandiose—way that Comte conceived of this special science of the social, however, was unique. Comte saw this new science, sociology, as the last and greatest of all sciences, one which would include all other sciences and integrate and relate their findings into a cohesive whole. It has to be pointed out, however, that there was a seventh science, one even greater than sociology. Namely, Comte considered "Anthropology, or true science of Man [to be] the last gradation in the Grand Hierarchy of Abstract Science."

Comte's explanation of the Positive philosophy introduced the important relationship between theory, practice and human understanding of the world. On page 27 of the 1855 printing of Harriet Martineau's translation of *The Positive Philosophy of Auguste Comte,* we see his observation that, "If it is true that every theory must be based upon observed facts, it is equally true that facts can not be observed without the guidance of some theories. Without such guidance, our facts would be desultory and fruitless; we could not retain them: for the most part we could not even perceive them."

Comte is generally regarded as the first Western sociologist (Ibn Khaldun having preceded him in North Africa by nearly four centuries). Comte's emphasis on the interconnectedness of social elements was a forerunner of modern functionalism. Nevertheless, as with many others of Comte's time, certain elements of his work are now viewed as eccentric and unscientific, and his grand vision of sociology as the centerpiece of all the sciences has not come to fruition. His emphasis on a quantitative, mathematical basis for decision-making remains with us today.

It is a foundation of the modern notion of Positivism, modern quantitative statistical analysis, and business decision-making. His description of the continuing cyclical relationship between theory and practice is seen in modern business systems of Total Quality Management and Continuous Quality Improvement where advocates describe a continuous cycle of theory and practice through the four-part cycle of plan, do, check, and act. Despite his advocacy of quantitative analysis, Comte saw a limit in its ability to help explain social phenomena.

The early sociology of Herbert Spencer came about broadly as a reaction to Comte; writing after various developments in evolutionary biology, Spencer attempted (in vain) to reformulate the discipline in what we might now describe as socially Darwinistic terms. (Spencer was in actual fact a proponent of Lamarckism rather than Darwinism).

Comte's fame today owes in part to Emile Littre, who founded *The Positivist Review* in 1867. Debates continue to rage, however, as to how much Comte appropriated from the work of his mentor, Henri de Saint-Simon.

4

Early Thinkers and Pioneers of Sociological Theory

INTRODUCTION

Social theory is an essential tool used by scholars in the analysis of society; through the use of theoretical frameworks social structures and phenomena are analyzed and placed in context within a particular school of thought. The field is interdisciplinary, drawing ideas from and contributing to such disciplines as anthropology, economics, history, human geography, literary theory, mass communications, philosophy, sociology, and theology. It is argued by many that the beginnings of social theory are difficult to pinpoint, many arguments return to Ancient Greece. Berch Berberlogu cites Plato, Socrates and Aristotle as some of the totemic figures amongst the Greek thinkers and traces their influence upon social theory throughout the enlightenment up to the late nineteenth and early twentieth century. "Critical" social theories, such as neomarxist theories and feminist theories, argue that as theories are generally based on premises that entail normative positions, it is necessary to critique the ideological aspects of theories and related oppressive social relations.

Social Theory as a Discipline

Harrington (2005) discusses the etymology of social theory, stating that while the term did not exist in any language before the twentieth century, its origins are ancient and lie in two words; 'social' from the Latin socius and 'theory' from the Greek theoria. Social theorising aided the Greeks in making sense of their lives, and in questioning the value and meaning of things around them. Social theory as a discipline emerged with the period which we now consider to be modernity and was largely equated with an attitude of critical thinking, based on rationality, logic and objectivity, and the desire for knowledge through 'aposteriori' methods of discovery, rather than 'apriori' methods of tradition. With this in mind it is easy to link social theory to deeper seated philosophical discussions.

Social Theory in Relation to Natural Science

Social theory always had an uneasy relationship with academic disciplines; many of its key thinkers never held a university position. Compared to workers in disciplines within the "objective" natural sciences — such as physics or chemistry — social theorists may make less use of the scientific method and of other fact-based methods to prove a point. Instead, they tackle very large-scale social trends and structures using hypotheses that they cannot easily prove, except over the course of time. Criticism from opponents of social theories often objects to this. Extremely critical theorists, such as deconstructionists or postmodernists, may argue that any type of research or method has inherent flaws. Often, however, thinkers may present their ideas as social theory because the social reality that those ideas describe appears so overarching as to remain unprovable. The social theories of modernity or anarchy can exemplify this.

However, social theories still play a major part in the sciences of sociology, anthropology, economics, and others. Objective science-based research often begins with a hypothesis formed from a social theory. Likewise, science-based research can often provide support for social theories or can spawn new ones.

For instance, statistical research grounded in the scientific method that finds a severe income disparity between women and men performing the same occupation can complement the underlying premises of the complex social theories of feminism or of patriarchy. In general, and in particular among adherents of pure sociology, social theory has appeal because it takes the focus away from the individual (the way in which most westerners look at the world) and focuses it on the society itself and the social forces which control individuals' lives. This sociological insight (often termed the sociological imagination) has appealed to students and others dissatisfied with the *status quo* because it looks beyond the assumption of societal structures and patterns as purely random.

HISTORY OF PRE-CLASSICAL SOCIAL THEORISTS

Prior to 19th century, social theory took largely narrative and normative traits. Expressed in story form, it both assumed ethical principles and recommended moral acts. Thus one can regard religious figures as the earliest social theorists. Saint Augustine (354-430) and St. Thomas Aquinas (*circa* 1225-1274) concerned themselves exclusively with a just society. St. Augustine describes late Ancient Roman society but through a lens of hatred and contempt for what he saw as false Gods, and in reaction theorized The City of God. Similarly, in China, Master Kong (otherwise known as Confucius) (551-479 BCE) envisaged a just society that went beyond his contemporary society of the Warring States. Later on, also in China, Mozi (*circa* 470-*circa* 390 BCE) recommended a more pragmatic sociology, but ethical at base. In the 18th century, after Montesquieu's The Spirit of Law that prove social elements influences on the human nature, pre-classical period of social theories have changed to a new form that provide the basic ideas for social theory. Such as: evolution, philosophy of history, social life and social contract, public and general will, competition in social space, organistic pattern for social description and... Jean-Jacques Rousseau in this time played a significant role in social theory. He revealed the origin of inequality, analyze the social contract(and social compact) that forms social integration and define the social sphere or civil society. He also emphasized that man has the liberty to change his world, a revolutionary assertion that made it possible to program and change society.

Classical Social Theory

The first "modern" social theories (known as classical theories) that begin to resemble the analytic social theory of today developed almost simultaneously with the birth of the science of sociology. Auguste Comte (1798-1857), known as the 'father of sociology', laid the groundwork for one of the first social theories-social evolutionism. In the 19th century three great classical theories of social and historical change emerged: the social evolutionism theory (of which Social Darwinism forms a part), the social cycle theory and the Marxist historical materialism theory.

Another early modern theorist, Herbert Spencer (1820-1903), coined the term "survival of the fittest" (and incidentally recommended avoidance of governmental action on behalf of the poor (socialism) as a positive act). Some Post-Modern social theorists like Shepard Humphries, draw heavily upon Spencer's work and argue that many of his observations are timeless (just as relevant in 2008 as 1898). Vilfredo Pareto (1848-1923) and Pitirim A. Sorokin argued that 'history goes in cycles', and presented the social cycle theory to illustrate their point. Ferdinand Tönnies (1855-1936) made *community* and *society* (*Gemeinschaft and Gesellschaft*, 1887) the special topics of the new science of "sociology", both of them based on different modes of will of social actors. Emile Durkheim postulated a number of major theories regarding anomie and functionalism. Max Weber theorized on bureaucracy, religion, and authority. Karl Marx theorized on the class struggle and social progress towards communism and laid the groun work for the theory that became known as Marxism. Marxism became more than a theory, of course, carrying deep implications over the course of 20th century history (including the Russian Revolution of 1917).

Most of the 19th century pioneers of social theory and sociology, like Saint-Simon, Comte, Marx, John Stuart Mill or Spencer, never held university posts. Most people regarded them as philosophers, because much of the their thinking was interdisciplinary and "outside the box" of the existing disciplines of their time (eg:, philology, law, and history).

Many of the classical theories had one common factor: they all agreed that the history of humanity is pursuing a certain fixed path. They differed on where that path would lead: social progress, technological progress, decline or even fall, etc. Social cycle theorists were much more skeptical of the Western achievements and technological progress, however, arguing that progress is but an illusion in of the ups and downs of the historical cycles. The classical approach has been criticized by many modern sociologists and theorists, among them Karl Popper, Robert Nisbet, Charles Tilly and Immanuel Wallerstein.

Modern Social Theory

Although the majority of 19th-century social theories now class as obsolete, they have spawned new, modern social theories. Some modern social theories represent some advanced version of the classical theories, like Multilineal theories of evolution (neoevolutionism, sociobiology, theory of modernization, theory of post-industrial society) and various strains of Neo-Marxism. In the late 19th and early 20th centuries, by a more or less arbitrary division of topics, the social theory became most closely related to academic sociology while other subjects such as anthropology, philosophy, and social work branched out into their own disciplines. Such subjects as "philosophy of history" withered, and their subject matter became part of social theory as taught in sociology.

Attempts to recapture a space for discussion free of disciplines began in earnest in the late 1920s and early 1930s. The Frankfurt Institute for Social Research provides the most successful example. The Committee on Social Thought at the University of Chicago followed in the 1940s. In the 1970s, programs in Social and Political Thought were established at Sussex and York. Others followed, with various different emphases and structures, such as Social Theory and History (University of California, Davis). Cultural Studies programs, notably that of Birmingham University, extended the concerns of social theory into the domain of culture and thus anthropology. A chair and undergraduate program in social theory was established at the University of Melbourne and a number of universities now specialize in social theory (UC-Santa Cruz is one example). Finally social theory seems to be gaining more acceptance as a classical academic discipline.

In modern times, generally speaking, social theory began to stress free will, individual choice, subjective reasoning, and the importance of unpredictable events in place of the classic determinism – thus social theory become much more complex. Rational Choice Theory and Symbolic Interactionism furnish two examples. Most modern sociologists deem there are no great unifying 'laws of history', but rather smaller, more specific, and more complex laws that govern society.

Post-modern Social Theory

Scholars and historians most commonly hold postmodernism to be a movement of ideas arising from, but also critical of elements of modernism. Because of the wide range of uses of the term, different elements of modernity are chosen as being continuous, and different elements of modernity are held to be critiqued. Each of the different uses also is rooted in some argument about the nature of knowledge, known in philosophy as epistemology. Individuals who use the term are arguing that either there is something fundamentally different about the transmission of meaning, or that modernism has fundamental flaws in its system of knowledge.

The argument for the necessity of the term states that economic and technological conditions of our age have given rise to a decentralized, media-dominated society in which ideas are simulacra and only inter-referential representations and copies of each other, with no real original, stable or objective source for communication and meaning. Globalization, brought on by innovations in communication, manufacturing and transportation, is often cited as one force which has driven the decentralized modern life, creating a culturally pluralistic and interconnected global society lacking any single dominant center of political power, communication, or intellectual production. The postmodern view is that inter-subjective knowledge, and not objective knowledge is the dominant form of discourse under such conditions, and the ubiquity of copies and dissemination fundamentally alters the relationship between reader and what is read, between observer and the observed, between those who consume and those who produce. Not all people who use the term postmodern or postmodernism see these developments as positive. Users of the term often argue that their ideals have arisen as the result of particular economic and social conditions, including what is described as "late capitalism" and the growth of broadcast media, and that such conditions have pushed society into a new historical period.

In 1971, the term Postmodernism was coined by the Arab American Theorist Ihab Hassan in his book: The

Dismemberment of Orpheus: Toward a Postmodern Literature. In 1979 Jean-François Lyotard wrote a short but influential work *The Postmodern Condition: A report on knowledge*. Jean Baudrillard, Michel Foucault, and Roland Barthes were influential in 1970s in developing postmodern theory.

HERBERT SPENCER (1820-1903)

A Victorian biologist and philosopher, Herbert Spencer was born April 27th, 1820, at the height of British industrialism. He was educated at home in mathematics, natural science, history and English, among some other languages. Spencer was sickly in his youth, all eight of his other siblings dying at a young age. His constitution remained weak throughout his life, and he would later suffer from nervous breakdowns which he never recovered from, and he wandered about London never in a complete state of good health. He suffered from chronic insomnia, could only work a few hours a day, and used fairly substantial amounts of opium. He experienced a strange sensation in his head which he called "the mischief", and was known for eccentricities like the wearing of ear-plugs to avoid over-excitement, especially when he could not hold his ground in an argument. He obtained a job as a civil engineer on the railways at sixteen and wrote during his spare time. This vocation of his took up ten years of his life, and imbued him with a healthy optimism for life and society.

Spencer became the sub-editor of The Economist in 1848, an important financial weekly at the time for the upper-middle class. He interacted with famous people like Thomas Huxley and John Tyndall, among many other leading intellectuals of Victorian Britain. Spencer published numerous articles in the radical press of his time, like The Leader, The Fortnightly and The Westminster Review, largely concerning the government, pushing for limiting its role as a mediator in society. He advocated the abolishment of Poor Laws, national education and a central church; he wanted the lifting of all restrictions on commerce and factory legislation. Across the street from where he worked was John Chapman's office, and that was where he first met his assistant Marian Evans, later known as George Eliot. They developed a very close friendship, and talked of marriage but never actually married. Even so, they remained intimate companions up till her death. His book Social Statics was published in 1851 to great acclaim, but his quietly influential Principles Of Psychology released in 1855 met with much criticism. Although one of the most influential figures in sociology and psychology, Spencer was overshadowed because of his somewhat controversial ideas. In fact, his theory of evolution actually preceded Charles Darwin's, when he wrote The Developmental Hypothesis in 1852, 7 years before Darwin's Origin Of Species! His theory was not taken into serious consideration largely because of a lack of an effective theoretical system for natural selection. Nevertheless, it was Spencer and not Darwin who first popularized the term "Evolution", and few people outside the field realize that the oft-used phrase "survival of the fittest" was actually coined by Spencer!

His evolutionary stance led to his most famous idea, "Social Darwinism." It influenced early evolutionary economists like Thorstein Veblen, as well as the members of the American apologist school like William Graham Sumner. He projected his theory of biological evolution onto a social plane, emphasizing the importance of organic analogy, i.e. the similarities between Organism and State. He saw evolution as the change from a homogeneous condition that was innately unstable, to a heterogenous and stable one. He highlighted four main concepts: Growth, Differentiation, Integration and Adaptation, ideas commonly present in developmental biology, and which could easily be brought into the context of a developing, growing society. Spencer's last years were characterized by a collapse of his initial optimism, replaced instead by a pessimism regarding the future of mankind. Nevertheless, he devoted much of his efforts in reinforcing his arguments and preventing the mis-interpretation of his monumental theory of non-interference. He was admired by many intellectuals, including American philosopher William James, but was frequently accused of being petty, hypochondriacal, and maudlin. He died in 1903, and is buried at High Gate Cemetery near George Eliot and Karl Marx.

HERBERT SPENCER: THE WORK

Herbert Spencer was a theorist whose valuable insights have often been drowned in a sea of irrelevance and specious reasoning. What is relevant in his work will therefore have to be selected in a manner recommended by Richard Hofstadter when he wrote about Frederick Jackson Turner, "The most valid procedure with a historical thinker of his kind is not to try to have sport with his marginal failings but to rescue whatever is viable by cutting out what has proved wrong, tempering what is overstated, tightening what is loosely put, and setting the whole in its proper place among usable perspectives." This account of Spencer's work will be severely selective. Here, as elsewhere in this book, only the writer's sociological contributions, and among these only the central ones, will be considered. Spencer's general metaphysics, or antimetaphysics, will be touched upon only tangentially. This is all the easier since critics now seem to be of the opinion that deep down Spencer was a rather shallow philosopher. Some historians of sociology tend to see Spencer as a continuator of Comte's organicist and evolutionary approach. Although Spencer seems to have protested too much in disclaiming any profound influence of Comte's thought on his own, it is true that his general orientation differs significantly from Comte's. Spencer described their different approaches in this way:

What is Comte's professed aim? To give a coherent account of the progress of *human conceptions*. What is my aim? To give a coherent account of the progress of the *external world.* Comte proposes to describe the necessary, and the actual, filiation of *ideas*. I propose to describe the necessary, and the actual, filiation of *things*. Comte professes to interpret the genesis of our *knowledge of nature*. My aim is to interpret... the genesis of the *phenomena which constitute nature*, The one is subjective. The other is objective..

Comte was, of course, not only interested in the development of ideas but also in the correlative changes in social organization, and he dealt with social order as well as with progress. Nevertheless, Spencer correctly perceived the essential differences between them. Spencer's first and foremost concern was with evolutionary changes in social structures and social institutions rather than with the attendant mental states. To Spencer, like to Marx, ideas were epiphenomenal. "The average opinion in every age and country," he writes, "is a function of the social structure in that age and country."

Evolution, that is, "a change from a state of relatively indefinite, incoherent, homogeneity to a state of relatively definite, coherent, heterogeneity," was to Spencer that universal process, which explains alike both the "earliest changes which the universe at large is supposed to have undergone... and those latest changes which we trace in society and the products of social life." Once this master key to the riddles of the universe is used, it becomes apparent, Spencer argued, that the evolution of human societies, far from being different from other evolutionary phenomena, is but a special case of a universally applicable natural law. Sociology can become a science only when it is based on the idea of natural, evolutionary law. "There can be no complete acceptance of sociology as a science, so long as the belief in a social order not conforming to natural law, survives."

It is axiomatic to Spencer that ultimately all aspects of the universe, whether organic or inorganic, social or nonsocial, are subject to the laws os evolution. His sociological reflections concentrate, however, on the parallels between organic and social evolution, between similarities in the structure and evolution of organic and social units. Biological analogies occupy a privileged position in all of Spencer's sociological reasoning although he was moved to draw attention to the limitations o such analogies. Because Spencer was a radical individualist organic analogies caused him some sociological and philosophica difficulties, which Comte, with his collective philosophy, wa spared.

Spencer's most fruitful use of organic analogies was hi notion that with evolutionary growth come changes in an unit's structure and functions, that increases in size bring i their wake increases in differentiation. What he had in min here, to use a homely example, is the idea that if men wer suddenly to grow to the size of elephants, only majo modifications in their bodily structures would allow them t continue being viable organisms.

EVOLUTION

The first clear articulation of Spencer's evolutionar perspective occurred in his essay, 'Progress: Its Law and Cause published in Chapman's *Westminster Review* in 1857, and whic later formed the basis of the *First Principles of a New System of Philosophy* (1862). In it he expounded a theory of evolution which combined insights from Samuel Taylor Coleridge's essay 'The Theory of Life'—itself derivative from Friedrich von Schelling's Naturphilosophie—with a generalization of von Baer's law of embryological development. Spencer posited that all structures in the universe develop from a simple, undifferentiated, homogeneity to a complex, differentiated, heterogeneity, while being accompanied by a process of greater integration of the differentiated parts. This evolutionary process could be found at work, Spencer believed, throughout the cosmos. It was a universal law, applying to the stars and the galaxies as much as to biological organisms, and to human social organization as much as to the human mind. It differed from other scientific laws only by its greater generality, and the laws of the special sciences could be shown to be illustrations of this principle.

This attempt to explain the evolution of complexity was radically different from that to be found in Darwin's *Origin of Species* which was published two years later. Spencer is often, quite erroneously, believed to have merely appropriated and generalized Darwin's work on natural selection. But although after reading Darwin's work he coined the phrase 'survival of the fittest' as his own term for Darwin's concept, and is often misrepresented as a thinker who merely applied the Darwinian theory to society, he only grudgingly incorporated natural selection into his preexisting overall system. The primary mechanism of species transformation that he recognized was Lamarckian use-inheritance which posited that organs are developed or are diminished by use or disuse and that the resulting changes may be transmitted to future generations. Spencer believed that this evolutionary mechanism was also necessary to explain 'higher' evolution, especially the social development of humanity. Moreover, in contrast to Darwin, he held that evolution had a direction and an end-point, the attainment of a final state of equilibrium. He tried to apply the theory of biological evolution to sociology. He proposed that society was the product of change from lower to higher forms, just as in the theory of biological evolution, the lowest forms of life are said to be evolving into higher forms. Spencer claimed that man's mind had evolved in the same way from the simple automatic responses of lower animals to the process of reasoning in the thinking man. Spencer believed in two kinds of knowledge: knowledge gained by the individual and knowledge gained by the race. Intuition, or knowledge learned unconsciously, was the inherited experience of the race.

THE DEVELOPMENT OF HERBERT SPENCER'S CONCEPT OF EVOLUTION

The scientific controversies surrounding the theory of evolution in the nineteenth century were primarily concerned with the interpretation of the geological, paleontological, and biological evidence. The public debate, on the other hand, centered above all on man's place in nature and the implications of evolution for the immortal soul, the mind, and it organ, the brain. It is somewhat surprising to find that the writings of historians and indeed of Darwin himself fail to pay close attention to the effects of the theory of evolution on the study of mind and brain. If we do turn our attention directly to this topic, we find that the major nineteenth century figures are Herbert Spencer, John Hughlings Jackson, and George J. Romanes. In this brief paper I want to confine my attention to the development and influence of Spencer's concept of evolution. Unlike Darwin, Spencer was never much of an observer or indeed a reader, and his independent formulation of a theory of evolution developed from his speculations in social theory and psychology. The idea of evolution itself was not, of course, original. He was converted to a belief in the so-called "development hypothesis" by reading Charles Lyell, whose supposed refutation of Lamarck led Spencer to the opposite conclusion. Spencer also took part in the debates surrounding the anonymous *Vestiges of the Natural History of Creation* (1844) and discussed this book with T. H. Huxley, who later said of the period 1851—1858, "...the only person known to me whose knowledge and capacity compelled respect, and who was, at the same time, a through-going evolutionist, was Mr. Herbert Spencer... Many and prolonged were the battles we fought on this topic. But even my friend's rare dialectic skill and copiousness of apt illustration could not drive me from my agnostic position." 1 What was original and interesting about Spencer's theory was three-fold: the traditions on which it drew, the areas in which he applied it, and the tenacity with which he clung to belief in the inheritance of acquired characteristics. I want to point out that the origins, applications and influences of Spencer's evolutionism were not only different from those of Darwin but that they were also more significant for the development of our conception of mind and brain.

Spencer's first serious intellectual endeavours were devoted to the study of phrenology, and it was from phrenology that he drew the conception of society as an organism in which interdependent, specialized structures serve diverse functions. Similarly, his concept of the adaptation of the faculties of men to their organic, psychological and social needs was based on a phrenological view of man. These ideas were used as the basis of his attempt to refute Utilitarian social and ethical theory in his first book, *Social Statics* (1851), and he later reflected that two passages in that work were "the earliest foreshadowing of the general doctrine of Evolution. In the next two years his reflections on odd phrases encountered in his desultory reading led him to generalize his evolutionism from organic phenomena to embrace absolutely everything. He declared his advocacy of "The Development Hypothesis" in an article which appeared in 1852, and these ideas were then developed further until they became the universal formula which appeared in his *First Principles* (1862). Rather than pursue the development of this rather fruitless cosmic cliche, I want to turn to the application of evolution to psychology.

The second tradition which played an important part in Spencer's thinking was the theory of the association of ideas. Associationism is the only serious alternative to belief in innate ideas that has been proposed. It is based on two assumptions:

1) that complex mental phenomena are formed from simple sensations, and
2) that this occurs by means of habit or repetition.

Modern Associationism began as an afterthought in Locke's *Essay* and was developed by David Hartley into a comprehensive explanatory principle in psychology. By the nineteenth century it had become the reigning psychological theory. Its modern form is the theory of conditioning of stimulus-response psychology, and it also provides the associationist principle in psychoanalysis. Thus, Associationism remains the basic assumption of psychological theory.

In one sense, Spencer's psychology of evolutionary associationism was a simple synthesis of "use inheritance" and the law of association. As he put it, "The familiar doctrine of association here undergoes a great extension; for it is held that not only in the individual do ideas become connected when in experience the things producing them have repeatedly occurred together, but that such results of repeated occurrences accumulate in successions of individuals: the effects of associations are supposed to be transmitted as modifications of the nervous system." That is, Spencer's psychology extends the theory of association from the *tabula rasa* of the individual to that of the race. What was novel in Spencer's view of psychological evolution was the implication which he took it to have for the place of mind in nature. When he was making notes for *The Principles of Psychology* in 1853, he was struck by the importance of adaptation for mental as well as bodily life. "There at once followed the idea that the growth of a correspondence between inner and outer actions had to be traced up from the beginning; so as to show the way in which Mind gradually evolves out of Life.

This was, I think, the thought which originated the book and gave it its most distinctive character;..." Thus, two ideas were at the heart of his psychology: first, the continuity of all mental phenomena — extending from the first contractions of a sensitive polyp to the evolution of the forms of thought; 10 and second, the emphasis on progressive adaptation as "increasing adjustment of inner subjective relations to outer objective relations..." Mental phenomena are therefore defined as "incidents of the correspondence between the organism and its environment."

It would be difficult to overestimate the significance of this view for later psychological work. As it was increasingly applied, psychology was progressively seen as a biological science, and mental phenomena be came one — albeit the most highly evolved — among the many functions of the organism which bring about adaptation to its physical and social environment. For the present, there is only time to note that it significantly influenced modern neurology, neurophysiology and psychoanalysis. Spencer's conception of the mind as an adaptive function was also a crucial influence on the development of the pragmatic philosophy and functional psychology of William James and John Dewey. James said that "few recent formulas have done more real service of a rough sort in psychology than the Spencerian one that the essence of mental life and of bodily life are one, namely, 'the adjustment of inner to outer relations'" Although he had grave reservations about Spencer's speculative bent, James praised him lavishly for insisting that "since mind and its environment have evolved together, they must be studied together."

There is, unfortunately, a very serious flaw in this rosy picture: Spencer's life-long belief in the inheritance of acquired characteristics. Since the 1880s, the temptation to dismiss Spencer because of his advocacy of this erroneous mechanism has overwhelmed most biologists, psychologists, and historians. As a scientific judgement this is unimpeachable, but it is not very enlightening for the historian, whose first duty is to understand the past. Spencer could point triumphantly to Darwin's own writings to show that he had allowed an increasing role for use-inheritance at the expense of natural selection, just as Spencer had granted a role for natural selection in the early stages of evolution. In the 1880s, Spencer was right to argue that on the evidence then available, this was a matter of emphasis, and the relative weight to be attached to various factors was very much an open question. However, these mitigating circumstances cannot fully account for the immense weight which Spencer attached to the role of use inheritance. He argued, for example, that it was the chief factor in the evolution of civilised man. Much more was at stake than a simple debate over a biological mechanism. He prefaced his analysis of *The Factors of Organic Evolution* by pointing out that while its direct bearings are biological, "it has indirect bearings upon Psychology, Ethics and Sociology. My belief in the profound importance of these indirect bearings, was originally a chief prompter to set forth the argument;... " He was convinced that the evolution of complex mental phenomena was inexplicable unless one resorted to belief in the inheritance of functionally-produced modifications. But, most important of all, he could not bear to believe that institutions and circumstances do not affect a nation *en masse*. It was, therefore, Spencer's belief in rapid social progress which most strongly influenced the way he viewed the biological evidence. Lest we remember Spencer too unkindly, we should recall that there have been more recent examples of this view, based on similar convictions about the improvement of society, for example, the genetic theory of Lysenko and Michurin. I submit, therefore, that we should be sympathetic toward Spencer's so-called "Lamarckianism", on the grounds that Victorian meliorism was too powerful a presupposition for him to overcome. The idea of progress was at the heart of his life's work, and we should attend to the heuristic value of the "indirect bearings" of his evolutionism at least as carefully as we do to his biological accuracy.

If we still want to fault Spencer's evolutionism, we can easily do so on a number of counts. Even so, the net effect of his influence leads one to reiterate the full text of Darwin's cryptic statement of the most important consequence of his theory. You will recall the sentence, "Light will be thrown on the origin of man and his history." In the sixth edition the preceding sentences read as follows: "In the future I see open fields for far more important researches. Psychology will be securely based on the foundation already well laid by Mr. Herbert Spencer, that of the necessary acquirement of each mental power and capacity by gradation."

EMILE DURKHEIM

David Emile Durkheim (April 15, 1858 – November 15, 1917) was a French sociologist. He formally established the academic discipline and, with Karl Marx and Max Weber, is commonly cited as the principal architect of modern social science. Durkheim set up the first European department of sociology at the University of Bordeaux in 1895, publishing his *Rules of the Sociological Method*. In 1896, he established the journal *L'Annee Sociologique*. Durkheim's seminal monograph, *Suicide* (1897), a study of suicide rates amongst Catholic and Protestant populations, pioneered modern social research and served to distinguish social science from psychology or political philosophy. His classic work, *The Elementary Forms of Religious Life* (1912), compared the socio-cultural lives of aboriginal and modern societies, further establishing his reputation.

Durkheim refined the positivism originally set forth by Auguste Comte, promoting epistemological realism and the hypothetico-deductive model. For him, sociology was the science of institutions, its aim being to discover structural "social facts". Durkheim was a major proponent of structural functionalism, a foundational perspective in both sociology and anthropology. In his view, social science should be purely holistic; that is, sociology should study phenomena attributed to society at large, rather than being limited to the specific actions of individuals.

Durkheim remained a dominant force in French intellectual life until his death in 1917, presenting numerous lectures and published works on a variety of topics, including, the sociology of knowledge, morality, social stratification, religion, law, education, and deviance. Marcel Mauss, a notable social anthropologist of the pre-war era, was his nephew. Durkheimian terms such as "collective conscience" have since entered the popular discourse.

SOCIAL FACT

In sociology, social facts are the values, cultural norms, and social structures external to the individual. For French sociologist Emile Durkheim, sociology was 'the science of social facts'. The task of the sociologist, then, was to search for correlations between social facts to reveal laws. Having discovered the laws of social structure, it is posited that the sociologist is then able to determine whether any given society is 'healthy' or 'pathological' and prescribe appropriate remedies. Durkheim made two main distinctions between social facts—material and nonmaterial social facts. Material social facts, he explained, have to do with the physical social structures which exerts influence on the individual. It is something that can be touched emerging because of society's shared belief that it serves a purpose. Nonmaterial social facts are the values, norms and other conceptually held beliefs. Among the most known of Durkheim's work is his discovery of the 'social fact' of suicide rates. By carefully examining police suicide statistics in different districts, Durkheim was able to 'demonstrate' that the suicide rate of Catholic communities is lower than that of Protestant communities. He ascribed this to a *social* (as opposed to individual) cause. This was considered groundbreaking and remains a much-cited work even today.

Initially, Durkheim's 'discovery of social facts' was seen as significant because it promised to make it possible to study the behaviour of entire societies, rather than just of particular individuals. Modern sociologists refer to Durkheim's studies for two quite different purposes, however:

- As graphic demonstrations of how careful the social researcher must be to ensure that data gathered for analysis is accurate. Durkheim's reported suicide rates were, it is now clear, largely an artifact of the way in which particular deaths were classified as 'suicide' or 'non-suicide' by different communities. What he had actually discovered then was not different *suicide rates* at all—it was different ways of *thinking about suicide.*
- As an entry point into the study of social meaning, and the way in which apparently identical individual acts often cannot be classified empirically. Social *acts* (even such an apparently private and individual act as suicide), in this modern view, are always seen (and classified) by social *actors*. Discovering the 'social facts', it follows, is generally neither possible nor desirable, but discovering the way in which individuals perceive and classify particular acts is what offers insight.

A total social fact [fait social total] is "an activity that has implications throughout society, in the economic, legal, political, and religious spheres." (Sedgewick 2002: 95) "Diverse strands of social and psychological life are woven together through what he [Marcel Mauss] comes to call 'total social facts'. A total social fact is such that it informs and organises seemingly quite distinct practices and institutions." The term was popularized by Marcel Mauss in his classic The Gift where he wrote, "These phenomena are at once legal, economic, religious, aesthetic, morphological and so on. They are legal in that they concern individual and collective rights, organized and diffuse morality; they may be entirely obligatory, or subject simply to praise or disapproval. They are at once political and domestic, being of interest both to classes and to clans and families. They are religious; they concern true religion, animism, magic and diffuse religious mentality. They are economic, for the notions of value, utility, interest, luxury, wealth, acquisition, accumulation, consumption and liberal and sumptuous expenditure are all present...".

THE DIVISION OF LABOUR IN SOCIETY

The Division of Labour in Society is the dissertation of French sociologist Emile Durkheim, written in 1893. It was influential in advancing sociological theories and thought, with ideas which in turn were influenced by Auguste Comte. Durkheim described how social order was maintained in societies based on two very different forms of solidarity (mechanical and organic), and the transition from more "primitive" societies to advanced industrial societies.

Durkheim suggested that in a "primitive" society, *mechanical solidarity,* with people acting and thinking alike and with a collective or common conscience, is what allows social order to be maintained. In such a society, Durkheim viewed crime as an act that "offends strong and defined states of the collective conscience." Because social ties were relatively homogeneous and weak throughout society, the law had to be repressive and penal, to respond to offences of the common conscience.

In an advanced, industrial, capitalist society, the complex division of labour means that people are allocated in society according to merit and rewarded accordingly: social inequality reflects natural inequality. Durkheim argued that moral regulation was needed, as well as economic regulation, to maintain order (or *organic solidarity*) in society with people able to "compose their differences peaceably". In this type of society, law would be more restitory than penal, seeking to restore rather than punish excessively.

He thought that transition of a society from "primitive" to advanced may bring about major disorder, crisis, and anomie. However, once society has reached the "advanced" stage, it becomes much stronger and is done developing. Unlike Karl Marx, Durkheim did not foresee any different society arising out of the industrial capitalist division of labour. He regards conflict, chaos, and disorder as pathological phenomena to modern society, whereas Marx highlights class conflict.

SUICIDE (BOOK)

Suicide was one of the groundbreaking books in the field of sociology. Written by French sociologist Emile Durkheim and published in 1897 it was a case study of suicide, a publication unique for its time which provided an example of what the sociological monograph should look like.

Findings

Durkheim established that:

- Suicide rates are higher in men than women (although married women who remained childless for a number of years ended up with a high suicide rate)
- Suicide rates are higher for those who are single than those who are married
- Suicide rates are higher for people without children than people with children
- Suicide rates are higher among Protestants than Catholics and Jews
- Suicide rates are higher among soldiers than civilians
- Suicide rates are higher in times of peace than in times of war (the suicide rate in France fell after the *coup d'etat* of Louis Bonaparte, for example. War also reduced the suicide rate, after war broke out in 1866 between Austria and Italy, the suicide rate fell by 14% in both countries.)
- Suicide rates are higher in Scandinavian countries
- the higher the education level, the more likely it was that an individual would commit suicide, however Durkheim established that religion was more important than education; Jewish people were generally highly educated but had a low suicide rate.

Types of Suicide

- Egoistic suicide reflects a prolonged sense of not belonging, of not being integrated in a community, an experience, of not having a tether, an absence that can give rise to meaninglessness, apathy, melancholy, and depression.

- Altruistic suicide: is characterized by a sense of being overwhelmed by a group's goals and beliefs.
- Anomic suicide: reflects an individual's moral confusion and lack of social direction, which is related to dramatic social and economic upheaval.
- Fatalistic suicide: the opposite of anomic suicide, when a person is excessively regulated, when their futures are pitilessly blocked and passions violently choked by oppressive discipline.

RULES OF THE SOCIOLOGICAL METHOD

Rules of the Sociological Method, is a book by Emile Durkheim, first published in 1895. It is recognized for being the direct result of Durkheim's own project of establishing sociology as a positivist social science. It thus suggests two central theses, without which sociology would not be a science:

1. It must have a specific object of study. Unlike philosophy or psychology, sociology's proper object of study is the social fact.
2. It must respect and apply a recognized objective, scientific method, bringing it as close as possible to the other exact sciences. This method must at all cost avoid prejudice and subjective judgment.

SOCIAL FACTS AND SUICIDE

Durkheim defined social facts as things external to, and coercive of, the actor. These are created from collective forces and do not emanate from the individual. While they may not seem to be observable, social facts are things, and "are to be studied empirically, *not* philosophically". They cannot be deduced from pure reason or thought, but require a study of history and society in order to observe their effects and understand the nature of these social facts. In *The Rules of Sociological Method*, Durkheim begins by noting features such as the following (quote 3):

Social Facts. When I fulfil my obligations as brother, husband, or citizen, when I execute my contracts, I perform duties which are defined, externally to myself and my acts, in law and in custom. Even if they conform to my own sentiments and I feel their reality subjectively, such reality is still objective, for I did not create them; I merely inherited them through my education. As examples of social facts, Durkheim cites religious beliefs, currency used to undertake transactions, and factors such as "the practices followed in my profession".

These types of conduct or thought are not only external to the individual but are, moreover, endowed with coercive power, by virtue of which they impose themselves upon him, independent of his individual will..

While obligations, values, attitudes, and beliefs may appear to be individual, Durkheim argues that these social facts exist at the level of society as a whole, arising from social relationships and human association. They exist as a result of social interactions and historical developments over long periods of time, and come from "varying collective representations and diverse forms of social organization". As individuals who are born and raised in a society, these social facts are learned (through socialization) and generally accepted, but the individual has nothing to do with establishing these.

While society is composed of individuals, society is not just the sum of individuals, and these facts exist at the level of society, not at the individual level. As such, these social facts do exist, they are the social reality of society, a reality that constitutes the proper study of sociology. The study of social facts is the "distinct object or subject matter of sociology". Durkheim distinguishes social facts from psychological, biological, or economic facts by noting that these are social and rooted in group sentiments and values. At the same time, he distinguishes the study of social facts from philosophy by noting that the real effects of social facts are "manifested in external indicators of sentiments such as religious doctrines, laws, moral codes" and these effects can be observed and studied by the sociologist. The study of social facts is thus a large part of the study of sociology. In order to do this, the sociologist must "rid themselves of preconceptions" and undertake objective study which can "focus on objective, external indicators such as religious doctrines or laws".

Each social fact is real, something that is constraining on the individual and external to the actor. The social fact is not just in the mind of the individual – that is, these facts are more than psychological facts. That these exist in society as a whole, over time, and sometimes across societies, provides some proof of this. At the same time they are in the minds of individuals so they are also mental states. Ritzer notes that social facts can be considered to be mental phenomena that are external to and coercive of psychological facts, such as human instincts. The individual mental state could be considered to intervene between social fact and action. Durkheim may not have provided a sufficient analysis of the assumptions underlying, or the characteristics of, these mental states. For Durkheim the study of sociology should be the study of social facts, attempting to find the causes of social facts and the functions of these social facts.

Social facts regulate human social action and act as constraints over individual behaviour and action. They may be enforced with law, with clearly defined penalties associated with violation of the sentiments and values of the group. Sanctions may be associated with social facts, for example as in religion, where resistance may result in disapproval from others or from spiritual leaders. Individuals may be unaware of social facts and generally accept them. In this case, individuals may accept the values and codes of society and accept them as their own.

Two types of social facts are material and non-material social facts. Material social facts are features of society such as social structures and institutions. These could be the system of law, the economy, church and many aspects of religion, the state, and educational institutions and structures. They could also include features such as channels of communication, urban structures, and population distribution. While these are important for understanding the structures and form of interaction in any society, it is nonmaterial social facts that constitute the main subject of study of sociology.

Nonmaterial social facts are social facts which do not have a material reality. They consist of features such as norms, values, and systems of morality. Some contemporary examples are the norm of the one to three child family, the positive values associated with family structures, and the negative associations connected to aggression and anger. In Durkheim's terminology, some of these nonmaterial social facts are morality, collective consciousness, and social currents. An example of the latter is Durkheim's analysis of suicide.

Social facts can also be divided into normal and pathological social facts. Normal social facts are the most widely distributed and useful social facts, assisting in the maintenance of society and social life. Pathological social facts are those that we might associate with social problems and ills of various types. Suicide is one example of this, where social facts ought to be different. For Durkheim, the much greater frequency of the normal is proof of the superiority of the normal.

Durkheim later modified the notion of a single collective consciousness, and adopted the view that there were collective representations as part of specific states of substrata of the collective. That is, there may be different norms and values for different groups within society. These collective representations are also social facts because they are in the consciousness of some collective and are not reducible to individual consciousnesses. The social structures, institutions, norms and values that have become part of the study of sociology can be derived from Durkheim's approach, and today there is little difficulty distinguishing sociology from psychology.

Suicide

After Durkheim wrote *The Rules of Sociological Method*, he tackled the subject of suicide as an example of how a sociologist can study a subject that seems extremely personal, with no social aspect to it – even being anti-social. It could be argued that suicide is such a personal act that it involves only personal psychology and purely individual thought processes. Durkheim's aim was not to explain or predict an individual tendency to suicide, but to explain one type of nonmaterial social facts, social currents. Social currents are characteristics of society, but may not have the permanence and stability that some parts of collective consciousness or collective representation have. They may be associated with movements such as "enthusiasm, indignation, and pity.". Hadden notes that Durkheim wished to show that sociological factors were "capable of explaining much about such anti-social phenomena".

In the case of suicide, these social currents are expressed as suicide rates, rates that differ among societies, and among different groups in society. These rates show regularities over time, with changes in the rates often occurring at similar times in different societies. Thus these rates can be said to be social facts (or at least the statistical representation of social facts) in the sense that they are not just personal, but are societal characteristics. This can be seen in the following quote (quote 12):

Suicide Rates as Social Facts. At each moment of its history, therefore, each society has a definite aptitude for suicide. The relative intensity of this aptitude is measured by taking the proportion between the total number of voluntary deaths and the population of every age and sex. We will call this numerical datum *the rate of mortality through suicide, characteristic of the society under consideration*.... The suicide-rate is therefore a factual order, unified and definite, as is shown by both its permanence and its variability. For this permanence would be inexplicable if it were not the result of a group of distinct characteristics, solidary with one another, and simultaneously effective in spite of different attendant circumstances; and this variability proves the concrete and individual quality of these same characteristics, since they vary with the individual character of society itself. In short, these statistical data express the suicidal tendency with which each society is collectively afflicted.... Each society is predisposed to contribute a definite quota of voluntary deaths. This predisposition may therefore be the subject of a special study belonging to sociology.

Durkheim takes up the analysis of suicide in a very quantitative and statistical manner. While he did not have available to him very precise or complete data or sophisticated statistical techniques, his method is exemplary in showing how to test hypotheses, reject incorrect explanations for suicide, sort through a great variety of possible explanations, and attempt to control for extraneous factors. Some of the factors that others had used to explain suicide were heredity, climate, race, individual psychopathic states (mental illness), and imitation.

As an example of Durkheim's method, consider how he analyzes cosmic factors, such as weather or season. Durkheim notes that in all countries suicide is greater in the summer months, that no country is an exception to this, and that the proportion of suicides in the six warmer months to the six colder months is very similar in each country. Durkheim notes that this has led some commentators to say the "heat increases the excitability of the nervous system". But suicide may result from depression as much as from over-excitement, and heat cannot possibly act the same way on both causes. Further, a closer analysis by Durkheim considers temperature variations and shows that while suicides increase in number as temperature increases, suicides reach a peak before the temperature does. In addition, if temperature is a cause of suicide, warm countries might be expected to have more suicides than cold countries, but the opposite tends to be the case.

A related explanation that Durkheim considers is that great changes in temperature are associated with suicide, but again he finds that there is no correlation between suicide rates and the fact of temperature change. Rather, the causes must be in some factor that has continuity over time. He then notes that the rates are more closely connected to the length of day, with suicides increasing as the days grow longer, and decreasing in number as the length of day declines. But it is not the sun itself which is the cause, because at noontime there are fewer suicides than at other times of the day. What Durkheim finds is that the factors associated with higher numbers of suicides must be those that relate to "the time when social life is at its height". The time of day, the day of week, the season of the year, and so on, are not in themselves the reason for the changes in the number of suicides. Rather, the times when social life and interaction among people are greater, are also those associated with increased suicide. Durkheim concludes this section by saying (quote 13):

Social Explanation. If voluntary deaths increase from January to July, it is not because heat disturbs the organism, but because social life is more intense. To be sure, this greater intensity derives from the greater ease of development of social life in the Summer than in the Winter, owing to the sun's position..., the state of the atmosphere, etc. But the physical environment does not stimulate it directly; above all, it has no effect on the progression of suicide. The latter depends on social conditions.. While this is not a proof or determination of what causes suicide yet, Durkheim notes that the causes must relate to collective life and must be such that these time factors can be incorporated into an explanation. But the explanation must be social in nature, and cannot be simply related to natural factors, these natural factors must work socially, and affect some social aspects which are related to suicide.

Note that Durkheim 's method here is very empirical, and he searches through various sorts of data and evidence to find factors associated with suicide. But the explanation is not simply a relation between these data and suicides. Rather he is searching for social causes or conditions that are expressed through these. That is, he uses data to discover patterns, but the patterns themselves are not the cause of the phenomenon. Rather the cause is social, and the observed, empirical patterns constitute a means of finding underlying causes.

Another factor that Durkheim considers is religion. While he does find that religion is associated with suicide, in the sense that Protestant countries and regions have higher suicide rates than do Catholic ones, religious doctrines are not an important factor in explaining these differences. That is, suicide is condemned more or less equally in each religion, and doctrinal statements concerning suicide are all negative. If there is a difference between the two religions with respect to suicide rates, it must be in some aspect of social organization that differs between the two churches. But if this is the factor related to suicide, then it is the social organization that is the cause of the difference, not religion in itself. Giddens notes that Durkheim finds further proof of this in other factors related to social organization, that is, family structure. Where there is more integration in family structure, the suicides are lesser in number.

Durkheim argues that the most important aspects of social organization and collective life for explaining differences in suicide rates are the degree of integration into and regulation by society. For Durkheim, integration is the "degree to which collective sentiments are shared" and regulation refers to "the degree of external constraint on people.". Catholicism is a more highly integrated religion than Protestantism, and it is in this that the difference in suicide rates is expressed. That is, it is not the religious doctrines themselves but the different social organization of the two religions. As Giddens notes, degree of integration of family structure is related in the same way to suicides. Those in larger families are less likely to commit suicide, whereas those in smaller families, or single, are more likely.

Over time, various social factors also make their influence felt. Durkheim notes that there was a decline in the number of suicides in all the European countries in 1848, a year of revolution and political change throughout Europe. Times of political crisis, war, and economic change are also associated with changes in the rate of suicide. Each of these great social movements could be considered to be examples of social currents that have widespread impact within and across societies.

Ritzer notes that Durkheim was making two arguments. First, he argued that different collectivities have different collective consciousness or collective representation. These produce different social currents, and these lead to different suicide rates. By studying different groups and societies, some of these currents can be analyzed, and the effect of these on suicide can be determined. Second, changes in the collective consciousness lead to changes in social currents. These are then associated with changes in suicide rates (quote 14):

Sociological Explanation. The conclusion from all these facts is that the social suicide-rate can be explained only sociologically. At any given moment the moral constitution of society established the contingent of voluntary deaths. There is, therefore, for each people a collective force of a definite amount of energy, impelling men to self-destruction. The victim's acts which at first seem to express only his personal temperament are really the supplement and prolongation of a social condition which they express externally.

... Each social group really has a collective inclination for the act, quite its own, and the source of all individual inclination, rather than the result. It is made up of the currents of egoism, altruism or anomy running through the society under consideration with the tendencies to languorous melancholy, active renunciation or exasperated weariness derivative from these currents. These tendencies of the whole social body, by affecting individuals, cause them to commit suicide. The private experiences usually thought to be the proximate causes of suicide have only the influence borrowed from the victim's moral predisposition, itself and echo of the moral state of society..

Four Types of Suicide

The manner in which social integration and regulation work can be better seen by examining the four fold classification of suicides that Durkheim developed. Durkheim ends his discussion of the organic-psychic and physical environmental factors by concluding that they cannot explain "each social group[s]... specific tendency to suicide.". By eliminating other explanations, Durkheim claims that these tendencies must depend on social causes and must be collective phenomena. The key to each type is a social factor, with the degrees of integration and regulation into society being either too high or too low.

Egoistic Suicide. This is the type of suicide that occurs where the degree of social integration is low, and there is a sense of meaningless among individuals. In traditional societies, with mechanical solidarity, this is not likely to be the cause of suicide. There the strong collective consciousness gives people a broad sense of meaning to their lives. Within modern society, the weaker collective consciousness means that people may not see the same meaning in their lives, and unrestrained pursuit of individual interests may lead to strong dissatisfaction. One of the results of this can be suicide. Individuals who are strongly integrated into a family structure, a religious group, or some other type of integrative group are less likely to encounter these problems, and that explains the lower suicide rates among them.

The factors leading to egoistic suicide can be social currents such as depression and disillusionment. For Durkheim, these are social forces or social facts, even though it is the depressed or melancholy individual who takes his or her life voluntarily. "Actors are *never* free of the force of the collectivity: 'However individualized a man may be, there is always something collective remaining – the very depression and melancholy resulting from this same exaggerated individualism.'" Also, on p. 214 of *Suicide*, Durkheim says "Thence are formed currents of depression and disillusionment emanating from no particular individual but expressing society's state of disillusionment." Durkheim notes that "the bond attaching man to life relaxes because that attaching him to society is itself slack.... The individual yields to the slightest shock of circumstance because the state of society has made him a ready prey to suicide."

Altruistic Suicide. This is the type of suicide that occurs when integration is too great, the collective consciousness too strong, and the "individual is forced into committing suicide." Integration may not be the direct cause of suicide here, but the social currents that go along with this very high degree of integration can lead to this.

The followers of Jim Jones of the People's Temple or the members of the Solar Temple are an example of this, as are ritual suicides in Japan. Ritzer notes that some may "feel it is their duty" to commit suicide. Examples in primitive society cited by Durkheim are suicides of those who are old and sick, suicides of women following the death of their husband, and suicides of followers after the death of a chief. According to Durkheim this type of suicide may actually "springs from hope, for it depends on the belief in beautiful perspectives beyond this life."

Anomic Suicide. Anomie or anomy come from the Greek meaning lawlessness. *Nomos* means usage, custom, or law and *nemein* means to distribute. Anomy thus is social instability resulting from breakdown of standards and values.

This is a type of suicide related to too low a degree of regulation, or external constraint on people. As with the anomic division of labour, this can occur when the normal form of the division of labour is disrupted, and "the collectivity is temporarily incapable of exercising its authority over individuals." This can occur either during periods associated with economic depression (stock market crash of the 1930s) or over-rapid economic expansion. New situations with few norms, the regulative effect of structures is weakened, and the individual may feel rootless. In this situation, an individual may be subject to anomic social currents. People that are freed from constraints become "slaves to their passions, and as a result, according to Durkheim's view, commit a wide range of destructive acts, including killing themselves in greater numbers than they ordinarily would." In addition to economic anomie, Durkheim also spends time examining domestic anomie. For example, suicides of family members may occur after the death of a husband or wife.

Fatalistic Suicide. When regulation is too strong, Durkheim considers the possibility that "persons with futures pitilessly blocked and passions violently choked by oppressive discipline" may see no way out. The individual sees no possible manner in which their lives can be improved, and when in a state of melancholy, may be subject to social currents of fatalistic suicide.

Summary. Durkheim's analysis of suicide shows the manner in which the social as opposed to the psychological and biological can be emphasized, and how it results in some useful ways of analyzing the actions of individuals. Suicide rates as expressions of social currents are social facts that affect societies and individuals within those societies. The study of psychology is still useful in attempting to determine individual motives and the manner in which the specific circumstances can lead to an individual deciding to voluntarily end their life. But an analysis of these circumstances should be set within the context of the social currents to which that individual is subject.

The method of analysis of Durkheim should prove useful even today. In terms of suicide, the social causes are now well recognized, and any analysis of suicide would have to include these. Some combination of egoistic, anomic, and fatalistic types of suicide may help explain and understand this phenomenon. More generally, the method of *Suicide* is exemplary in providing researchers with a means of understanding the social factors that are associated with particular phenomena. Durkheim examines patterns on the data in an attempt to determine how social factors can play a role in explaining these phenomena. This might be applied to sociobiological arguments today. The trends themselves are not the cause, but indicative of a cause, a social explanation has to be found.

CONCLUSIONS ABOUT DURKHEIM

Social Facts and Social Aspects. These are real things that do affect people. He had a strong structural view of society, and the manner in which each of us is influenced by these social facts and how we must fit into these. Durkheim attempted to see a role for the social as distinguished from the economic, psychological and biological. This can be seen in his view of the social influences on suicide rates, where he takes a wide variety of factors and considers their influence on the tendency or aptitude for suicide. The effect of each of these factors is not a simple connection between the factor and the tendency to suicide, but must be mediated by social factors. In particular, the social factors that he identified were the degree of integration and the degree of regulation. For modern theories of sociobiology, and the influence of genetics, Durkheim's approach could prove a useful counter.

Division of Labour and forms of solidarity. Durkheim again shows how the division of labour is set within a social context, so that economic relationships are governed by social conventions that may not always be apparent. Durkheim's view that the division of labour does not result in a disintegration of society, but changes the form of social solidarity provides a useful way of examining modern society.

The last few pages of Giddens' discussion of Durkheim examines individuality and individual freedom within an overall structure. Durkheim notes that individualism is a product of long historical developments within western society, with the French Revolution giving a "decisive impetus to the growth of moral individualism." Part of this view is the sanctity of the individual, the worth of the human individual, individual rights and the encouragement of individual action and initiative. But Durkheim notes that these themselves are social facts in the sense that these ideas are social products, created by society. Durkheim further argues that they are not the product of egoism, that is, self-interest as the basic motivation for human action. While the development of individualism will promote self-interest and egoism, this is not the source of individualism, and an unchecked development of egoism would destroy society. This is not what happens though, except perhaps under exceptional circumstances.

What Durkheim argues is that freedom is not to be identified with liberation from all restraints, this results in anomie. Rather, freedom exists in being "master of oneself" by "putting oneself under the wing of society." That is, freedom is achieved within a set of moral rules, and discipline within this set of rules is an essential aspect of freedom. The notion of rights and responsibilities may be a means of tying these together.

Sociological Approaches. Many of common approaches to sociology derive from Durkheim. The method of attempting to determine social facts and their influence, along with concepts such as norms, values, socialization, institutions, etc. could be considered to come at least partly from Durkheim.

Problems

At the same time as Durkheim made a number of important contributions to sociology, there are a number of problems with his analysis. Some of these are as follows.

Action. As noted above, Durkheim has a particular view of human freedom and this may be regarded as too limited. Or even if this approach is adopted, it is not clear what is the basis for individual human motivation and action. Durkheim's view is a very strong structural view. Society and social facts more or less determine our behaviour, and we have little option but to accept those. He favours such an approach, and considers deviations from this as abnormal. This could allow his approach to be used to identify any behaviour that is not part of the common morality as abnormal and perhaps deviant, something that has to be corrected or eliminated. For example, immigrants, youth culture, etc.

While there are many aspects of a common morality in our society, there are also many opportunities for individuals acting in a variety of ways in similar situations. Durkheim might recognize this as possible, but he seems to have little to say concerning the nature of human motivation. He is too concerned with the larger structural issues. Durkheim and Marx are similar in this sense, they both have a very strong structural view, with limited possibility for human action, or little theory of human action. Weber's model of action or some of the more recent approaches such as symbolic interaction would prove more useful here.

Consensus, Solidarity and Common Consciousness. While Durkheim makes a useful contribution in presenting ideas concerning the source of societal solidarity, this often appears to be his only concern. One difficulty with Durkheim and the structural functional approach is that the latter almost completely ignore conflict and power differences. Durkheim may have constructed his approach in part to negate the Marxian or conflict approach to the study of society. Durkheim treats the anomic and forced forms of the division of labour as unusual, and devotes little time to their analysis.

FERDINAND TÖNNIES

Ferdinand Tönnies (26 July 1855, near Oldenswort (Eiderstedt, North Frisia)-9 April 1936, Kiel, Germany) was a German sociologist. He was a major contributor to sociological theory and field studies, best known for his distinction between two types of social groups, Gemeinschaft and Gesellschaft. He was also a prolific writer and co-founder of the German Society for Sociology (being its president 1909-1933, when he was ousted by the Nazis).

Life

Ferdinand Tönnies was born into a wealthy farmer's family in Nordfriesland in Schleswig-Holstein, then under Danish rule. He studied at the universities of Jena, Bonn, Leipzig, Berlin, and Tübingen. He received a doctorate in Tübingen in 1877 (with a Latin thesis on the ancient Siwa Oasis). Four years later he became a private lecturer at the University of Kiel. Because he had sympathized with the Hamburg dockers' strike of 1896, the conservative Prussian government considered him to be a social democrat, and Tönnies was not called to a professorial chair until 1913. He held this post at the university of Kiel for only three years. He returned to the university as a professor emeritus in 1921 and taught until 1933 when he was ousted by the Nazis, due to his earlier publications that criticized them.

Tönnies, the first German sociologist proper, published over 900 works and contributed to many areas of sociology and philosophy. Many of his writings on sociological theories — including *Gemeinschaft und Gesellschaft* (1887) — furthered pure sociology. He coined the term *Voluntarism*. Tönnies also contributed to the study of social change, particularly on public opinion, customs and technology, crime, and suicide. He also had a vivid interest in methodology, especially statistics, and sociological research, inventing his own technique of statistical association.

Gemeinschaft and Gesellschaft

Tönnies distinguished between two types of social groupings. *Gemeinschaft* — often translated as *community* (or left untranslated)— refers to groupings based on feelings of togetherness and on mutual bonds, which are felt as a goal to be kept up, their members being means for this goal. *Gesellschaft* — often translated as *society* — on the other hand, refers to groups that are sustained by it being instrumental for their members' individual aims and goals.

Gemeinschaft may be exemplified historically by a family or a neighborhood in a pre-modern (rural) society; *Gesellschaft* by a joint-stock company or a state in a modern society, i.e. the society when Tönnies lived. *Gesellschaft* relationships arose in an urban and capitalist setting, characterized by individualism and impersonal monetary connections between people. Social ties were often instrumental and superficial, with selfinterest and exploitation increasingly the norm. Examples are corporations, states, or voluntary associations.

His distinction between social groupings is based on the assumption that there are only two basic forms of an actor's will, to approve of other men. (For Tönnies, such an approval is by no means self-evident, he is quite influenced by Thomas Hobbes). Following his "essential will" ("*Wesenwille*"), an actor will see himself as a means to serve the goals of social grouping; very often it is an underlying, subconscious force. Groupings formed around an essential will are called a *Gemeinschaft*. The other will is the "arbitrary will" ("*Kürwille*"): An actor sees a social grouping as a means to further his individual goals; so it is purposive and future-oriented. Groupings around the latter are called *Gesellschaft*. Whereas the membership in a *Gemeinschaft* is self-fulfilling, a *Gesellschaft* is instrumental for its members. In pure sociology — theoretically —, these two normal types of will are to be strictly separated; in applied sociology — empirically — they are always mixed.

Tönnies' distinction between *Gemeinschaft* and *Gesellschaft*, like others between tradition and modernity, has been criticized for over-generalizing differences between societies, and implying that all societies were following a similar evolutionary path, which he has never proclaimed.

GEMEINSCHAFT AND GESELLSCHAFT

Gemeinschaft are sociological categories introduced by the German sociologist Ferdinand Tönnies for two normal types of human association. (A *normal type*, as coined by Tönnies, is a purely conceptual tool to be built up logically, whereas an *ideal type*, as coined by Max Weber, is a concept formed by accentuating main elements of a historic/social change.) *Gemeinschaft und Gesellschaft* sparked a major revival of corporatist thinking including sparking the rise of Neo-medievalism, rise of support for guild socialism, and caused major changes in the field of sociology.

Tönnies' concepts of both terms *"Gemeinschaft und Gesellschaft"* were published first 1887. Seven more German editions came out during his life time, the last 1935. The second edition of 1912 turned out to be an unexpected but lasting success, and the antagonism of these two terms belonged to the general stock of concepts German pre-1933 intellectuals were quite familiar with and quite often misunderstood.

Gemeinschaft

Gemeinschaft (often translated as *community*) is an association in which individuals are oriented to the large association as much if not more than to their own self interest. Furthermore, individuals in Gemeinschaft are regulated by common mores, or beliefs about the appropriate behaviour and responsibility of members of the association, to each other and to the association at large; associations marked by "unity of will" (Tönnies, 22). Tönnies saw the family as the most perfect expression of Gemeinschaft; however, he expected that Gemeinschaft could be based on shared place and shared belief as well as kinship, and he included globally dispersed religious communities as possible examples of Gemeinschaft. Gemeinschaft community is ascribed status. You are given a status by birth. For example, born of farmer, will stay a farmer until death.

Gemeinschaften are broadly characterized by a moderate division of labour, strong personal relationships, strong families, and relatively simple social institutions. In such societies there is seldom a need to enforce social control externally, due to a collective sense of loyalty individuals feel for society.

Gesellschaft

In contrast, *Gesellschaft* (often translated as *society* or *civil society* or 'association') describes associations in which, for the individual, the larger association never takes on more importance than the individual's self interest, and lack the same level of shared mores. Gesellschaft is maintained through individuals acting in their own self interest. A modern business is a good example of Gesellschaft, the workers, managers, and owners may have very little in terms of shared orientations or beliefs, they may not care deeply for the product they are making, but it is in all their self interest to come to work to make money, and thus the business continues. Gesellschaft society is achieved status. You reach your status by education and work. I.e. University.

Unlike *Gemeinschaften*, *Gesellschaften* emphasize secondary relationships rather than familial or community ties, and there is generally less individual loyalty to society. Social cohesion in *Gesellschaften* typically derives from a more elabourate division of labour. Such societies are considered more susceptible to class conflict as well as racial and ethnic conflicts. The sociological upheavals during the Reconstruction era of the United States complicated the sociological category of *Gemeinschaft* because former slaves, whose kinship ties were complicated under slavery, forged new communities that shared aspects of both *Gemeinschaft* and *Gesellschaft*.

Since, for Tönnies, *Gemeinschaft* and *Gesellschaft* are *normal types*, he considered them a matter of Pure Sociology, whereas in Applied Sociology, on doing empirical research, he expected to find nothing else than a mix of them. Nevertheless, following Tönnies, without *normal types* one might not be able to analyze this mix.

5

Pioneer Thinkers

DIALECTICAL MATERIALISM

Dialectical materialism is a strand of Marxist theorizing, composed of a synthesis of Hegel's dialectics and Ludwig Andreas Feuerbach's materialism, based upon an interpretation of Karl Marx's work. According to certain followers of Karl Marx's thinking, it is the philosophical basis of Marxism, although this remains a controversial assertion due to the disputed status of science and naturalism in Marx's thought. The basic idea of dialectical materialism is that every economic order grows to a state of maximum efficiency, while at the same time developing internal contradictions or weaknesses that contribute to its decay.

The Term

Dialectical materialism was coined in 1887 by Joseph Dietzgen, a socialist tanner who corresponded with Marx both during and after the failed 1848 German Revolution. Dietzgen had himself constructed dialectical materialism independently of Marx and Friedrich Engels. Casual mention of the term is also found in Kautsky's *Frederick Engels*, written in the same year. Marx himself had talked about the "materialist conception of history", which was later referred to as "historical materialism" by Engels. Engels further exposed the "materialist dialectic" — not "dialectical materialism" — in his *Dialectics of Nature* in 1883. Georgi Plekhanov, the father of Russian Marxism, later introduced the term dialectical materialism to Marxist literature. Joseph Stalin further codified it as *Diamat* and imposed it as the doctrine of Marxism-Leninism.

The term was not used by Marx in any of his works, and the actual presence of "dialectical materialism" within his thought remains the subject of significant controversy, particularly regarding the relationship between dialectics, ontology and nature. For scholars working on these issues from a variety of perspectives see the works of Bertell Ollman, Chris Arthurs, Roger Albritton, and Roy Bhaskar.

Aspects

Dialectical materialism originates from two major aspects of Marx's philosophy. One is his transformation of Hegel's idealistic understanding of dialectics into a materialist one, an act commonly said to have "put Hegel's dialectics back on its feet". Marx's materialism developed through his engagement with Feuerbach. Marx sought to base human social organization within the context of the material reproduction of their daily lives, which he calls sensous practice in his early works (Marx 1844, 1845). From this material context men develop certain ideas about their world, thereby leading to the core materialist conception that social being determines social consciousness. The dialectical aspect retains the Hegelian method within this materialist framework, and emphasizes the process of historical change arising from contradiction and class struggle based in a particular social context.

Hegel

Dialectical materialism is essentially characterized by the thesis that history is the product of class struggles and follows the general Hegelian principle of philosophy of history, that is the development of the thesis into its antithesis which is sublated by the *Aufhebung* ("synthesis"). The term *Aufhebung* was not used by Hegel to describe his dialectics. The *Aufhebung* conserves the thesis and the antithesis and transcends them both (*Aufheben* — this contradiction explains the difficulties of Hegel's thought). Hegel's dialectics aims to explain the development of human history. He considered that truth was the product of history and that it passed through various moments, including the moment of error; error and negativity are part of the development of truth. Hegel's idealism considered history a product of the Spirit (Geist or also Zeitgeist — the

"Spirit of the Time"). By contrast, Marx's dialectical materialism considers history as a product of material class struggle in society. Thus, theory has its roots in the materiality of social existence.

Materialism in Dialectical Materialism

Marx's doctoral thesis concerned the atomism of Epicurus and Democritus, which (along with stoicism) is considered the foundation of materialist philosophy.

Marx was also familiar with Lucretius's theory of clinamen. Materialism asserts the primacy of the material world: in short, matter precedes thought. Materialism is a realist philosophy of science, which holds that the world is material; that all phenomena in the universe consist of "matter in motion," wherein all things are interdependent and interconnected and develop according to natural law; that the world exists outside us and independently of our perception of it; that thought is a reflection of the material world in the brain, and that the world is *in principle* knowable.

"The ideal is nothing else than the material world reflected by the human mind, and translated into forms of thought." — Karl Marx, *Das Kapital*, Vol. 1.

Marx endorsed this materialist philosophy against Hegel's idealism; he "turned Hegel's dialectics upside down." However, Marx also criticized classical materialism as another idealist philosophy due to its transhistorical understanding of material contexts. According to the famous *Theses on Feuerbach* (1845), philosophy had to stop "interpreting" the world in endless metaphysical debates, in order to start "changing" the world, as was being done by the rising workers' movement observed by Engels in England (Chartist movement) and by Marx in France and Germany.

Thus, dialectical materialists tend to accord primacy to class struggle. The ultimate sense of Marx's materialist philosophy is that philosophy itself must take a position in the class struggle based on objective analysis of physical and social relations. Otherwise, it will be reduced to spiritualist idealism, such as the philosophies of Kant or Hegel, which are only ideologies, that is the material product of social existence.

Dialectics in Dialectical Materialism

Dialectics is the science of the general and abstract laws of the development of nature, society, and thought. Its principal features are:

- The universe is an integral whole in which things are interdependent, rather than a mixture of things isolated from each other.
- The natural world or cosmos is in a state of constant motion:

"All nature, from the smallest thing to the biggest, from a grain of sand to the sun, from the protista to man, is in a constant state of coming into being and going out of being, in a constant flux, in a ceaseless state of movement and change." —Friedrich Engels, *Dialectics of Nature*.

- Development is a process whereby insignificant and imperceptible quantitative changes lead to fundamental, qualitative changes. Qualitative changes occur not gradually, but rapidly and abruptly, as leaps from one state to another. A simple example from the physical world is the heating of water: a one degree increase in temperature is a quantitative change, but between water of 100 degrees and steam of 100 degrees (the effect latent heat) there is a qualitative change.

"Merely quantitative differences, beyond a certain point, pass into qualitative changes." —Karl Marx, *Capital*, Vol. 1.

- All things contain within themselves internal dialectical contradictions, which are the primary cause of motion, change, and development in the world. It is important to note that 'dialectical contradiction' is not about simple 'opposites' or 'negation'. For formal approaches, the core message of 'dialectical opposition / contradiction' must be understood as 'some sense' opposition between the objects involved in a directly associated context.

For the application of the dialectic to history see Historical materialism.

Engels' Laws of Dialectics

As mentioned above, Engels determined three laws of dialectics from his reading of Hegel's Science of Logic. Engels elucidated these laws in his work Dialectics of Nature:

1. The law of the unity and conflict of opposites;
2. The law of the passage of quantitative changes into qualitative changes;
3. The law of the negation of the negation.

The first law was seen by both Hegel and Lenin as the central feature of a dialectical understanding of things and originates with the ancient Ionian philosopher Heraclitus.

The second law Hegel took from Aristotle, and it is equated with what scientists call phase transitions. It may be traced to the ancient Ionian philosophers (particularly Anaximenes), from whom Aristotle, Hegel and Engels inherited the concept. For all these authors, one of the main illustrations is the phase transitions of water. There has also been an effort to apply this mechanism to social phenomena, whereby population increases result in changes in social structure. The law of the passage of quantitative changes into qualitative changes can also be applied to the process of social change and class conflict..

The third law is Hegel's own. It was the expression through which (amongst other things) Hegel's dialectic became fashionable during his life-time. In drawing up these laws, Engels presupposes a holistic approach outlined above and in Lenin's three elements of dialectic below, and emphasizes elsewhere that all things are in motion.

Lenin's Elements of Dialectics

After reading Hegel's Science of Logic in 1914, Lenin made some brief notes outlining three "elements" of logic. They are:

1. The determination of the concept out of itself [the thing itself must be considered in its relations and in its development];
2. The contradictory nature of the thing itself (the other of itself), the contradictory forces and tendencies in each phenomenon;
3. The union of analysis and synthesis.

Such apparently are the elements of dialectics. — *Lenin, Summary of dialectics*

Lenin develops these in a further series of notes, and appears to argue that "the transition of quantity into quality and vice versa" is an example of the unity and opposition of opposites expressed tentatively as "not only the unity of opposites, but the transitions of every determination, quality, feature, side, property into every other [into its opposite?]."

HISTORY OF DIALECTICAL MATERIALISM

Dialectical materialism was first elabourated by Lenin in *Materialism and Empiriocriticism* in 1908 around three axes: the "materialist inversion" of Hegelian dialectics, the historicity of ethical principles ordered to class struggle and the convergence of "laws of evolution" in physics (Helmholtz), biology (Darwin) and in political economics (Marx). Lenin hence took position between a historicist Marxism (Labriola) and a determinist Marxism, close to "social Darwinism" (Kautsky). New discoveries in physics, including x-rays, electrons, and the beginnings of quantum mechanics challenged previous conceptions of matter and materialism. Matter seemed to be disappearing. Lenin disagreed:

'Matter disappears' means that the limit within which we have hitherto known matter disappears and that our knowledge is penetrating deeper; properties of matter are disappearing that formerly seemed absolute, immutable and primary, and which are now revealed to be relative and characteristic only of certain states of matter. For the *sole* 'property' of matter with whose recognition philosophical materialism is bound up is the property of *being an objective reality*, of existing outside of the mind.

Lenin was following on from the work of Friedrich Engels, who had noted that "with each epoch-making discovery even in the sphere of natural science, materialism has to change its form." One of Lenin's challenges was distancing materialism as a viable philosophical outlook from what he referred to as the "vulgar materialism" expressed in statements like "the brain secretes thought in the same way as the liver secretes bile" (attributed to 18th century physician Pierre Jean Georges Cabanis, 1757-1808); "metaphysical materialism" (matter is composed of immutable, unchanging particles); and 19th-century "mechanical materialism" (matter was like little molecular billiard balls interacting according to simple laws of mechanics). Lenin's (and Engels') solution to this challenge was "dialectical materialism", where matter was understood in the broader sense of "objective reality" and consistent with new developments in science.

Lukács' Additions

Georg Lukács, who had been minister of Culture in Bela Kun's short-lived Hungarian Soviet Republic (1919), published *History and Class Consciousness* in 1923. This book defined dialectical materialism as the knowledge of society as a whole, knowledge which in itself was immediately the class consciousness of the proletariat. In the first chapter, "What is Orthodox Marxism?", Lukács defined orthodoxy as the fidelity to the "Marxist method", and not to the "dogmas":

"Orthodox Marxism, therefore, does not imply the uncritical acceptance of the results of Marx's investigations. It is not the 'belief' in this or that thesis, nor the exegesis of a 'sacred' book. On the contrary, orthodoxy refers exclusively to method. It is the scientific conviction that dialectical materialism is the road to truth and that its methods can be developed, expanded and deepened only along the lines laid down by its founders."

Lukács criticized revisionist attempts by calling for the return to this Marxist method. In much the same way that Althusser would later define Marxism and psychoanalysis as "conflictual sciences", Lukács conceives "revisionism" and political splits as inherent to Marxist theory and praxis, insofar as dialectical materialism is, according to him, the product of class struggle:

"For this reason the task of orthodox Marxism, its victory over Revisionism and utopianism can never mean the defeat, once and for all, of false tendencies. It is an ever-renewed struggle against the insidious effects of bourgeois ideology on the thought of the proletariat. Marxist orthodoxy is no guardian of traditions, it is the eternally vigilant prophet proclaiming the relation between the tasks of the immediate present and the totality of the historical process."

Furthermore, he stated that "The premise of dialectical materialism is, we recall: 'It is not men's consciousness that determines their existence, but on the contrary, their social existence that determines their consciousness.'... Only when the core of existence stands revealed as a social process can existence be seen as the product, albeit the hitherto unconscious product, of human activity." In line with Marx's thought, he thus criticized the individualist bourgeois philosophy of the subject, which founds itself on the voluntary and conscious subject. Against this ideology, he asserts the primacy of social relations. Existence — and thus the world — is the product of human activity; but this can be seen only if the primacy of social process on individual consciousness is accepted. He classified this consciousness as an effect of ideological mystification. His thesis doesn't entail that Lukács restrains human liberty on behalf of some kind of sociological determinism: to the contrary, this production of existence is the possibility of *praxis*.

However, this heterodox definition, that "orthodox Marxism" is fidelity to the Marxist "method", and not to "dogmas", was condemned, along with Karl Korsch's work, in July 1924, during the 5th Comintern Congress, by Grigory Zinoviev.

Dialectical Materialism

Some evolutionary biologists, such as Richard Lewontin and the late Stephen Jay Gould have employed dialectical materialism in their approach, playing a precautionary heuristic role in their work. For example, from Lewontin's perspective, Dialectical materialism is not, and never has been, a programmatic method for solving particular physical problems. Rather, a dialectical analysis provides an overview and a set of warning signs against particular forms of dogmatism and narrowness of thought. It tells us, "Remember that history may leave an important trace. Remember that being and becoming are dual aspects of nature. Remember that conditions change and that the conditions necessary to the initiation of some process may be destroyed by the process itself. Remember to pay attention to real objects in time and space and not lose them in utterly idealized abstractions. Remember that qualitative effects of context and interaction may be lost when phenomena are isolated". And above all else, "Remember that all the other caveats are only reminders and warning signs whose application to different circumstances of the real world is contingent."

Stephen Jay Gould shared similar views regarding a heuristic role for dialectical materialism. He wrote "Dialectical thinking should be taken more seriously by Western scholars, not discarded because some nations of the second world have constructed a cardboard version as an official political doctrine." Further when presented as guidelines for a philosophy of change, not as dogmatic percepts true by fiat, the three classical laws of dialectics embody a holistic vision that views change as interaction among components of complete systems, and sees the components themselves not as a priori entities, but as both products and inputs to the system. Thus, the law of "interpenetrating opposites" records the inextricable interdependence of components: the "transformation of quantity to quality" defends a systems-based view of change that translates incremental inputs into alterations of state; and the "negation of negation" describes the direction given to history because complex systems cannot revert exactly to previous states.

This heuristic was also applied to the theory of punctuated equilibrium proposed by Niles Eldredge and Gould. They wrote "History, as Hegel said, moves upward in a spiral of negations," and that "puncuated equilibria is a model for discontinuous tempos of change (in) the process of speciation and the deployment of species in geological time." They noted that "the law of transformation of quantity into quality", "holds that a new quality emerges in a leap as the slow accumulation of quantitative changes, long resisted by a stable system, finally forces it rapidly from one state into another," a phenomenon described in some disciplines as a paradigm shift. Apart from the commonly cited example of water turning to steam with increased temperature, Gould and Eldredge noted another analogy in information theory, "with its jargon of equilibrium, steady state, and homeostasis maintained by negative feedback," and "extremely rapid transitions that occur with positive feedback."

Lewontin, Gould, and Eldredge, were thus more interested in dialectical materialism as a heuristic, than as a dogmatic form of 'truth', or as a statement of their politics. Nevertheless, they found a readiness for critics especially, to "seize upon" key statements and quite literally portray punctuated equilibrium and exercises associated with it, such as public exhibitions, as a "Marxist plot"

HISTORICAL MATERIALISM

Historical materialism is a methodological approach to the study of society, economics, and history, first articulated by Karl Marx (1818-1883). Marx himself never used the term but referred to his approach as "the materialist conception of history." Historical materialism looks for the causes of developments and changes in human society in the means by which humans collectively produce the necessities of life. The non-economic features of a society (e.g. social classes, political structures, ideologies) are seen as being an outgrowth of its economic activity. The classic brief statement of the theory was made by Marx in the Preface to *A Contribution to the Critique of Political Economy* (1859):

"My inquiry led me to the conclusion that neither legal relations nor political forms could be comprehended whether by themselves or on the basis of a so-called general development of the human mind, but that on the contrary they originate in the material conditions of life, the totality of which Hegel, following the example of English and French thinkers of the eighteenth century, embraces within the term "civil society"; that the autonomy of this civil society, however, has to be sought in political economy. The study of this, which I began in Paris, I continued in Brussels, where I moved owing to an expulsion order issued by M. Guizot. The general conclusion at which I arrived and which, once reached, became the guiding principle of my studies can be summarised as follows:

In the social production of their existence, men inevitably enter into definite relations, which are independent of their will, namely relations of production appropriate to a given stage in the development of their material forces of production. The totality of these relations of production constitutes the economic structure of society, the real foundation, on which arises a legal and political superstructure, and to which correspond definite forms of consciousness. The mode of production of material life conditions the general process of social, political, and intellectual life. It is not the consciousness of men that determines their existence, but their social existence that determines their consciousness. At a certain stage of development, the material productive forces of society come into conflict with the existing relations of production or — this merely expresses the same thing in legal terms — with the property relations within the framework of which they have operated hitherto. From forms of development, of the productive forces, these relations turn into their fetters. Then begins an era of social revolution. The changes in the economic foundation lead, sooner or later, to the transformation of the whole, immense, superstructure.

In studying such transformations, it is always necessary to distinguish between the material transformation of the economic conditions of production, which can be determined with the precision of natural science, and the legal, political, religious, artistic, or philosophic — in short, ideological forms in which men become conscious of this conflict and fight it out. Just as one does not judge an individual by what he thinks about himself, so one cannot judge such a period of transformation by its consciousness, but, on the contrary, this consciousness must be explained from the contradictions of material life, from the conflict existing between the social forces of production and the relations of production. "

Since Marx's time, the theory has been modified and expanded by thousands of Marxist thinkers. It now has many variants.

Key Ideas

Historical materialism started from a fundamental underlying reality of human existence: that in order for human beings to survive and continue existence from generation to generation, it is necessary for them to produce and reproduce the material requirements of life. While this may seem obvious it was only with Marx that this was seen as foundation for understanding human society and historical development. Marx then extended this premise by asserting the importance of the fact that, in order to carry out production and exchange, people have to enter into very definite social relations, most fundamentally *production relations*.

However, production does not get carried out in the abstract, or by entering into arbitrary or random relations chosen at will. Human beings collectively work on nature but do not do the same work; there is a division of labour in which people not only do different jobs, but according to Marxist theory, some people live from the work of others by owning the means of production. How this is accomplished depends on the type of society. Production is carried out through very definite relations between people. And, in turn, these production relations are determined by the level and character of the productive forces that are present at any given time in history. For Marx, productive forces refer to the means of production such as the tools, instruments, technology, land, raw materials, and human knowledge and abilities in terms of using these means of production.

Writers who identify with historical materialism usually postulate that society has moved through a number of types or modes of production. That is, the character of the production relations is determined by the character of the productive forces; these could be the simple tools and instruments of early human existence, or the more developed machinery and technology of present age. The main modes of production Marx identified generally include primitive communism or tribal society (a prehistoric stage), ancient society, feudalism and capitalism. In each of these social stages, people interact with nature and produce their living in different ways. Any surplus from that production is allotted in different ways. Ancient society was based on a ruling class of slave owners and a class of slaves; feudalism based on landowners and serfs; and capitalism based on the capitalist class and the working class. The capitalist class privately owns the means of production, distribution and exchange (e.g. factories, mines, shops and banks) while the working class live by exchanging their socialized labour with the capital class for wages.

Marx identified the production relations of society (arising on the basis of given productive forces) as the economic base of society. He also explained that on the foundation of the economic base there arise certain political institutions, laws, customs, culture, etc., and ideas, ways of thinking, morality, etc. These constituted the political/ideological superstructure of society. This superstructure not only has its origin in the economic base, but its features also ultimately correspond to the character and development of that economic base, i.e. the way people organize society is determined by the economic base and the relations that arise from its mode of production.

Historical materialism can be seen to rest on the following principles:

- The basis of human society is how humans work on nature to produce the means of subsistence.
- There is a division of labour into social classes (relations of production) based on property ownership where some people live from the labour of others.
- The system of class division is dependent on the mode of production.
- The mode of production is based on the level of the productive forces.
- Society moves from stage to stage when the dominant class is displaced by a new emerging class, by overthrowing the "political shell" that enforces the old relations of production no longer corresponding to the new productive forces. This takes place in the superstructure of society, the political arena in the form of revolution, whereby the underclass "liberates" the productive forces with new relations of production, and social relations, corresponding to it.

Marx's clearest formulation of his "Materialist Conception of History" was in the 1859 Preface to his book *A contribution to the Critique of Political Economy*, whose relevant passage is reproduced here:

"In the social production of their existence, men inevitably enter Into definite relations, which are independent of their will, namely relations of production appropriate to a given stage in the development of their material forces of production. The totality of these relations of production constitutes the economic structure of society, the real foundation, on which arises a legal and political superstructure and to which correspond definite forms of consciousness. The mode of production of material life conditions the general process of social, political and intellectual life. It is not the consciousness of men that determines their existence, but their social existence that determines their consciousness. At a certain stage of development, the material productive forces of society come into conflict with the existing relations of production or — this merely expresses the same thing in legal terms — with the property relations within the framework of which they have operated hitherto. From forms of development of the productive forces these relations turn into their fetters. Then begins an era of social revolution.

The changes in the economic foundation lead sooner or later to the transformation of the whole immense superstructure. In studying such transformations it is always necessary to distinguish between the material transformation of the economic conditions of production, which can be determined with the precision of natural science, and the legal, political, religious, artistic or philosophic — in short, ideological forms in which men become conscious of this conflict and fight it out. Just as one does not judge an individual by what he thinks about himself, so one cannot judge such a period of transformation by its consciousness, but, on the contrary, this consciousness must be explained from the contradictions of material life, from the conflict existing between the social forces of production and the relations of production."

Perhaps the most influential recent defense of this passage, and of relevant Marxian and Marxist assertions is G.A. Cohen's *Karl Marx's Theory of History: A Defence*.

Key Implications

Many writers note that historical materialism represented a revolution in human thought, and a break from previous ways of understanding the underlying basis of change within various human societies.

The theory shows what Marx called a "coherence" in human history, because each generation inherits the productive forces developed previously and in turn further develops them before passing them on to the next generation. Further that this coherence increasingly involves more of humanity the more the productive forces develop and expand to bind people together in production and exchange. This understanding counters the notion that human history is simply a series of accidents, either without any underlying cause or caused by supernatural beings or forces exerting their will on society. This posits that history is made as a result of struggle between different social classes rooted in the underlying economic base.

Marx's Materialism

While the "historical" part of historical materialism does not cause a comprehension problem (i.e., it means the present is explained by analysing the past), the term materialism is more difficult. Historical materialism uses "materialism" to make two separate points, where the truth or falsehood of one point does not affect the others. Firstly there is metaphysical or philosophical materialism, in which matter-in-motion is considered primary and thought about matter-in-motion, or thought about abstractions, secondary. Secondly, there is the notion that economic processes form the material base of society upon which institutions and ideas rest and from which they derive. While the economy is the base structure of society, it does not follow that everything in history is determined by the economy, just as every feature of a house is not determined by its foundations. Thus, there is the idea that in the capitalist mode of production the behaviour of actors in the market economy (means of production, distribution and exchange, the relations of production) plays the major role in configuring society.

Historical Materialism and the Future

In his analysis of the movement of history, Marx predicted the breakdown of capitalism (as a result of class struggle and the falling rate of profit), and the establishment in time of a communist society in which class-based human conflict would be overcome. The means of production would be held in the common ownership and used for the common good.

Marxist Beliefs about History

"Society does not consist of individuals, but expresses the sum of interrelations, the relations within which these individuals stand." — Karl Marx, *Grundrisse, 1858*

According to Marxist theorists, history develops in accordance with the following observations:

1. Social progress is driven by progress in the material, productive forces a society has at its disposal (technology, labour, capital goods, etc.)
2. Humans are inevitably involved in production relations (roughly speaking, economic relationships or

institutions), which constitute our most decisive social relations.

3. Production relations progress, with a degree of inevitability, following and corresponding to the development of the productive forces.
4. Relations of production help determine the degree and types of the development of the forces of production. For example, capitalism tends to increase the rate at which the forces develop and stresses the accumulation of capital.
5. Both productive forces and production relations progress independently of mankind's strategic intentions or will.
6. The superstructure — the cultural and institutional features of a society, its ideological materials—is ultimately an expression of the mode of production (which combines both the forces and relations of production) on which the society is founded.
7. Every type of state is a powerful institution of the ruling class; the state is an instrument which one class uses to secure its rule and enforce its preferred production relations (and its exploitation) onto society.
8. State power is usually only transferred from one class to another by social and political upheaval.
9. When a given style of production relations no longer supports further progress in the productive forces, either further progress is strangled, or 'revolution' must occur.
10. The actual historical process is not predetermined but depends on the class struggle, especially the organization and consciousness of the working class.

This sketch is abstract-real historical understanding needed for developing political strategy and tactics must involve "concrete analysis of concrete conditions" (V.I. Lenin).

Alienation and Freedom

Hunter-gatherer societies were structured so that the economic forces and the political forces were one and the same. The elements of force and relation operated together, harmoniously. In the feudal society, the political forces of the kings and nobility had their relations with the economic forces of the villages through serfdom. The serfs, although not free, were tied to both forces and, thus, not completely alienated. Capitalism, Marx argued, completely separates the economic and political forces, leaving them to have relations through a limiting government. He takes the state to be a sign of this separation-it exists to manage the massive conflicts of interest which arise between classes in all those societies based on property relations.

The History of Historical Materialism

Marx's attachment to materialism arose from his doctoral research on the philosophy of Epicurus, as well as his reading of Adam Smith and other writers in classical political economy. Historical materialism builds upon the idea that became current in philosophy from the sixteenth to eighteenth centuries that the development of human society has moved through a series of stages, from hunting and gathering, through pastoralism and cultivation, to commercial society.

Friedrich Engels wrote: "I use 'historical materialism' to designate the view of the course of history, which seeks the ultimate causes and the great moving power of all important historic events in the economic development of society, in the changes in the modes of production and exchange, with the consequent division of society into distinct classes and the struggles of these classes."

Warnings against Misuse

"One has to "leave philosophy aside", one has to leap out of it and devote oneself like an ordinary man to the study of actuality, for which there exists also an enormous amount of literary material, unknown, of course, to the philosophers... Philosophy and the study of the actual world have the same relation to one another as masturbation and sexual love." Marx himself took care to indicate that he was only proposing a guideline to historical research (*Leitfaden* or *Auffassung*), and was not providing any substantive "theory of history" or "grand philosophy of history", let alone a "master-key to history". Numerous times, he and Engels expressed irritation with dilettante academics who sought to knock up their skimpy historical knowledge as quickly as possible into some grand theoretical system that would explain "everything" about history.

To their great annoyance, the materialist outlook was used as an excuse for not studying history.

In the 1872 Preface to the French edition of Das Kapital Vol. 1, Marx also emphasised that "There is no royal road to science, and only those who do not dread the fatiguing climb of its steep paths have a chance of gaining its luminous summits". Reaching a scientific understanding was hard work. Conscientious, painstaking research was required, instead of philosophical speculation and unwarranted, sweeping generalisations.

But having abandoned abstract philosophical speculation in his youth, Marx himself showed great reluctance during the rest of his life about offering any generalities or universal truths about human existence or human history. The first explicit and systematic summary of the materialist interpretation of history published, *Anti-Dühring*, was written by Friedrich Engels. One of the aims of Engels's polemic *Herr Eugen Dühring's Revolution in Science* (written with Marx's approval) was to ridicule the easy "world schematism" of philosophers, who invented the latest wisdom from behind their writing desks. Towards the end of his life, in 1877, Marx wrote a letter to the editor of the Russian paper *Otetchestvennye Zapisky*, which significantly contained the following disclaimer: "(...) If Russia is tending to become a capitalist nation after the example of the Western European countries, and during the last years she has been taking a lot of trouble in this direction-she will not succeed without having first transformed a good part of her peasants into proletarians; and after that, once taken to the bosom of the capitalist regime, she will experience its pitiless laws like other profane peoples. That is all. But that is not enough for my critic. He feels himself obliged to metamorphose my historical sketch of the genesis of capitalism in Western Europe into an historico-philosophic theory of the marche generale imposed by fate upon every people, whatever the historic circumstances in which it finds itself, in order that it may ultimately arrive at the form of economy which will ensure, together with the greatest expansion of the productive powers of social labour, the most complete development of man. But I beg his pardon. (He is both honouring and shaming me too much.)"

Marx goes on to illustrate how the same factors can in different historical contexts produce very different results, so that quick and easy generalisations are not really possible. To indicate how seriously Marx took research, it is interesting to note that when he died, his estate contained several cubic metres of Russian statistical publications (it was, as the old Marx observed, in Russia that his ideas gained most influence).

But what is true is that insofar as Marx and Engels regarded historical processes as law-governed processes, the possible future directions of historical development were to a great extent *limited* and *conditioned* by what happened before. Retrospectively, historical processes could be understood to have happened by *necessity* in certain ways and not others, and to some extent at least, the most likely variants of the future could be specified on the basis of careful study of the known facts.

Towards the end of his life, Engels commented several times about the abuse of historical materialism. In a letter to Conrad Schmidt dated August 5, 1890, he stated that "And if this man (i.e., Paul Barth) has not yet discovered that while the material mode of existence is the *primum agens* this does not preclude the ideological spheres from reacting upon it in their turn, though with a secondary effect, he cannot possibly have understood the subject he is writing about. (...) The materialist conception of history has a lot of [dangerous friends] nowadays, to whom it serves as an excuse for not studying history. Just as Marx used to say, commenting on the French "Marxists" of the late 70s: "All I know is that I am not a Marxist." (...) In general, the word "materialistic" serves many of the younger writers in Germany as a mere phrase with which anything and everything is labelled without further study, that is, they stick on this label and then consider the question disposed of. But our conception of history is above all a guide to study, not a lever for construction after the manner of the Hegelian. All history must be studied afresh, the conditions of existence of the different formations of society must be examined individually before the attempt is made to deduce them from the political, civil law, aesthetic, philosophic, religious, etc., views corresponding to them. Up to now but little has been done here because only a few people have got down to it seriously. In this field we can utilize heaps of help, it is immensely big, anyone who will work seriously can achieve much and distinguish himself. But instead of this too many of the younger Germans simply make use of the phrase historical materialism (and everything can be turned into a phrase) only in order to get their own relatively scanty historical knowledge — for economic history is still in its swaddling clothes! — constructed into a neat system as quickly as possible, and they then deem themselves something very tremendous. And after that a Barth can come along and attack the thing itself, which in his circle has indeed been degraded to a mere phrase."

Finally, in a letter to Franz Mehring, Frederick Engels dated 14 July 1893, Engels stated: "...there is only one other point lacking, which, however, Marx and I always failed to stress enough in our writings and in regard to which we are all equally guilty. That is to say, we all laid, and were bound to lay, the main emphasis, in the first place, on the derivation of political, juridical and other ideological notions, and of actions arising through the medium of these notions, from basic economic facts. But in so doing we neglected the formal side — the ways and means by which these notions, etc., come about — for the sake of the content. This has given our adversaries a welcome opportunity for misunderstandings, of which Paul Barth is a striking example."

Historical Materialism in Marxist Thought

In 1880, about three years before Marx died, Friedrich Engels indicated that he accepted the usage of the term "historical materialism". Recalling the early days of the new interpretation of history, he stated: "We, at that time, were all materialists, or, at least, very advanced free-thinkers, and to us it appeared inconceivable that almost all educated people in England should believe in all sorts of impossible miracles, and that even geologists like Buckland and Mantell should contort the facts of their science so as not to clash too much with the myths of the book of Genesis; while, in order to find people who dared to use their own intellectual faculties with regard to religious matters, you had to go amongst the uneducated, the "great unwashed", as they were then called, the working people, especially the Owenite Socialists".

In a foreword to his essay *Ludwig Feuerbach and the End of Classical German Philosophy* (1886), three years after Marx's death, Engels claimed confidently that "In the meantime, the Marxist world outlook has found representatives far beyond the boundaries of Germany and Europe and in all the literary languages of the world." In his old age, Engels speculated about a new cosmology or ontology which would show the principles of dialectics to be universal features of reality. He also drafted an article on *The part played by labour in the transition from Ape to Man*, apparently a theory of anthropogenesis which would integrate the insights of Marx and Charles Darwin.

At the very least, Marxism had now been born, and "historical materialism" had become a distinct philosophical doctrine, subsequently elabourated and systematised by intellectuals like Eduard Bernstein, Karl Kautsky, Georgi Plekhanov and Nikolai Bukharin. Even so, up to the 1930s many of Marx's earlier works were still unknown, and in reality most self-styled Marxists had not read beyond Capital Vol. 1. Isaac Deutscher provides an anecdote about the knowledge of Marx in that era: "*Capital* is a tough nut to crack, opined Ignacy Daszyñski, one of the best known socialist "people's tribunes" around the turn of the 20th century, but anyhow he had not read it. But, he said, Karl Kautsky had read it, and written a popular summary of the first volume. He hadn't read this either, but Kazimierz Kelles-Krauz, the party theoretician, had read Kautsky's pamphlet and summarised it. He also had not read Kelles-Krauz's text, but the financial expert of the party, Hermann Diamand, had read it and had told him, i.e. Daszynski, everything about it".

After Lenin's death in 1924, Marxism was transformed into Marxism-Leninism and from there to Maoism or Marxism-Leninism-Mao Zedong Thought in China which some regard as the "true doctrine" and others as a "state religion". In the early years of the 20th century, historical materialism was often treated by socialist writers as interchangeable with dialectical materialism, a formulation never used by Friedrich Engels however. According to many Marxists influenced by Soviet Marxism, historical materialism is a specifically sociological method, while dialectical materialism refers to a more general, abstract, philosophy. The Soviet orthodox Marxist tradition, influential for half a century, based itself on Joseph Stalin's pamphlet *Dialectical and Historical Materialism* and on textbooks issued by the "Institute of Marxism-Leninism of the Central Committee of the Communist Party of the Soviet Union".

Recent Versions

Several scholars have argued that historical materialism ought to be revised in the light of modern scientific knowledge. Jürgen Habermas believes historical materialism "needs revision in many respects", especially because it has ignored the significance of communicative action. Göran Therborn has argued that the method of historical materialism should be applied to historical materialism as intellectual tradition, and to the history of Marxism itself. In the early 1980s Paul Hirst and Barry Hindess elabourated a structural Marxism interpretation of historical materialism. Regulation theory, especially in the work of Michel Aglietta draws extensively on historical materialism. Spiral dynamics shows similarities to historical materialism.

Criticisms

Philosopher of science Karl Popper, in his Conjectures and Refutations, critiqued such claims of the explanatory power or valid application of historical materialism by arguing that it could explain or explain away any fact brought before it, making it unfalsifiable. Underlying the dispute among historians are the different assumptions made about the definition or concept of "history" and "historiography". Different historians take a different view of what it is all about, and what the possibilities of historical and social scientific knowledge are.

Broadly, the importance of the study of history lies in the ability of history to explain the present. According to its adherents, historical materialism is important in explaining history from a scientific perspective, by following the scientific method, as opposed to belief-system theories like creationism and intelligent design which explain the present from a belief-system point of view.

BASIC THEORIES OF KARL MARX

Outside his specific economic theories, Marx's main contribution to the social sciences has been his theory of historical materialism. Its starting point is anthropological. Human beings cannot survive without social organisation. Social organisation is based upon social labour and social communication. Social labour always occurs within a given framework of specific, historically determined, social relations of production. These social relations of production determine in the last analysis all other social relations, including those of social communication. It is social existence which determines social consciousness and not the other way around.

Historical materialism posits that relations of production which become stabilised and reproduce themselves are structures which can no longer be changed gradually, piecemeal. They are modes of production. To use Hegel's dialectical language, which was largely adopted (and adapted) by Marx: they can only change qualitatively through a complete social upheaval, a social revolution or counter-revolution. Quantitative changes can occur within modes of production, but they do not modify the basic structure. In each mode of production, a given set of relations of production constitutes the basis (infrastructure) on which is erected a complex superstructure, encompassing the state and the law (except in a classless society), ideology, religion, philosophy, the arts, morality, etc. Relations of production are the sum total of social relations which human beings establish among themselves in the production of their material lives. They are therefore not limited to what actually happens at the point of production. Humankind could not survive, i.e. produce, if there did not exist specific forms of circulation of goods, e.g. between producing units (circulation of tools and raw materials) and between production units and consumers. A priori allocation of goods determines other relations of production than does allocation of goods through the market. Partial commodity production also implies other relations of production than does generalised commodity production.

Except in the case of classless societies, modes of production, centred around prevailing relations of production, are embodied in specific class relations which, in the last analysis, over-determine relations between individuals. Historical materialism does not deny the individual's free will, his attempts to make choices concerning his existence according to his individual passions, his interests as he understands them, his convictions, his moral options etc. What historical materialism does state is: (1) that these choices are strongly predetermined by the social framework (education, prevailing ideology and moral 'values', variants of behaviour limited by material conditions etc.); (2) that the outcome of the collision of millions of different passions, interests and options is essentially a phenomenon of social logic and not of individual psychology. Here, class interests are predominant.

There is no example in history of a ruling class not trying to defend its class rule, or of an exploited class not trying to limit (and occasionally eliminate) the exploitation it suffers. So outside classless society, the class struggle is a permanent feature of human society. In fact, one of the key theses of historical materialism is that 'the history of humankind is the history of class struggles'. The immediate object of class struggle is economic and material. It is a struggle for the division of the social product between the direct producers (the productive, exploited class) and those who appropriate what Marx calls the social surplus product, the residuum of the social product once the producers and their offspring are fed (in the large sense of the word; i.e. the sum total of the consumer goods consumed by that class) and the initial stock of tools and raw materials is reproduced (including the restoration of the initial fertility of the soil). The ruling class functions as a ruling class essentially through the appropriation of the social surplus product. By getting possession of the social surplus product, it acquires the means to foster and maintain most of the superstructural activities mentioned above; and by doing so, it can largely determine their function-to maintain and reproduce the given social structure, the given mode of production-and their contents.

We say 'largely determine' and not 'completely determine'. First, there is an 'immanent dialectical', i.e. an autonomous movement, of each specific superstructural sphere of activity. Each generation of scientists, artists, philosophers, theologists, lawyers and politicians finds a given corpus of ideas, forms, rules, techniques, ways of thinking, to which it is initiated through education and current practice, etc. It is not forced to simply continue and reproduce these elements. It can transform them, modify them, change their interconnections, even negate them. Again: historical materialism does not deny that there is a specific history of science, a history of art, a history of philosophy, a history of political and moral ideas, a history of religion etc., which all follow their own logic. It tries to explain why a certain number of scientific, artistic, philosophical, ideological, juridical changes or even revolutions occur at a given time and in given countries, quite different from other ones which occurred some centuries earlier elsewhere. The nexus of these 'revolutions' with given historical periods is a nexus of class interests.

Second, each social formation (i.e. a given country in a given epoch) while being characterised by predominant relations of production (i.e. a given mode of production at a certain phase of its development) includes different relations of production which are largely remnants of the past, but also sometimes nuclei of future modes of production. Thus there exists not only the ruling class and the exploited class characteristic of that prevailing mode of production (capitalists and wage earners under capitalism). There also exist remnants of social classes which were predominant when other relations of production prevailed and which, while having lost their hegemony, still manage to survive in the interstices of the new society. This is, for example, the case with petty commodity producers (peasants, handicraftsmen, small merchants), semi-feudal landowners, and even slave-owners, in many already predominantly capitalist social formations throughout the 19th and part of the 20th centuries. Each of these social classes has its own ideology, its own religious and moral values, which are intertwined with the ideology of the hegemonic ruling class, without becoming completely absorbed by that ideology.

Third, even after a given ruling class (e.g. the feudal or semi-feudal nobility) has disappeared as a ruling class, its ideology can survive through sheer force of social inertia and routine (custom). The survival of traditional ancien regime catholic ideology in France during a large part of the 19th century, in spite of the sweeping social, political and ideological changes ushered in by the French revolution, is an illustration of that rule.

Finally, Marx's statement that the ruling ideology of each epoch is the ideology of the ruling class-another basic tenet of historical materialism-does not express more than it actually says. It implies that other ideologies can exist side by side with that ruling ideology without being hegemonic. To cite the most important of these occurrences: exploited and (or) oppressed social classes can develop their own ideology, which will start to challenge the prevailing hegemonic one. In fact, an ideological class struggle accompanies and sometimes even precedes the political class struggle properly speaking. Religious and philosophical struggles preceding the classical bourgeois revolutions; the first socialist critiques of bourgeois society preceding the constitution of the first working-class parties and revolutions, are examples of that type.

The class struggle has been up to now the great motor of history. Human beings make their own history. No mode of production can be replaced by another one without deliberate actions by large social forces, i.e. without social revolution (or counter-revolution). Whether these revolutions or counter-revolutions actually lead to the long-term implementation of deliberate projects of social reorganization is another matter altogether. Very often, their outcome is to a large extent different from the intention of the main actors. Human beings act consciously, but they can act with false consciousness. They do not necessarily understand why they want to realise certain social and (or) political plans, why they want to maintain or to change economic or juridical institutions; and especially, they rarely understand in a scientific sense the laws of social change, the material and social preconditions for successfully conserving or changing such institutions. Indeed, Marx claims that only with the discovery of the main tenets of historical materialism have we made a significant step forward towards understanding these laws, without claiming to be able to predict 'all' future developments of society.

Social change, social revolutions and counter-revolutions are furthermore occurring within determined material constraints. The level of development of the productive forces-essentially tools and human skills, including their effects upon the fertility of the soil-limits the possibilities of institutional change. Slave labour has shown itself to be largely incompatible with the factory system based upon contemporary machines. Socialism would not be durably built upon the basis of the wooden plough and the potter's wheel. A social revolution generally widens the scope for the development of the productive forces and leads to social progress in most fields of human activity in a momentous way. Likewise, an epoch of deep social crisis is ushered in when there is a growing conflict between the prevailing mode of production (i.e. the existing social order) on the one hand, and the further development of the productive forces on the other. Such a social crisis will then manifest itself on all major fields and social activity: politics, ideology, morals and law, as well as in the realm of the economic life properly speaking.

Historical materialism thereby provides a measuring stick for human progress: the growth of the productive forces, measurable through the growth of the average productivity of labour, and the number, longevity and skill of the human species. This measuring stick in no way abstracts from the natural preconditions for human survival and human growth (in the broadest sense of the concept). Nor does it abstract from the conditional and partial character of such progress, in terms of social organisation and individual alienation. In the last analysis, the division of society into antagonistic social classes rejects, from the point of view of historical materialism, an inevitable limitation of human freedom. For Marx and Engels, the real measuring rod of human freedom, i.e. of human wealth, is not 'productive labour'; this only creates the material pre-condition for that freedom. The real measuring rod is leisure time, not in the sense of 'time for doing nothing' but in the sense of time freed from the iron necessity to produce and reproduce material livelihood, and therefore disposable for all-round and free development of the individual talents, wishes, capacities, potentialities, of each human being.

As long as society is too poor, as long as goods and services satisfying basic needs are too scarce, only part of society can be freed from the necessity to devote most of its life to 'work for a livelihood' (i.e. of forced labour, in the anthropological/ sociological sense of the word, that is in relation to desires, aspirations and talents, not to a juridical status of bonded labour). That is essentially what represents the freedom of the ruling classes and their hangers-on, who are 'being paid to think', to create, to invent, to administer, because they have become free from the obligation to bake their own bread, weave their own clothes and build their own houses. Once the productive forces are developed far enough to guarantee all human beings satisfaction of their basic needs by 'productive labour' limited to a minor fraction of lifetime (the half work-day or less), then the material need of the division of society in classes disappears. Then, there remains no objective basis for part of society to monopolise administration, access to information, knowledge, intellectual labour. For that reason, historical materialism explains both the reasons why class societies and class struggles arose in history, and why they will disappear in the future in a classless society of democratically self-administering associated producers.

Historical materialism therefore contains an attempt at explaining the origin, the functions and the future withering away of the state as a specific institution, as well as an attempt to explain politics and political activity in general, as an expression of social conflicts centred around different social interests (mainly, but not only, those of different social classes; important fractions of classes, as well as non-class social groupings, also come into play). For Marx and Engels, the state is not existent with human society as such, or with 'organised society' or even with 'civilised society' in the abstract, neither is it the result of any voluntarily concluded 'social contract' between individuals. The state is the sum total of apparatuses, i.e. special groups of people separate and apart from the rest (majority) of society, that appropriate to themselves functions of a repressive or integrative nature which were initially exercised by all citizens. This process of alienation occurs in conjunction with the emergence of social classes. The state is an instrument for fostering, conserving and reproducing a given class structure, and not a neutral arbiter between antagonistic class interests.

The emergence of a classless society is therefore closely intertwined, for adherents to historical materialism, with the process of withering away of the state, i.e. of gradual devolution to the whole of society (self-management, self-administration) of all specific functions today exercised by special apparatuses, i.e. of the dissolution of these apparatuses. Marx and Engels visualised the dictatorship of the proletariat, the last form of the state and of political class rule, as an instrument for assuring the transition from class society to classless society. It should itself be a state of a special kind, organising its own gradual disappearance.

We said above that, from the point of view of historical materialism, the immediate object of class struggle is the division of the social product between different social classes. Even the political class struggle in the final analysis serves that main purpose; but it also covers a much broader field of social conflicts. As all state activities have some bearing upon the relative stability of a given social formation, and the class rule to which it is submitted, the class struggle can extend to all fields of politics from foreign policy to educational problems and religious conflicts. This has of course to be proven through painstaking analysis, and not proclaimed as an axiom or a revealed truth. When conducted successfully, such exercises in class analysis and class definition of political, social and even literary struggles becomes impressive works of historical explanation, as for example Marx's *Class Struggles in France 1848-50*, Engels' *The German Peasant War*, Franz Mehring's *Die Lesssing-Legende*, Trotsky's *History of the Russian Revolution*, etc.

VILFREDO PARETO: LOGICAL AND NONLOGICAL ACTION

Pareto defines logical actions as those "that use means appropriate to ends and which logically link means with ends." This logical conjunction of means with ends must hold not only for the subject performing them, "but [also] from the standpoint of other persons who have a more extensive knowledge." Logical actions are those actions that are both subjectively and objectively logical. Nonlogical action is simply taken to mean all action not falling within Pareto's explicit definition of the logical; it is a residual category.

Pareto follows what he sees as an inductive procedure in developing his conceptual framework for the analysis of the nonlogical element in human action. After considering a wide array of cases in both past and contemporary history, and taking as his evidence many types of ideologies—beliefs and doctrines that have allegedly moved men to action—Pareto concluded that these nonscientific belief systems and theories were only rarely determinants of action but instead were most frequently the expression of deep-seated sentiments. Pareto argued that although men most often fail to engage in logical action, they have a strong tendency to "logicalize" their behaviour, that is, to make it appear as the logical result of a set of ideas. In fact, what accounts for most action is not the set of beliefs that is used to rationalize or "logicalize" it, but rather a pre-existing state of mind, a basic human sentiment. For example, a man has a horror of murder. Therefore, he will not commit murder. He tells himself, however, that "the Gods punish murderers" and imagines that this is why he refrains from murder. If we designate human sentiments, the basic Sources of nonlogical action, as A, the theories relating to action as B, and action itself as C, we realize that, although A, B, and C are mutually inter-related, A independently influences B and C far more than B influences C. To think otherwise, Pareto argues, is to fall into the rationalistic fallacy that has been the bane of most previous social theory.

Whereas B and C, nonlogical theories and overt acts respectively, are directly observable, human sentiments or states of mind can only be inferred. Pareto was not prepared to analyze these basic sentiments, but left this task to psychologists. "Nonlogical actions originate chiefly in definite psychic states, sentiments, subconscious feelings, and the like. It is the province of psychology to investigate such psychic states. Here we start with them as data of fact, without going beyond that."

Pareto concentrated his attention on conduct that reflects these psychic states, and, more particularly, the theories and belief systems that serve to justify and rationalize nonlogical action. One of his central concerns is with an exhaustive critique of nonscientific theories associated with action. He submits metaphysical, religious, and moral systems to a destructive analysis and shows to his own satisfaction that all of them, despite their pretensions to the contrary, have nothing at all in common with scientific theories. Notions such as "liberty," "equality," "progress," or "the General Will" are as vacuous as the myths and magical incantations with which savages rationalize their actions. None is verifiable, all are fictions that serve mainly to clothe and make respectable the actions of men. Even though Pareto does not deny that such myths may upon occasion influence conduct, he mainly highlights those instances in which they serve merely as masks. He sees unmasking as one of the main tasks of the social analyst. "We have to see to what extent reality is disfigured in the theories and descriptions of it that one finds in the literature of thought. We have an image in a curved mirror; our problem is to discover the form of the object so altered by refraction." As will become clear later, such unmasking served Pareto's ideological purposes and not only his scientific aims.

THEORETICAL CONTENT

With an understanding of the historical antecedents and the assumptions that informed Pareto's knowledge in mind, we can now turn to his theory proper. We have compiled his "propositions" from the major works mentioned earlier, *The Socialist Systems* and *The Mind and Society*. Two volumes of selections from Pareto's *Treatise* edited by Joseph Lopreato (1965) and the work on Pareto by S. E. Finer (1966) are also important references. The general logic of Pareto's work follows from his conception of society as a systematic whole made up of interdependent parts. He argued forcefully that the introduction of change at any point affecting any part will necessarily produce change in other parts, as well as in the total system. Forces within society work to maintain the existing form of social organization and to ensure that change is orderly and compatible with the nature of the social system. Hence, for Pareto, change is not conceived in terms of dramatic institutional response. To the contrary, action and reaction within the system represent a process of *maintaining* order in the presence of threats. As with homeostasis in physiology, the components of society compensate automatically for alterations or strain in the external environment.

The relationships among variables in Pareto's system are not unilateral. As a rule, relationships involve *reciprocal dependence*. For this reason Pareto rejected the traditional conception of cause and effect as both one-sided and simplistic. He believed that the association of social variables could be best understood as *functional*, but he appears to have employed a mathematical conception of function. By this we mean that the state of the variable depends on the changes with another (or other) variable(s). In a quantitative sense, fluctuations in the system can best be conceived as correlational, as a matter of the degree of relative correspondence. This is different from Durkheimian functionalism, where the focus is on the purposes of social practices. For Pareto, the most important elements of a social system are those that are universal, that is, found in all systems. These constant elements tend to be regular and uniform and to demonstrate continuity over time. He argued that the *identification* and *measurement* of the constant components that comprise the social system represent sociology's reason for being.

Turning his attention to the members of society, Pareto held that human action within the system can be classified as either *logical* or *nonlogical*. Logical action occurs when a preponderance of rigorous evidence is employed by the actor to assess (1) whether an end can be realistically achieved, and if so, (2) what the best means are to reach that goal. Influenced heavily be Machiavelli, Pareto argued that logical action is unusual (confined typically to such rational behavior as economic and scientific conduct). Rather, it is nonlogical action, reflective of underlying human sentiments or innate instincts, that dominates the range of human behaviour. Pareto did not separate human action from the social system. Rather, he incorporated both the logical and nonlogical within its internal dynamics.

Pareto held that systemic equilibrium is a consequence of the constancies of external conditions and internal elements. External conditions consist of two major categories: the impact upon society by its natural environment (geography) and the influences represented by other systems or by the same system at an earlier historical stage. Internal elements can be classified into principle types. These are *economic interests, residues, derivations, social stratification,* and *the circulation of the elite*. For Pareto, economic interests represent logical action directed toward the maximization of satisfaction. He did *not* consider this internal element of value in the understanding of the social system. Another internal element consists of nonlogical actions that are manifestations of underlying mental or psychic states of sentiments. Termed *residues*, such manifestations correspond with innate dispositions that appear to be bioinstinctual in essence. At the individual level, residues seem synonymous with drives or basic impulses that ordinarily culminate in social interaction. Such an interpretation has to be inferred from Pareto's classification of residues as well as his general usage of the concept.

Pareto identified 51 residues and combined them into six distinct classes: (1) *combinations*, or the impulse to form associations and categories of things, events, and ideas; (2) *persistence of aggregates*, or the impulse to preserve abstractions, symbols, and social relationships over time; (3) *sentiments through exterior acts*, or the impulse to express powerful underlying emotions through religious rituals, political agitation, and so forth; (4) *sociability*, or the impulse to impose uniform standards of behaviour to realize popularity, prestige, and standing; (5) *integrity of personality*, or the impulse to preserve the personality; and *sexuality*, or the impulse toward all sexually related action.

Derivations constitute the next constant and internal element of social systems. Derivations are a form of nonlogical action. And just as residues are manifestations of sentiments, so too are derivations manifestations of residues. Derivations are in effect ideologies or "pseudo-logical" defenses that are subject to further classification. These are *assertions, appeals to authority, claims that are in accordance with prevailing sentiments or the conventional wisdom,* and *verbal proofs that employ ambiguity, abstractions, and analogies in lieu of hard evidence.*

It is crucial at this juncture to make note of Pareto's theoretical intent. By means of his residues and derivations, he sought not only to identify constant elements of the social system but to construct a basis for criticizing rival theories that did not measure up to his "logico-experimental" conception of science. Thus, for Pareto, both the social system and his theoretical attempts to explain it were based on logical action. Alternative theories, especially those that seemed to offer an alternative vision of society, were dismissed as mere "derivations," ideologies masquerading as science. They sought legitimacy through assertion, authority, "what everybody knows," and verbal obtuseness.

For Pareto, still another constant element found in all social systems is *social stratification*. By such, Pareto meant that residues are differentially distributed among individuals, groups, and classes in society. Such a state of affairs, when combined with real moral, intellectual, and physical differences, represents the basis for inequality. This fundamental component of society means that all theories of political democracy, classlessness, and mass government are contradicted by the systemic imperative of social stratification. Therefore, egalitarian conceptions of society can be nothing more than derivations (unfounded ideologies) used by ruling circles to control the lower strata.

The final internal element for Pareto is the *circulation of the elite*. History, he argued, is the "cemetery of aristocracies." By this he sought to show that although stratification is a part of the natural order of things, the composition of its elite circles does not remain unchanged.

According to Pareto, those on the top often resort to measures of repression that sustain them for long periods. However, sooner or later the "more fit" members of the subject classes will demand their place. If they are not assimilated into the existing elite, then the historical stage is set for the revolution or coup d'etat.

As expected, Pareto found specific residues at the base of the circulation of the elite. These are the residues of *combinations* and *persistence*. Combination residues are the basis for the grand schemes of political and financial empire building, or the bringing together of state power and the interests of economic enterprise. The elite act in the style of Machiavelli's *foxes*, and although they are willing to innovate and assume risks, they prefer deception to force.

Persistence residues, on the other hand, dominate a contending body of elite. For Pareto, these were Machiavelli's *lions* with their strong and enduring attachment to family, class, country, and other traditional social relationships. Here we find the patriots and nationalists who fear neither the use of violence nor the raw exercise of power. Pareto's world saw the predominance of foxes. Soon, he predicted, the day of the lion would dawn.

THE THEORY OF ELITES AND THE CIRCULATION OF ELITES

It is a basic axiom for Pareto that people are unequal physically, as well as intellectually and morally. In society as a whole, and in any of its particular strata and groupings, some people are more gifted than others. Those who are most capable in any particular grouping are the elite.

Let us assume that in every branch of human activity each individual is given an index which stands as a sign of his capacity, very much the same way grades are given... in examinations in school. The highest type of lawyer, for instance, will be given 10. The man who does not get a client will be given 1—reserving zero for the man who is an out-and-out idiot. To the man who has made his millions—honestly or dishonestly as the case may be—we will give 10. To the man who has earned his thousands we will give 6; to such as will just manage to keep out of the poor-house, 1, keeping zero for those who get in. To the woman "in politics"... who has managed to infatuate a man of power and play a part in the man's career, we shall give some higher number such as 8 or 9; to the strumpet who merely satisfies the senses of such a man and exerts no influence on public affairs, we shall give zero. To the clever rascal who knows how to fool people and still keep clear of the penitentiary, we shall give 8, 9, or 10, according to the number of geese he has plucked.... To the sneak-thief who snatches a piece of silver from a restaurant table and runs away into the arms of a policeman, we shall give 1. The term elite has no moral or honorific connotations in Pareto's usage. It denotes simply "a class of the people who have the highest indices in their branch of activity." Pareto argues that "It will help if we further divide that [elite] class into two classes: a governing elite, comprising individuals who directly or indirectly play some considerable part in government, and a non-governing elite, comprising the rest." His main discussion focuses on the governing elite.

There is a basic ambiguity in Pareto's treatment of the notion of the elite. In some passages, as in the one quoted above, it would appear that those occupying elite positions are, by definition, the most qualified. But there are many other passages where Pareto asserts that people are assigned elite positions by virtue of being so labelled. That is, men assigned elite positions may not have the requisite capabilities, while others not so labelled may have them. The label "lawyer" is affixed to a man who is supposed to know something about the law and often does, though sometimes again he is an ignoramus. So the governing elite contains individuals who wear labels appropriate to political offices of a certain altitude—ministers, Senators, Deputies... and so on—making the apposite exceptions for those who have found their way into that exalted community without possessing qualities corresponding to the labels they wear.... Wealth, family, or social connections also help in many other cases to win the label of the elite in general, or of the governing elite in particular, for persons who otherwise hold no claim upon it.

It would seem that Pareto believed that only in perfectly open societies, those with perfect social mobility, would elite position correlate fully with superior capacity. Only under such conditions would the governing elite, for example, consist of the people most capable of governing. The actual social fact is that obstacles such as inherited wealth, family connections, and the like prevent the free circulation of individuals through the ranks of society, so that those wearing an elite label and those possessing highest capacity tend to diverge to greater or lesser degrees. Given the likelihood of divergencies between ascribed elite position and actual achievement and capacity, Pareto is a passionate advocate of maximum social mobility and of careers open to all. He saw the danger that elite positions that were once occupied by men of real talent would in the course of time be preempted by men devoid of such talent.

In the beginning, military, religious, and commercial aristocracies and plutocracies... must have constituted parts of the governing elite and sometimes made up the whole of it. The victorious warrior, the prosperous merchant, the opulent plutocrat, were men of such parts, each in his own field, as to be superior to the average individual. Under those circumstances the label corresponded to an actual capacity. But as time goes by, considerable, sometimes very considerable, differences arise between the capacity and the label.... Aristocracies do not last.... History is a graveyard of aristocracies.... They decay not in numbers only. They decay also in quality, in the sense that they lose their vigour, that there is a decline in the proportions of the residues which enabled them to win their power and hold it. The governing class is restored not only in numbers, but... in quality, by families rising from the lower classes and bringing with them the vigour and the proportions of residues necessary for keeping themselves in power.... Potent cause of disturbance in the equilibrium is the accumulation of superior elements in the lower classes and, conversely, of inferior elements in the higher classes.

When governing or nongoverning elites attempt to close themselves to the influx of newer and more capable elements from the underlying population, when the circulation of elites is impeded, social equilibrium is upset and the social order will decay. Pareto argued that if the governing elite does not "find ways to assimilate the exceptional individuals who come to the front in the subject classes," an imbalance is created in the body politic and the body social until this condition is rectified, either through a new opening of channels of mobility or through violent overthrow of an old ineffectual governing elite by a new one that is capable of governing.

Not only are intelligence and aptitudes unequally distributed among the members of society, but the residues as well. Under ordinary circumstances, the "conservative" residues of Class II preponderate in the masses and thus make them submissive. The governing elite, however, if it is to be effective, must consist of individuals who have a strong mixture of both Class I and Class II elements. A predominance of interests that are primarily industrial and commercial enriches the ruling class in individuals who are shrewd, astute, and well-provided with combination instincts; and divests it of individuals of the sturdy impulsive type.... One might guess that if cunning, chicanery, combinations were all there was to government, the dominion of the class in which Class I residues by far predominate would last over a very, very long period.... But governing is also a matter of force, and as Class I residues grow stronger and Class II residues weaker, the individuals in power become less and less capable of using force, so that an unstable equilibrium results and revolutions occur.... The masses, which are strong in Class II residues, carry them upwards into the governing class either by gradual infiltration or in sudden spurts through revolutions.

The ideal governing class contains a judicious mixture of lions and foxes, of men capable of decisive and forceful action and of others who are imaginative, innovative, and unscrupulous.

When imperfections in the circulation of governing elites prevent the attainment of such judicious mixtures among the governing, regimes either degenerate into hidebound and ossified bureaucracies incapable of renewal and adaptation, or into weak regimes of squabbling lawyers and rhetoricians incapable of decisive and forceful action. When this happens, the governed will succeed in overthrowing their rulers and new elites will institute a more effective regime.

What applies to political regimes applies to the economic realm as well. In this field, "speculators" are akin to the foxes and "rentiers" to the lions. Speculators and rentiers do not only have different interests but they reflect different temperaments and different residues. Neither is very good at using force, but they both otherwise fall roughly into the same dichotomous classes that explain political fluctuations.

In the speculator group Class I residues predominate, in the rentier group, Class II residues.... The two groups perform functions of differing utility in society. The [speculator] group is primarily responsible for change, for economic and social progress. The [rentier] group, instead, is a powerful element in stability, and in many cases counteracts the dangers attending the adventurous capers of the [speculators]. A society in which the [rentiers] almost exclusively predominate remains stationary and, as it were, crystallized. A society in which [the speculators] predominate lacks stability, lives in a state of shaky equilibrium that may be upset by a slight accident from within or from without.

Like in the governing elite where things work best when both residues of Class I and Class II are represented, so in the economic order maximum effectiveness is attained when both rentiers and speculators are present, each providing a balance by checking the excesses of the other. Pareto implies throughout that a judicious mixture in top elites of men with Class I and Class II residues makes for the most stable economic structure, as well as for the most enduring political structure.

THE CIRCULATION OF THE ELITE

Vilfredo Pareto was born in Paris in 1848, the year of the revolution that brought the fall of the House of Bourbon and the rise of Louis Napoleon. Pareto's father was an Italian nobleman and political exile, and his mother was French. With the issuance of a general amnesty, the family returned to Italy in 1868. Vilfredo graduated from the Polytechnic Institute in Turin with a degree in engineering. He first worked for two Italian railways and then served as general superintendent of iron mines owned by a bank in Florence.

Pareto's contributions to sociology were matched by his early efforts in the field of economics. He was greatly influenced by the works of Leon Walras on economic equilibrium and, in a personal meeting with the Swiss academician, succeeded in demonstrating his command of Walras's work. In 1893 Walras resigned from the University of Lausanne, and Pareto became his successor. Five years later, he became heir to a sizable fortune and through the remainder of his life left Switzerland only rarely. We can identify two major turning points in the intellectual life of Pareto. Over time, the engineer–economist became convinced of the limitations of narrowly drawn conceptions of economic systems and advanced the need for a general theory of society. So inspired, in 1902-1903 he published *The Socialist Systems* and some years later added to a long list of publications his *General Treatise on Sociology* (1915). A refined and reorganized version of the latter was published in 1935 under the title *The Mind and Society*. Throughout his writing career, the thrust of Pareto's work was toward an equilibrium model of society. His conception of the social systems came to be highly influential at Harvard University, particularly in the work of Talcott Parsons and George Homans.

Another watershed in the life of Pareto was more clearly political and ideological. In his youth he was swayed by the democratic and humanitarian ethic. He opposed the authority of the church and the ready resort to military force that swept European history. However, Pareto's early sentiments were to change. In the last decade of the nineteenth century, he wrote scores of articles calling for the reorganization of society along the lines of laissez-faire economics. In the current of Italian politics, the ideals of democracy came to assume a socialist face. Pareto fiercely retained his "liberal" conception of free trade, while repudiating political equality.

Before publication of *The Socialist Systems*, Pareto had decided that his own prior reasoning in support of political liberty was more emotional than rational. Both this work and his later *Treatise* were to contain polemical assaults on democratic structure and ideology. Pareto drew fire from his critics who labelled him variously the "Karl Marx of the bourgeoisie" and the "Marx of fascism." One of his admirers was Benito Mussolini, who offered him a seat in the Italian senate shortly before his Pareto's death in 1923.

History and Biography

A brief sketch of the historical milieu in which Pareto's life was shaped will bring us back to a familiar theme: Sociological theories of order were typically a conservative response to conditions of disorder. In the nineteenth century, Italy (like European society in general) was divided and fragmented. With the fall of Bonaparte in the early years of the era, the French Bourbons and the Austrian emperor came to rule various republics and duchies in Italy, with Pope Pius VII regaining the Papal States. Hence the specter of foreign domination coexisted with the division of the nation, a separation that inhibited the commercial interests of the rising bourgeoisie. This was a time for the formation of shadowy organizations predicated on political resistance, which succeeded in touching off popular rebellions throughout the nation. New leaders were to appear, such as Mazzini, Gioberti, and Garibaldi, each of whom sought to unite Italy through half a century of fire and blood. One year after Pareto graduated from the Polytechnic Institute in Turin, Rome became the capital of a newly unified Kingdom of Italy. However, there proved to be more to unification than lines drawn on maps.

Divisions in the new Italy were as always political, economic, and social. However, these conformed to some extent with the major geographical regions of the country. In the north, modernization had taken the form of political bureaucratization and industrial development. The largely agrarian south featured widespread poverty, misery, and illiteracy. The forces of the right, based in the more affluent north, controlled the kingdom until 1876. Its panaceas of free trade, unequal taxation, a balanced budget, and an austere attitude toward public work expenditures alienated large segments of the population. Riding the tide of disaffection, the predominantly southern political left swept to a parliamentary victory. Although promising progressive taxation, public services, and wider suffrage, the liberal government ruled by patronage and corruption until the First World War. Some industrial development in Italy was evident in the latter part of the nineteenth century, particularly in textiles. However, the level of that development lagged behind other European states such as France and England. In the south, the larger owners successfully opposed the land reform desperately wanted by the peasants. Laws calling for compulsory education were not implemented, taxation remained regressive, and the governmental bureaucracy remained bloated and ineffective. Popular insurrections flourished, the intellectuals became disaffected, and the liberal democratic ideals withered in the dust of economic stagnation. On October 28, 1922, Benito Mussolini marched on Rome.

Within a short time, the vision of peace gave way to the glorification of war. The interests of the owning class were preserved under a system of centralized state control while the dream of political enfranchisement succumbed to one-party rule. The diversity of unions, minority groups, and political opposition collapsed under the press of nationalism. Together, these conditions marked the advent of the iron fist of Italian fascism.

Assumptions

Pareto's theory, written in the positivist tradition, fits almost too well the ideal type that is the order paradigm. To begin, he assumed sociology to be an empirical discipline, meant to follow the methodical lead of the natural sciences. He called for the establishment of the "logico-experimental" method by which investigation would be based solely on experience and observation. Moreover, the construction of his theory, particularly in its major terms, reflected his view of order in the universe. Pareto believed that the highest form human organization is the social system. It logically follows that the natural state of society is one of dynamic equilibrium.

In some important ways, Pareto was influenced by the works of Comte and Spencer. He embraced Spencer's position on noninterference (especially as it applied to laissez-faire economics). The concepts of greater differentiation and interrelationships developed by both Spencer and Durkheim appear to have also informed the work of the Italian, especially in his early sociology. However, by the time that his *Treatise* was published (1915), Pareto was to condemn Spencer and Comte along two lines. First, he rejected the earlier positivists for their lack of scientific sophistication. Second, he faulted their vision of evolutionary progress.

It must be admitted that Pareto's conception of the social system was quite mature when compared with the efforts of his contemporaries. He drew on his engineering background to substitute a mechanical image (system) for a biological one (organism). Of crucial importance was Pareto's conception of society as a system of elements or variables in a state of reciprocal and mutual interdependence. His systemic explanation of how a society works, and its interpenetration with the minds of its members, rendered organicism quite crude in comparison. However, Pareto's intellectual break with Spencer and Comte went beyond the question of sophistication.

Pareto imagined in the work of his intellectual ancestors the unacceptable tainting of the Enlightenment philosophies. In the *Treatise* he called for the abandonment of the ideal of unilinear progress, a principle he had discerned in the evolutionary conceptions of his predecessors. As we have seen, neither Comte nor Spencer assumed the perfectability of human nature. They held fast to the Hobbesian conception of the antisocial being saved from mutual destruction only through reason. However, Pareto went beyond Hobbes. When the promise of progress in his native Italy fell far short of fruition, he was drawn to perhaps the starkest portrait of human nature in Western philosophy, that of Niccolo Machiavelli.

In an attempt to end his exile at the hands of the Medici conquerors of his native Florence, Machiavelli (1469 – 1527) wrote *The Prince*. In it, he argued that the ordinary sentiments of humankind are those of greed and selfishness. In concrete terms, those who are subject to political authority are without gratitude, honesty, and courage. The subject population by nature is unable to resist to passions of the moment and will violate both principles and the rights of others. At an intellectual level, there is no creative thought but only the imitation of authority. It is this imitation of authority, together with the desire for self-preservation, that represents the only hope for human redemption.

Machiavelli did not specify precisely how those in power came to avoid the disaster of such a nature. However, he found in the despicable condition of the subject population a mandate for political action. He wrote that rulers are required to employ means that are beyond the pale of personal morality. These include a mastery of legal forms of social control but may also include deception, brute force, and the evaluation of all strategies by means of the ultimate end to which they are put. Therefore, the ruler is advised to give the appearance of virtue, piety, and thrift, thus behaving as the *fox*. Or when necessary, the ruler must resort to power and cruelty as does the *lion*. In the words of Machiavelli, it is "safer to be feared than loved." The power of such imagery had a striking impact on Vilfredo Pareto, as we shall soon discover.

One final point is in order. As we suggested earlier in the case of Auguste Comte, it is not necessary to conclude that the events of his era somehow converted Pareto from democrat to elitist. The ideological alliance between economic "liberalism" (then laissez-faire capitalism) and democracy was weak throughout the turbulence of eighteenth-and nineteenth-century Europe. It was inconceivable to the new owners of property that the fading aristocracy should retain its political privilege. It was also unacceptable that the crown heads continue to use their power to grant economic charters only to those persons and firms that enjoyed royal pleasure. Adam Smith's *Wealth of Nations* became the manifesto of the rising bourgeoisie simply because it called for laissez-faire economics. This meant in effect an end to the mercantile system whereby the crown frequently conferred monopoly status on favoured enterprises.

Calls for bourgeoisie democracy in this historical context did *not* mean universal suffrage, political representation of the whole people, or the recognition of common rights in governmental affairs. Ultimately, it meant state assurance of a free economic order whereby the demands of the marketplace would determine what should be produced, who should produce it, how it should be produced, and how the production should be distributed. Of course, the new owners would be the definers and executives of the "will of the market."

For Pareto, when disenfranchised workers and peasants pressed for land reform, union organization, and public works, democracy had been carried too far. In the situation of his times, the Italian (like Comte and Spencer before him) was a laissez-faire revolutionary. However, he perceived little economic gain and great turmoil to be had should political freedom be expanded. Indeed, before Mussolini's rise to power, the bourgeois agenda was under serious attack by the adherents of an alternative: democratic socialism. Given such conditions, Pareto's "antidemocratic" shift, as seen in his turn to the heritage of Machiavelli, represented a logical step, not a dramatic conversion.

PORTIONS OF PARETO'S ORIGINAL WORK: THE CIRCULATION OF ELITES

2026. *Social elites and their circulation.* Suppose we begin by giving a theoretical definition of the thing we are dealing With, making it as exact as possible, and then go on to see what practical consideration we can replace it with to get a first approximation. Let us for the moment completely disregard considerations as to the good or bad, useful or harmful, praiseworthy or reprehensible character of the various traits in individuals, and confine ourselves to degrees—to whether, in other words, the trait in a given case be slight, average, intense, or more exactly, to the index that may be assigned to each individual with reference to the degree, or intensity, in him of the trait in question.

Let us assume that in every branch of human activity each individual is given an index which stands as a sign of his capacity, very much the way grades are given in the various subjects in examinations in school. The highest type of lawyer, for instance, will be given 10. The man who does not get a client will be given 1—reserving zero for the man who is an out-and-out idiot. To the man who has made his millions—honestly or dishonestly as the case may be—we will give 10. To the man who has earned his thousands we will give 6; to such as just manage to keep out of the poor-house, 1, keeping zero for those who get in. To the woman "in politics," such as the Aspasia of Pericles, the Maintenon of Louis XIV, the Pompadour of Louis XV, who has managed to infatuate a man of power and play a part in the man's career, we shall give some higher number, such as 8 or 9; to the strumpet who merely satisfies the senses of such a man and exerts no influence on public affairs, we shall give zero. To a clever rascal who knows how to fool people and still keep clear of the penitentiary, we shall give 8, 9, or 10, according to the number of geese he has plucked and the amount of money he has been able to get out of them. To the sneak-thief who snatches a piece of silver from a restaurant table and runs away into the arms of a policeman, we shall give 1. To a poet like Carducci we shall give 8 or 9 according to our tastes; to a scribbler who puts people to rout with his sonnets we shall give zero. For chess-players we can get very precise indices, noting what matches, and how many, they have won. And so on for all the branches of human activity.

We are speaking, remember, of an actual, not a potential, state. If at an English examination a pupil says: "I could know English very well if I chose to; I do not know any because I have never seen fit to learn," the examiner replies: "I am not interested in your alibi. The grade for what you know is zero." If, similarly, someone says: "So-and-so does not steal, not because he couldn't, but because he is a gentleman," we reply: "Very well, we admire him for his self-control, but his grade as a thief is zero." There are people who worship Napoleon Bonaparte as a god. There are people who hate him as the lowest of criminals. Which are right? We do not choose to solve that question in connexion with a quite different matter. Whether Napoleon was a good man or a bad man, he was certainly not an idiot, nor a man of little account, as millions of others are. He had exceptional qualities, and that is enough for us to give him a high ranking, though without prejudice of any sort to questions that might be raised as to the ethics of his qualities or their social utility.

The facts just mentioned put us in the way of making a more general classification in which the preceding classification would be included and to which we shall have frequent occasion to refer in explaining social phenomena hereafter (Ss 2313f).

Suppose we put in one category, which we may call S, individuals whose incomes are essentially variable and depend upon the person's wide-awakeness in discovering sources of gain. In that group, generally speaking and disregarding exceptions, will be found those promoters of enterprise—those entrepreneurs—whom we were considering some pages back; and with them will be stockholders in industrial and commercial corporations (but not bondholders, who will more fittingly be placed in our group next following). Then will come owners of real estate in cities where building speculation is rife; and also landowners—on a similar condition that there be speculation in the lands about them; and then stock-exchange speculators and bankers who make money on governmental, industrial, and commercial loans. We might further add all persons depending upon such people—lawyers, engineers, politicians, working-people, clerks—and deriving advantage from their operations. In a word, we are putting together all persons who directly or indirectly speculate and in one way or another manage to increase their incomes by ingeniously taking advantage of circumstances.

And let us put into another category, which we may call R, persons who have fixed or virtually fixed incomes not depending to any great extent on ingenious combinations that may be conceived by an active mind. In this category, roughly, will be found persons who have savings and have deposited them in savings-banks or invested them in life-annuities; then people living on incomes from government bonds, certificates of the funded debt, corporation bonds, or other securities with fixed interest-rates; then owners of real estate and lands in places where there is no speculation; then farmers, working-people, clerks, depending upon such persons and in no way depending upon speculators. In a word, we so group together here all persons who neither directly nor indirectly depend on speculation and who have incomes that are fixed, or virtually fixed, or at least are but slightly variable.

Just to be rid of the inconvenience of using mere letters of the alphabet, suppose we use the term "speculators" for members of category S and the French term *rentiers* for members of category R. Now we can repeat of the two groups of persons more or less what we said above (S 2231) of mere owners of savings and *entrepreneurs*, and we shall find analogous conflicts, economic and social, between them. In the speculator group Class I residues predominate, in the *rentier* group, Class II residues. That that should be the case is readily understandable. A person of pronounced capacity for economic combinations is not satisfied with a fixed income, often a very small one. He wants to earn more, and if he finds a favourable opportunity, he moves into the S category. The two groups perform functions of differing utility in society. The S group is primarily responsible for change, for economic and social progress. The R group, instead, is a powerful element in stability, and in many cases counteracts the dangers attending the adventurous capers of the S's. A society in which R's almost exclusively predominate remains stationary and, as it were, crystallized. A society in which S's predominate lacks stability, lives in a state of shaky equilibrium that may be upset by a slight accident from within or from without.

Members of the R group must not be mistaken for "conservatives," nor members of the S group for "progressives," innovators, revolutionaries (Ss 226, 228-44). They may have points in common with such, but there is no identity. There are evolutions, revolutions, innovations, that the R's support, especially movements tending to restore to the ruling classes certain residues of group-persistence that had been banished by the S's. A revolution may be made against the S's—a revolution of that type founded the Roman Empire, and such, to some extent, was the revolution known as the Protestant Reformation. Then too, for the very reason that sentiments of group-persistence are dominant in them, the R's may be so blinded by sentiment as to act against their own interests. They readily allow themselves to be duped by anyone who takes them on the side of sentiment, and time and time again they have been the artisans of their own ruin (S 1873). If the old feudal lords, who were endowed with R traits in a very conspicuous degree, had not allowed themselves to be swept off their feet by a sum of sentiments in which religious enthusiasm was only one element, they would have seen at once that the Crusades were to be their ruin. In the eighteenth century, had the French nobility living on income, and that part of the French bourgeoisie which was in the same situation, not succumbed to the lure of humanitarian sentiments, they would not have prepared the ground for the Revolution that was to be their undoing. Not a few among the victims of the guillotine had for long years been continually, patiently, artfully grinding the blade that was to cut off their heads. In our day those among the R's who are known as "intellectuals" are following in the footprints of the French nobles of the eighteenth century and are working with all their might to encompass the ruin of their own class (S 2254).

Nor are the categories R and S to be confused with groupings that might be made according to economic occupation (Ss 1726-27). There again we find points of contact, but not full coincidence. A retail merchant often belongs to the R group, and a wholesale merchant too, but the wholesaler will more likely belong to the S group. Sometimes one same enterprise may change in character. An individual of the S type founds an industry as a result of fortunate speculations. When it yields or seems to be yielding a good return, he changes it into a corporation, retires from business, and passes over into the R group. A large number of stockholders in the new concern are also R's—the ones who bought stock when they thought they were buying a sure thing. If they are not mistaken, the business changes in character, moving over from the S type to the R type. But in many cases the best speculation the founder ever made was in changing his business to a corporation. It is soon in jeopardy, with the R's standing in line to pay for the broken crockery. There is no better business in this world than the business of fleecing the lambs—of exploiting the inexperience, the ingenuousness, the passions, of the R's. In our societies the fortunes of many many wealthy individuals have no other foundations.

The differing relative proportions in which S types and R types are combined in the governing class correspond to differing types of civilization; and such proportions are among the principal traits that have to be considered in social heterogeneity. Going back, for instance, to the protectionist cycle examined above (Ss 2209 f.), we may say that in modern democratic countries industrial protection increases the proportion of S's in the governing class. That increase in turn serves to intensify protection, and the process would go on indefinitely if counter-forces did not come into play to check it (S 2221).

6

Contemporary Thinkers

PITIRIM SOROKIN

Pitirim Alexandrovich Sorokin (January 21, 1889 – February 11, 1968) was a Russian-American sociologist born in Komi. Academic and political activist in Russia, he emigrated from Russia to the United States in 1923. He founded the Department of Sociology at Harvard University. He was a vocal opponent of Talcott Parsons' theories. Sorokin was an ardent opponent of communism, which he regarded as a "pest of man." He is best known for his contributions to the social cycle theory.

SOCIAL CYCLE THEORY

Social cycle theories are among the earliest social theories in sociology. Unlike the theory of social evolutionism, which views the evolution of society and human history as progressing in some new, unique direction(s), sociological cycle theory argues that events and stages of society and history are generally repeating themselves in cycles. Such a theory does not necessarily imply that there cannot be any social progress. In the early theory of Ssu-Ma Ch'ien and the more recent theories of long-term ("secular") political-demographic cycles as well as in the Varnic theory of P.R. Sarkar an explicit accounting is made of social progress.

Predecessors

Interpretation of history as repeating cycles of Dark and Golden Ages was a common belief among ancient cultures. Giorgio de Santillana, the former professor of the history of science at MIT, taught that over thirty ancient cultures held this view and associated the changing of the ages to the precession of the equinoxes. It was the dominant world belief prior to the Darwinian era which requires a linear viewpoint and discounts any mention of a long ago Golden Age.

The more limited cyclical view of history defined as repeating cycles of events was put forward in the academic world in the 19th century in historiosophy (a branch of historiography) and is a concept that falls under the category of sociology. However, Polybius, Ibn Khaldun, and Giambattista Vico can be seen as precursors of this analysis. The Saeculum was identified in Roman times. In recent times, P. R. Sarkar in his Social Cycle Theory has used this idea to elabourate his interpretation of history.

Classical Theories

Among the prominent historiosophers, Russian philosopher Nikolai Danilewski (1822-1885) is important. In *Rossiia i Europa* (1869) he differentiated between various smaller civilizations (Egyptian, Chinese, Persian, Greek, Roman, German, and Slav, among others). He wrote that each civilization has a life cycle, and by the end of the 19th century the Roman-German civilization was in decline, while the Slav civilization was approaching its Golden Age. A similar theory was put forward by Oswald Spengler (1880-1936) who in his *Der Untergang des Abendlandes* (1918) also expected that the Western civilization was about to collapse. The first social cycle theory in sociology was created by Italian sociologist and economist Vilfredo Pareto (1848-1923) in his *Trattato di Sociologia Generale* (1916). He centered his theory on the concept of an elite social class, which he divided into cunning 'foxes' and violent 'lions'. In his view of society, the power constantly passes from the 'foxes' to the 'lions' and vice versa.

Sociological cycle theory was also developed by Pitirim A. Sorokin (1889-1968) in his *Social and Cultural Dynamics* (1937, 1943). He classified societies according to their 'cultural mentality', which can be ideational (reality is spiritual), sensate (reality is material), or idealistic (a synthesis of the two). He interpreted the contemporary West as a sensate civilization dedicated to technological progress and prophesied its fall into decadence and the emergence of a new ideational or idealistic era.

Modern Theories

One of the most important recent findings in the study of the long-term dynamic social processes was the discovery of the political-demographic cycles as a basic feature of the dynamics of complex agrarian systems. The presence of political-demographic cycles in the pre-modern history of Europe and China, and in chiefdom level societies worldwide has been known for quite a long time, and already in the 1980s more or less developed mathematical models of demographic cycles started to be produced (first of all for Chinese "dynastic cycles") (Usher 1989). At the moment we have a very considerable number of such models.

Recently the most important contributions to the development of the mathematical models of long-term ("secular") sociodemographic cycles have been made by Sergey Nefedov, Peter Turchin, Andrey Korotayev, and Sergey Malkov. What is important is that on the basis of their models Nefedov, Turchin and Malkov have managed to demonstrate that sociodemographic cycles were a basic feature of complex agrarian systems (and not a specifically Chinese or European phenomenon).

The basic logic of these models is as follows:

- After the population reaches the ceiling of the carrying capacity of land, its growth rate declines toward near-zero values.
- The system experiences significant stress with decline in the living standards of the common population, increasing the severity of famines, growing rebellions etc.
- As has been shown by Nefedov, most complex agrarian systems had considerable reserves for stability, however, within 50–150 years these reserves were usually exhausted and the system experienced a demographic collapse (a Malthusian catastrophe), when increasingly severe famines, epidemics, increasing internal warfare and other disasters led to a considerable decline of population.

- As a result of this collapse, free resources became available, per capita production and consumption considerably increased, the population growth resumed and a new sociodemographic cycle started.

It has become possible to model these dynamics mathematically in a rather effective way. Note that the modern theories of political-demographic cycles do not deny the presence of trend dynamics and attempt at the study of the interaction between cyclical and trend components of historical dynamics.

Modern social scientists from different fields have introduced cycle theories to predict civilizational collapses in approaches that apply contemporary methods that update the approach of Spengler, such as the work of Joseph Tainter suggesting a civilizational life-cycle. In more micro-studies that follow the work of Malthus, scholars such as David Lempert have presented "alpha-helix" models of population, economics, and political response, including violence, in cyclical forms that add aspects of culture change into the model. Lempert has also modeled political violence in Russian society, suggesting that theories attributing violence in Russia to ideologies are less useful than cyclical models of population and economic productivity.

In Sarkar's Law of Social Cycle social progress is defined in terms of a new vision of human progress by placing an emphasis on human spiritual development. Integrated with that is Sarkar's theory of four basic ages of *warriors*, *intellectuals* and *acquisitors*, and a brief age of *labourers*. During such ages humanity has faced an eternal struggle with each epoch deteriorating into a harmful exploitative phase.

Sarkar devises an exit strategy from such a development, based on the role of enlightened moralists, the Sad-Vipras. It is their role, based on self-less virtues and ideation on the divine, to apply energy and accelerate social momentum when the evolutionary process is caught up in social stasis. If this is not done, the ruling class, after having abandoned its original virtues, by placing an intense focus on its own social agenda begins to inflict tremendous and unjustified misery on other sections of society. The downfall of Soviet Communism in 1990, the Great Depression of the 1930s and the Late-2000s recession are manifestations of such social stasis.

A PANORAMIC VIEW OF SOCIETY AND CULTURE

Sorokin's monumental *Social and Cultural Dynamics,* in which he at-tempted to develop a full explanatory scheme for social and cultural change (with supporting evidence based on detailed statistical investigations), must be taken as the major exhibit for assessing his view of social change. The work as a whole, as Louis Schneider has suggested, has a somewhat romantic cast: it presents a profusion of ideas and daring hypotheses, but lacks the poise, soberness, and careful marshalling of arguments that characterize the classical style. Such work is best approached by attention to its overall message and major contentions rather than by way of detailed criticism of particulars.

In this work, Sorokin attempts no less than a panoramic survey of the course of all human societies and cultures, supported by a series of general propositions to illuminate the historical variation in socio-cultural arrangements. He opposes any unilinear explanation of human evolution just as he opposes any approach that, as in the case of Spengler for example, conceives of the life cycle of cultures by way of quasi-biological analogies. Instead, he views socio-cultural phenomena as based on relatively coherent and integrated aggregates of cultural outlooks—which he calls *mentalities*—that impress their meanings on specific periods in the global history of humankind. What he is looking for, in his own words, is "the central principle [the reason] which permeates all the components" of a culture, "gives sense and significance to them, and in this way makes cosmos of a chaos of unintegrated fragments." He does not claim that any culture is ever fully integrated, and he is aware that it will always contain fragments that are not fully reconcilable. Still, he stresses that socio-cultural phenomena are not randomly distributed: rather, once analyzed from his specific angle of vision, they will reveal the operation of a few major *premises* that mark their overall character.

There are, according to Sorokin, only three fundamental premises for conceiving and apprehending the nature of reality. Either reality is felt to be directly accessible through the senses *(Sensate Culture)*: or it is felt to be disclosed only through a view that transcends the world of the senses and achieves a transcendent vision of the eternal, as in Platonic idealism

(Ideational Culture); or, finally, it takes an intermediate form *(Idealistic Culture)*, which attempts to fuse and synthesize the other two in a dialectical balance between opposite principles.

Correspondingly, there are three irreducible forms of truth: sensory, spiritual, and rational. At various periods of history, one of the three basic premises achieves preeminence over the others and stamps its character on the main ways of thinking, feeling, or experiencing that distinguish an epoch. That is why the principal institutions of society (law, art, philosophy, science, and religion) exhibit at any particular time a consistent mental outlook that is the reflection of the predominance of one or the other of the three major cultural premises. During a *Sensate* period, for example science will be rigidly empirical in its methods and procedures, art will strive for realism rather than for the imparting of transcendent visions, and religion will tend to be more concerned with the quest for concrete moral experience than for the truth of faith or reason.

Having been persuaded by his survey of world history that all the varieties of cultural constellations that have appeared on the human scene can be effectively encompassed as subvarieties of the three major *cultural* mentalities, Sorokin proceeds to explain why all major social change must be recurrent. The ceaseless flux of history, so he contends, has characteristic rhythms that are far from being random or subject to the whims of the Gods. Any culture, determined as it is by its major premises, follows a kind of inner necessity: it is subject to its own peculiar destiny. But the predominance of one fundamental *cultural mentality* carries within itself its own demise through the exhaustion of its own premises. This is what Sorokin, rejecting any explanation of social change through external factors, has called the principle of *immanent change.* As cultural systems reach the zenith of their full flowering, they "become less and less capable of serving as an instrument of adaptation, as an experience for real satisfaction of the needs of its bearers, and as foundation for their social and cultural life." At this point, a cultural system, by driving to the limits the premises that gave it birth, exceeds the mark, distorts the portion of truth it once embodied through one-sided exaggeration, and prepares its own demise, thereby giving birth to a new cultural system. This dialectic, which bears strong resemblances to the Hegelian, is at the heart of Sorokin's principle of *limits* and purports to explain the rhythmic periodicity of all socio-cultural phenomena. For Sorokin, just as for Hegel, change implies the rise of a new life at the same time as it imparts dissolution.

The three major types of *cultural mentalities*, Sorokin contends, follow each other in reliable sequence. *Sensate* forms will be followed by *Ideational,* and they in turn by *Idealistic* forms of cultural integration. After this cycle has been completed, the recurrence of a new *Sensate* culture will initiate a new cycle. Since the days of the early Greeks and their *Sensate* culture, Western culture has completed two cycles of this sequence. We are now living at the end of a *Sensate* phase which has lasted for several hundred years. This stage is now overripe, it has reached its limits, and we live in the shadow of twilight among the debris of a disintegrating culture that is no longer able to give meaning and significance to our lives. Ideas once dominant and organizing no longer serve as guideposts, having fallen apart. We can already discern the first harbingers of a new *Ideational* integration sprouting like seeds beneath the snow. Ours is a world in which the center no longer holds and where even the best lack all conviction. But those who have the vision can have intimations of glad tidings of future redemption from the tyranny of the senses.

This is not the place to discuss the enormous statistical labours that went into establishing trends in the fluctuation of art forms, of philosophical, ethical, and legal norms and values, or of social relationships in ordinary times as well as during wars and revolutions—all of which are to be found in the first three volumes of Sorokin's *magnum opus*. They have been scrutinized by experts in these areas and have frequently been found to be wanting. One especially telling overall criticism was made long ago by Hans Speier, who has said that Sorokin's study of history "is imbued with the spirit of the doctrine that he desires to refute," since the methods he uses to establish the impermanence of *Sensate* and empirical culture are in themselves extremely empirical. Sorokin would probably have answered that it is given to no man to step out of his time, that even an attempt to refute the preeminence of Sensate empiricism must still avail itself of the tools that his age and time put at his disposal. Nevertheless, Sorokin's "romantic" contribution will have to be judged in the future not by any isolated concrete result of his investigation, but by the fruitfulness of the theoretical leads he has imparted to succeeding scholars. Viewed in this light, at least some of these leads may well survive, even if a number of his general contentions will have been swept aside. Furthermore, even though he may have been wrong on many counts, some of Sorokin's anticipations, written in the 1930's indeed have a prophetic character. What he wrote then about the possible destruction of humankind by the pushing of buttons or about the coming celebration of hard-core pornography shows an almost uncanny sense of things to come in the world of the 1970's.

At a time when sociologists, under the impact of the debate about modernization and underdevelopment, have again begun to discuss the principles underlying the dynamics of socio-cultural change, Sorokin's stress on immanent change, as distinct from externally induced change may have renewed significance. When scholars have increasingly wondered why the external impact of Western culture has had so widely differing results in many Third World nations, it might be well to assume Sorokin's angle of vision and to ask whether cultures in their *Idealistic* or *Ideational* phases might be more resistant to the importation of the *Sensate* cultures of the West than cultures, such as the Japanese or the Korean, that are already largely conditioned by *Sensate* sets of ideas. Why, for example, are modern methods of birth control readily acceptable in those countries while they have failed in India or Egypt? Could it be that they are "out of phase" in the latter, but not in the former, countries?

Turning to Sorokin's *principle of limits*, one again has the impression that if it were shorn of the somewhat dogmatic and grandiose manner in which it was first formulated, it could have interesting possibilities as a hypothesis. In fact, it has been one of the mainstays of Claude Levi-Strauss's method of analysis. Whether or not Levi-Strauss is familiar with Sorokin's work, the resemblances are striking. For example, Levi-Strauss writes: "... In social un-dertakings mankind keeps manoeuvering within narrow limits. Social types are not isolated creations, wholly independent of each other, and each one an original entity, but rather the result of endless combinations, forever seeking to solve the same problems by manipulating the same fundamental elements." As should already be apparent, Sorokin's overall view is closely tied to his sociology of knowledge, a field to which, it is generally agreed, he made significant contributions.

SOCIOLOGY OF KNOWLEDGE

Sorokin's sociology of knowledge rejects any attempt to root ideas in the existential conditions of thinkers and their audiences. This contrasts sharply with most other sociological attempts to understand the rise and fall of ideas in relation to social structures, and is specifically in opposition to the theories of Marx, Weber and Mannheim, which have been examined earlier in this book. Although Sorokin has occasionally indicated that such an endeavour may be worthwhile, he himself did not take this route. Instead, his sociology of knowledge attempts to establish connections between concrete philosophical, religious, artistic, and scientific thought and the overall *cultural mentalities* in which this thought appears and flourishes. As has already been discussed, he attempts to document, for example, that in *Sensate* periods, scientific ideas tend to be based exclusively on sense experience and empirical proof and validation, whereas in periods of *Ideational* ascendancy, empirical science fails to develop, being replaced by varieties of *Naturphilosophien* that purport to attain intuitive insights into the nature of the universe.

Such attempts to link systems of ideas to supersystems and to drive every aspect of intellectual production from varying cultural mentalities, are open to the charge of tautological reasoning. As Merton has remarked, when Sorokin argues that "in a sensate society and culture the sensate system of truth based on the testimony of the organs of senses has to be dominant," he plainly argued in circles, "for sensate mentality has already been *defined* as one conserving of reality as only that which is presented to the sense organs.' " Sorokin's answer to such charges has not been very convincing. But even if his overall idealistic and emanationist explanation seems open to serious objections, this is not to say that his sociology of knowledge has been sterile. One need only dig beneath some of his grandiose characterizations of cultures to be re-warded by significant and worthwhile sets of concrete ideas.

Take, for example, Sorokin's discussion of the question which cultural values penetrate and diffuse more easily when imported into an alien culture? In an effort to answer this question he does not simply refer to the overall compatibility of values between donor and recipient cultures, though he does this also; rather he points to the character of the human agents that first come into contact with the donor culture. "The kind of values," he says "that pene-trate first depends, primarily, upon the kinds of human agents that first come into contact with the other culture. If they are merchants... then various commercial commodities penetrate first; if they are missionaries... then the ideological values' penetrate first. If they are conquerors and soldiers, then partly material, partly non-material values penetrate simultaneously. If they are students of philosophy or social science then they bring back and spread the theories and ideologies they studied." This is a significant insight worth further elabouration, an insight, moreover, which points to the connection of ideas with the existential conditions of their carriers, and is hence not subject to the charge of tautology that must beset all emanationist theories in the sociology of knowledge.

Or consider Sorokin's first adumbration of a sociological theory of scientific discovery and technological invention, namely the idea that "any important new invention... or any important new discovery in the natural sciences... is the result of a long process, with a multitude of small discoveries made step by step, [so that] the really new element in any important invention or discovery is comparatively a very modest one." In this case, Sorokin, to be sure, does not refer to the existential basis of scientific thought, yet he departs from his programmatic endeavours to link specific ideas to their matrix in overall cultural mentalities. He engaged, in fact, in an attempt to trace cumulative trends within scientific communities and to link specific innovators to the scientific tradition within which they operate.

Many of Sorokin's usable ideas in the sociology of knowledge do not come in his programmatic *magnum opus* but in a more modest companion volume, *Sociocultural Causality, Space,*

Time, published a few years later. Here, in a manner reminiscent of Durkheim and his school, Sorokin shows that the way a specific culture conceives of causality, space, and time is not identical with natural science conceptions and must be understood in relation to the specific socio-cultural context. Also following the Durkheimians, he argues moreover that even the space of the geometricians, for example, is "greatly conditioned and stamped by the sociocultural traits of the respective society and culture. The very units of the geometric distance—such as 'foot,' 'yard,' 'meter,' 'sajen,' 'finger,' 'rod,' and so on—bear the imprint of these [socio-cultural] conditions." Sorokin shows further how, with the increase in communications between local societies and the wider world, parochial systems of thought recede before more universal representations of space." 'To the right of Jones's house, about twenty rods' serves the purpose for a village where everyone knows where Jones's house is situated. But for the whole human population, such a point of spatial reference becomes indefinable and therefore unserviceable." The difference between universalistic and particularistic codes of communication, which has been highlighted in our days by Basil Bernstein and other scholars, can already be found *in nuce* in Sorokin's work.

It is worth noting Sorokin's observation that "the emergence of uniform... space of classical mechanics itself, with its system of reference, was conditioned by the sociocultural process of growth of cosmopolitan and international society and culture"; or his discussion of the fact that "when intercourse extends over many groups with different rhythms of sociocultural activities, and time indications, the concrete and local systems of sociocultural time cease to perform satisfactorily the functions of coordination and synchronization of their activities. Hence the urgent need to establish such a standardized system of time reckoning... as would serve equally all the groups as the uniform point of time reference for the coordination and synchronization of their activities." Here Sorokin succeeds in showing in convincing detail that notions such as time and space do not simply emanate from overall mentalities but are rooted in the concrete exigencies of human communities; that the~ are with apologies to Sorokin the emanist, existentially determined.

One further quotation will illustrate the great subtlety of Sorokin's sociological imagination. After having shown that in the modern world universal time-reckoning has largely replaced the community-rooted parochial ways of dealing with time, Sorokin turns around and makes the acute observation that the older qualitative time measures have by no means been fully replaced by quantitative time. In line with the art historian Wilhelm Pinder and reminiscent of what Mannheim called the "contemporaneity of the noncontempora-neous," Sorokin argues: "Within the same territorial aggregate composed of different religious, occupational, economic, national, and cultural groups, there are different rhythms and pulsations, and therefore different calendars and different conventions for the sociocultural time of these groups... Compare... a Harvard calendar with one operating, say, among factory workers.... The calendar of the Roman Catholics in Boston—in part, at least—is different from that of the Protestant Bostonians.... Side by side with quantitative time (which itself is in a degree a social convention), there exists a full-blooded sociocultural time, with all its 'earmarks': it is qualitative, it is not infinitely divisible..., it does not flow on evenly...; it is determined by social conditions, and reflects the rhythms and pulsations of the social life of a given group...

One ventures to think that this set of observations provides leads for several Ph.D. dissertations, even though the great French Durkheimian Maurice Halbwachs, probably unaware of Sorokin's work, has elabourated some of these ideas in his seminal work *The Social Framework of Memory* and elsewhere. Despite the fact that his ambitious overall scheme, like all closed total systems of sociological thought, may be found wanting, it should be apparent by now that Sorokin was a major force, a major thinker. Or, as a whimsical button worn by some graduate students at a recent convention of the American Sociological Association put it, "Sorokin lives."

SOCIAL STRATIFICATION AND SOCIAL MOBILITY

Sorokin holds a unique place in the study of social stratification and mobility. We owe to him the creation or definition of many of the terms that have become standard in this field. We also owe him a distinct vision of what the study of social mobility should be mainly concerned with, namely, the courses and consequences of demographic exchanges between groups, as distinct from the study of individuals who may move up or down or sideways in the social hierarchy. Sorokin defined social mobility in its broadest sense as the shifting of people in social space. He was not, however, interested in movements of individuals but in social metabolism, in the consequences of such movements for social groups differently located in the social structure.

"To find the position of a man or a social phenomenon in social space," Sorokin argued in the first place, "means to define his or its relations to other men or other social phenomena chosen as the point of reference.' " Methods appropriate for the study of mobility are somewhat reminiscent of the system of coordinates used for the location of an object in geometrical space. But the analytical task is not completed when one has established a person's relations to specific groups. What needs further exploration is "the relation of these groups to each other within a population, and the relation of this population to other populations." In other words, though the study of social mobility needs to concern itself with the movements of individuals, it also needs to pay close attention to the consequences of these movements for the social groups and the total structures that encompass these individual moves. Before considering social mobility we must know a good deal about the structure of stratification in which such movements occur.

Social stratification, to Sorokin, means "the differentiation of a given population into hierarchically superposed classes." Such stratification, he held, is a permanent characteristic of any organized social group. Stratification may be based on *economic* criteria—for example, when one focuses attention upon the differentials between the wealthy and the poor. But societies or groups are also *politically stratified* when their social ranks are hierarchically structured with respect to authority and power. If, however, the members of a society are differentiated into various occupational groups and some of these occupations are deemed more honourable than others, or if occupations are internally divided between those who give orders and those who receive orders, then we deal with *occupational stratification*. Though there may be other concrete forms of stratification, of central sociological importance are economic, political, and occupational stratification.

Sociological investigation must proceed to pay attention to the height and the profile of stratification pyramids. Of how many layers is it composed? Is its profile steep, or does it slope gradually ?

Whether one studies economic, political, or occupational stratification, Sorokin contended, one must always be attentive to two distinct phenomena: the rise or decline of a group as a whole and the increase or decrease of stratification within a group. In the first case we deal with increases of wealth, power, or occupational standing of social groups, as when we talk of the decline of the aristocracy or the rise of the bourgeoisie; in the second, we are concerned with the increase or decrease of the height and steepness of the stratification pyramid in regard to wealth, power, or occupational prestige within groups—for example, when we say that the American Black population now has a higher stratification profile than it had at the turn of the century.

In contrast to evolutionary and "progressive' thought, and in tune with his overall view of the course of human history, Sorokin argued that no consistent trend toward either the heightening or the flattening of stratificational pyramids can be discerned. Instead, all that can be observed is ceaseless fluctuation. At times, differences between the poor and the rich may be reduced through the impact of equalitarian forces, but at other times inequalitarian tendencies will again assert themselves. Or at one point democratic participation will reduce differences in political power, while at another aristocratic and dictatorial politics will successfully increase the height of the political pyramid. In similar ways, some groups decline and others rise in ceaseless fluctuation.

Exterior features of the architecture of social structures having been sketched, Sorokin proceeds to summarize their inner construction, to wit the character and disposition of the floors, the elevators, and the staircases that lead from one story to another; the ladders and accommodations for climbing up and going down from story to story. This brings him to the concrete details of his study of social mobility.

Social mobility is understood as the transition of people from one social position to another. There are two types of social mobility, *horizontal* and *vertical*. The first concerns movements from one social position to another situated on the same level, as in a movement from Baptist to Methodist affiliation, or from work as a foreman with Ford to similar work with Chrysler. The second refers to transitions of people from one social stratum to one higher or lower in the social scale, as in ascendant movements from rags to riches or in the downward mobility of inept children of able parents.

Both ascending and descending movements occur in two principal forms: the penetration of individuals of a lower stratum into an existing higher one, and the descent of individuals from a higher social position to one lower on the scale; or the collective ascent or descent of whole groups relative to other groups in the social pyramid. But—and this is what distinguished Sorokin's orientation from that of many contemporary students of stratification and mobility—his main focus was upon collective, not on individual phenomena. As he puts it, "The case of individual infiltration into an existing higher stratum or of individuals dropping from a higher social layer into a lower one are relatively common and comprehensible. They need no explanation. The second form of social ascending and descending, the rise and fall of groups, must be considered more carefully.

Groups and societies, according to Sorokin, may be distinguished according to their differences in the intensiveness and generality of social mobility. There may be stratified societies in which vertical mobility is virtually nil and others in which it is very frequent. We must therefore be careful to distinguish between the height and profile of stratification, and the prevalence or absence of social mobility. In some highly stratified societies where the membranes between strata are thin, social mobility is very high. In contrast other societies with various profiles and heights of stratification have hardly any stairs and elevators to allow members to pass from one floor to another, so that the strata are largely closed, rigidly separated, immobile, and virtually impenetrable. Assuming that there are no societies in which strata are absolutely closed and none where social mobility is absolutely free from obstacles, one must recognize that Sorokin's distinctions, even though stated too metaphorically, are of considerable heuristic value. In regard to degrees of openness and closure, Sorokin holds to his usual position. No perpetual trend toward either increase or decrease of vertical mobility can be discerned in the course of human history; all that can be noticed are variations through geographical space and fluctuations in historical time.

Attempting to identify the *channels of vertical mobility* and the mechanisms of social selection and distribution of individuals within different social strata, Sorokin identifies the army, the church, the school, as well as political, professional, and economic organizations, as principal conduits of vertical social circulation. They are the "sieves" that sift individuals who claim access to different social strata and positions. All these institutions are involved in social selection and distribution of the members of a society. They decide which people will climb and fall; they allocate individuals to various strata; they either open gates for the flow of individuals or create impediments to their movements.

Without minutely detailing the many ways in which Sorokin illustrates the operation of these institutions or the way in which he shows why at a given time certain stratification profiles have called for specific mechanisms of selection, we should take note, however, of what he considers a "permanent and universal" basis for interoccupational stratification, namely: "The importance of an occupation for the survival and existence of a group as a whole." The occupations that are considered most consequential in a society, he states, are those that "are connected with the functions of organization and control of a group."

In considering the impact of actual rates of social mobility, as well as the ideology of social mobility, on modern societies, we find Sorokin offers a fresh approach in the light of current experience. Far from indulging in unalloyed enthusiasm about high degrees of social mobility, Sorokin, like Durkheim, was at pains to highlight its dysfunctional and its functional aspects. He stressed, among other things, the heavy price in mental strain, mental disease, cynicism, social isolation, and loneliness of individuals cut adrift from their social moorings. He also stressed the increase in tolerance and the facilitation of intellectual life (as a result of discoveries and inventions) that were likely to occur with more frequency in highly mobile societies.

The analyst of social stratification, social mobility, and related matters can ignore Sorokin's work only at his or her expense. It still remains a veritable storehouse of ideas. Above all we need to take Sorokin's advice when he urges us to consider social mobility as a form of social exchange. Just as Levi-Strauss brought about a revolution in the study of kinship (stressing that marriage is to be seen as an exchange between elementary families), so Sorokin presents the innovative idea that social mobility does not primarily concern the placement of individuals but is to be understood as exchange between social groups. By fostering the circulation of individuals in social space, such exchange increases or decreases the specific weight and power of the groups and strata between which they move. This central idea, if more fully elabourated, could be the impetus for a great deal of research in social stratification.

THE SOCIAL PHILOSOPHY

In a work on the history of sociological theories, Sorokin's "integralist" philosophy can be discussed only in a peripheral way, even though it undoubtedly loomed very large among Sorokin's preoccupations, especially in the last third of his life.

All of Sorokin's tracts for the times that deal with his philosophy are imbued with a pervasive distaste, one may even say hatred, for modern urban culture and all that it stands for. The *Sensate* world of the city jungle and the world of modernity as a whole are, to Sorokin, compounds of utter depravity, which he castigates in the accents of Old Testament prophets or Russian itinerant preachers. Consider the following lines from the final chapter of his autobiography: "... In the human world around me the deadliest storm is raging. The very destiny of mankind is being weighed in the balance of life and death. The forces of the dying Sensate order are furiously destroying everything that stands in their way. In the name of 'God,' 'progress,' 'civilization,' communism,' 'democracy,' 'freedom,' 'capitalism,' 'the dignity of man,' and other shib-boleths they are uprooting these very values, murdering millions of human beings, threatening man's very survival and tending to turn this beautiful planet into an 'abomination of desolation.' " Sorokin's was an apocalyptic vision; he expected the fire next time. Yet, instilled as he was by a philosophy of history that rested on the notion of cyclical fluctuations in human affairs, he seems never to have doubted that the collapse of Western Sensate culture would be followed in its turn by a rebirth under different stars.

It is this new *Ideational* culture that Sorokin sought to anticipate in his Integralist philosophy. In times to come, the present desert of love would he superseded by a harmonious civilization in which altruistic love—which he studied intensely in the last period of his life—would overcome the competitive strivings of *Sensate* mentalities; here people would again find a secure footing in revitalized communities of their fellows. Then "the supreme Trinity of Truth, Goodness, and Beauty, wrongly divorced from one another by Sensate mentality" will be reinstalled in "one harmonious whole." Men and women, now mired in the slough of despond, will again grow to truly human stature. Sorokin fervently believed, that after the *Goetterdaemmerung* of the dying *Sensate* order, humankind would again enter into its true kingdom. Having "deliberately become a 'stranger' to the glittering vacuities, and short-lived 'successes' " of *Sensate* decay, having "alienated [himself] from its hollow values, sham-truths, and grandiose pretenses," Sorokin saw himself as another Moses who, even though he could not enter the promised land, was still able, owing to his cultural estrangement, to forecast its main features in his Integralist philosophy. Let him who has never dreamt of a redemptive Utopia of the future cast the first stone.

SOCIAL MOBILITY

By social mobility is understood any transition of an individual or social object or value—anything that has been created or modified by human activity—from one social position to another. There are two principal types of social mobility, *horizontal* and *vertical*.. By horizontal social mobility or shifting, is meant the transition of an individual or social object from one social group to another situated on the same level. Transitions of individuals, as from the Baptist to the Methodist religious group, from one citizenship to another, from one family (as a husband or wife) to another by divorce and remarriage, from one factory to another in the same occupational status, are all instances of social mobility. So too are transitions of social objects, the radio, automobile, fashion, Communism, Darwin's theory, within the same social stratum, as from lowa to California, or from any one place to another. In all these cases, "shifting" may take place without any noticeable change of the social position of an individual or social object in the vertical direction. By *vertical* social mobility is meant the relations involved in a transition of an individual (or a social object) from one social stratum to another. According to the direction of the transition there are two types of vertical social mobility: *ascending* and *descending*, or *social climbing* and *social sinking*. According to the nature of the stratification, there are ascending and descending currents of economic, political, and occupational mobility, not to mention other less important types. The ascending currents exist in two principal forms: as an *infiltration* of the individuals of a lower stratum into an existing higher one; and as a *creation of a new group by such individuals, and the insertion of such a group into a higher stratum instead of, or side by side with, the existing groups of this stratum.*. Correspondingly, the descending current has also two principal forms: the first consists in a dropping of individuals from a higher social position into an existing lower one, without a degradation or disintegration of the higher group to which they belonged; the second is manifested in *a degradation of a socia group as a whole, in an abasement of its rank among other groups, or in its disintegration as a social unit.*. The first case of "sinking" reminds one of an individual falling from a ship; the second of the sinking of the ship itself with all on board, or of the ship as a wreck breaking itself to pieces.

The cases of individual infiltration into an existing higher stratum or of individuals dropping from a higher social layer into a lower one are relatively common and comprehensible. They need no explanation. The second form of social ascending and descending, the rise and fall of groups, must be considered more carefully.

The following historical examples may serve to illustrate. The historians of India's caste-society tell us that the caste of the Brahmins did not always hold the position of indisputable superiority which it has held during the last two thousand years. In the remote past, the caste of the warriors and rulers, or the caste of the Kshatriyas, seems to have been not inferior to the caste of the Brahmins; and it appears that only after a long struggle did the latter become the highest caste. If this hypothesis be true, then this elevation of the rank of the Brahmin caste as a whole through the ranks of other castes is an example of the second type of social ascent.

The group as a whole being elevated, all its members, *in corpore*, through this very fact, are elevated also. Before the recognition of the Christian religion by Constantine the Great, the position of a Christian Bishop, or the Christian clergy, was not a high one among other social ranks of Roman society. In the next few centuries the Christian Church, as a whole, experienced an enormous elevation of social position and rank. Through this wholesale elevation of the Christian Church, the members of the clergy, and especially the high Church dignitaries, were elevated to the highest ranks of medieval society. And, contrariwise, a decrease in the authority of the Christian Church during the last two centuries has led to a relative abasement of the social ranks of the high Church dignitaries within the ranks of the present society.

The position of the Pope or a cardinal is still high, but undoubtedly it is lower than it was in the Middle Ages. The group of the legists in France is another example. In the twelfth century, this group appeared in France, as a group, and began to grow rapidly in significance and rank. Very soon, in the form of the judicial aristocracy, it inserted itself into the place of the previously existiug nobility. In this way, its members were raised to a much higher social position. During the seventeenth, and especially the eighteenth centuries, the group, as a whole, began to "sink," and finally disappeared in the conflagration of the Revolution. A similar process took place in the elevation of the Communal *Bourgeoisie* in the Middle Ages, in the privileged Six Corps or the *Guilda Mercatoria*, and in the aristocracy of many royal courts. To have a high position at the court of the Romanoffs, Hapsburgs, or Hohenzollerns before the revolutions meant to have one of the highest social ranks in the corresponding countries. The "sinking" of the dynasties led to a "social sinking" of all ranks connected with them. The group of the Communists in Russia, before the Revolution, did not have any high rank socially recognized. During the Rwolution the group climbed an enormous social distance and occupied the highest strata in Russian society. As a result, all its members have been elevated *en masse* to the place occupied by the Czarist aristocracy. Similar cases are given in a purely economic stratification. Before the "oil" and "automobile" era, to be a prominent manufacturer in this field did not mean to be a captain of industry and finance. A great expansion of these industries has transformed them into some of the most important kinds of industry. Correspondingly, to be a leading manufacturer in these fields now means to be one of the most important leaders of industry and finance. These examples illustrate the second collective form of ascending and descending currents of social mobility.

INTENSIVENESS OR VELOCITY AND GENERALITY OF VERTICAL SOCIAL MOBILITY

From the quantitative point of view, a further distinction must be made between the intensiveness and the generality of the vertical mobility. By its *intensiveness* is meant the vertical social distance, or the number of strata—economic or occupational or political— crossed by an individual in his upward or downward movement in a definite period of time. If, for instance, one individual in one year climbed from the position of a man with a yearly income of $500 to a position with an income of $50,000, while another man in the same period succeeded in increasing his income only from $500 to $1,000, in the first case the intensiveness of the economic climbing would be fifty times greater than in the second case. For a corresponding change, the intensiveness of the vertical mobility may be measured in the same way in the field to the political and occupational stratifications. By the generality of the vertical mobility, is meant the number of individuals who have changed their social position in the vertical direction in a definite period of time. The absolute number of such individuals gives the *absolute generality* of the vertical mobility in a given population; the proportion of such individuals to the total number of a given population gives the *relative generality of the vertical mobility*.

Finally, combining the data of intensiveness and relative generality of the vertical mobility in a definite field (e.g., in the economic), *the aggregate index of the vertical economic mobility of a given society* may be obtained. In this way a comparison of one society with another, or of the same society at different periods may be made, to find in which of them, or at what period, the aggregate mobility is greater. The same may be said about the aggregate index of the political and occupational vertical mobility.

Immobile and Mobile Types of Stratified Societies

On the basis of the above, it is easy to see that a social stratification of the same height and profile may have a different inner structure caused by the difference in the intensiveness and generality of the (horizontal and) vertical social mobility. Theoretically, there may be a stratified society in which the vertical social mobility is nil. This means that within it there is no ascending or descending, no circulation of its members; that every individual is forever attached to the social stratum in which he was bom; that the membranes or hymens which separate one stratum from another are absolutely impenetrable, and do not have any "holes" through which, nor any stairs and elevators with which, the dwellers of the different strata may pass from one floor to another. *Such a type of stratification may be styled as absolutely closed, rigid, impenetrable, or immobile.* The opposite theoretical type of the inner structure of the stratification of the same height and profile is that in which the vertical mobility is very intensive and general; here the membranes between the strata are very thin and have the largest holes to pass from one floor to another. Therefore, though the social building is as stratified as the immobile one, nevertheless, the dwellers of its different strata are continually challenging; they do not stay a very long time in the same "social story," and with the help of the largest staircases and elevators are *en masse* moving "up and down." *Such a type of social stratification may be styled open, plastic, penetrable, or mobile.* Between these two extreme types there may be many middle or intermediary types of stratification.

Having indicated these types and the types of the vertical mobility, turn now to an analysis of the different kinds of societies and the same society at different times, from the standpoint of the vertical mobility and penetrability of their strata.

Democracy and Vertical Social Mobility

One of the most conspicuous characteristics of the so-called "democratic societies" is a more intensive vertical mobility compared with that of the non-democratic groups. In democratic societies the social position of an individual, at least theoretically, is not determined by his birth; all positions are open to everybody who can get them; there are no judicial or religious obstacles to climbing or going down. All this facilitates a "greater vertical mobility" (capillarity, according to the expression of Dumont) in such societies. This greater mobility is probably one of the causes of the belief that the social building of democratic societies is not stratified, or is less stratified, than that of autocratic societies. We have seen that this opinion is not warranted by the facts. Such a belief is a kind of mental aberration, due to many causes, and among them to the fact that the strata in democratic groups are more open, have more holes and "elevators" to go up and down. This produces the illusion that there are no strata, even though they exist.

In pointing out this considerable mobility of the democratic societies, a reservation must be made at the same time, for not always, and not in all "democratic" societies, is the vertical mobility greater than in the "autocratic" ones. In some of the non-democratic groups mobility has been greater than in the democracies. This is not often seen because the "channels" and the methods of climbing and sinking in such societies are not "the elections," as in democracies, but other and somewhat different ones. While "elections" are conspicuous indications of mobility, its other outlets and channels are often overlooked Hence the impression of the stagnant and immobile character of all "non-electoral" societies. That this impression is far from being always true will be shown.

General Principles of Vertical Mobility

First Proposition.—There has scarcely been any society whose strata were absolutely closed, or in which vertical mobility in its three forms—economic, political and occupational—was not present.. That the strata of primitive tribes have been penetrable follows from the fact that within many of them there is no hereditary high position; their leaders often have been elected, their structures have been far from being quite rigid, and the personal qualities of an individual have played a decisive role in social ascent or descent. The nearest approach to an absolutely rigid society, without any vertical mobility, is the so-called caste-society. Its most conspicuous type exists in India. Here, indeed, vertical social mobility is very weak. But even here it has not been absolutely absent. Historical records show that in the past, when the caste-system had already been developed, it did happen that members of the highest Brahmin caste, or the king and his family, were overthrown or cast out for crimes. "Through a want of modesty many kings have perished, together with their belongings; through modesty even hermits in the forest have gained kingdoms.

Through a want of humility Vena perished, likewise king Nahusha, Sudas, Sumukha and Nevi," etc. On the other hand, the outcasts, after a suitable repentance, might be reinstated, or individuals born in a lower social stratum might succeed in entering the Brahmin caste, the top of the social cone of India. "By humility Prithu and Manu gained sovereignty, Kubera the position of the Lord of wealth and the son of Gandhi, the rank of a Brahmana." Because of the mixed intercaste marriages, it was possible slowly to climb or sink from caste to caste in several generations. Here are the juridical texts corroborating these statements. In Gautama we read: From a marriage of Brahmana and Kshatriya springs a Savarna, from a Brahmana and Vaisya a Nishada, from a Brahmana and Sudra a Parasava." In this way intercaste subdivision was appearing. But "In the seventh generation men obtain a change of caste either being raised to a higher or being degraded to a lower one." "By the power of austerities and of the seed from which they sprang the mixed races obtain here among men more exalted or lower rank in successive birth." Articles concerning the degradation and casting-out for the transgression of the caste rule are scattered throughout all the Sacred Books of India. The existence of the process of social climbing is certainly vouched for, too. At least, in the period of Early Buddhism, we find "many cases of Brahmans and Princes doing manual work and manual occupations. Among the middle classes we find not a few instances revealing anything but castebound heredity and groove, to wit, parents discussing the best profession for their son—no reference being made to the father's trade." "Social divisions and economic occupations were very far from being coinciding." "Labour was largely hereditary, yet there was, withal, a mobility and initiative anything but rigid revealed in the exercise of it." Moreover, at different periods, "slave-born kings are known in history but tabooed in Law." "The spectacle of the low-born man in power was never a rarity in India." The case of Chandragupta, a low-born son of Mura who became the founder of the great dynasty of the Maurya and the creator of the great and powerful Maurya Empire (321 to 297 B.C.) is only one conspicuous example among many.

For the last few decades we see a similar picture. The weak current of the vertical mobility has been active in different ways: "through enrolling in one of the more distinguished castes" by those who became wealthy and could obtain a sanction from the Brahmins; through creation of a new caste; through change of occupation; through intercaste marriages; through migration; and so on. Quite recently a considerable role began to be played by education, and by political and religious factors. It is evident, therefore, that, in spite of the fact that the caste-society of India is apparently the most conspicuous example of the most impenetrable and rigidly stratified body, nevertheless, even within it, the weak and slow currents of vertical mobility have been constantly present. If such is the case with the India caste-society, it is clear that in all other social bodies vertical mobility to this or that degree, must obviously be present. This statement is warranted by the facts. The histories of Greece, Rome, Egypt, China, Medieval Europe, and so on show the existence of a vertical mobility much more intensive than that of the Indian caste-society. The absolutely rigid society is a myth which has never been realized in history.

The Second Proposition.—There has never existed a society in which vertical social mobility has been absolutely free and the transition from one social stratum to another has had no resistance. This proposition is a mere corollary to the premises established above, that every organized society is a stratified body. If vertical mobility were absolutely free, in the resultant society there would be no strata. It would remind us of a building having no floors separating one story from another. But all societies have been stratified. This means that within them there has been a kind of "sieve" which has sifted the individuals, allowing some to go up, keeping others in the lower strata, and contrariwise.

Only in periods of anarchy and great disorder, when the entire social structure is broken and where the social strata are considerably demolished, do we have anything reminding us of a chaotic and disorganized vertical mobility *en masse.* But even in such periods, there are some hindrances to unlimited social mobility, partly in the form of the remnants of the "sieve" of the old regime, partly in the form of a rapidly growing "new sieve." After a short period, if such an anarchic society does not perish in anarchy, a modified "sieve" rapidly takes the place of the old one and, incidentally, becomes as tight as its predecessor. What is to be understood by the "sieve" will be explained further on. Here it is enough to say that it exists and functions in this or that form in any society. The proposition is so evident and in the future we shall indicate so many facts which warrant it, that there is no need to dwell on it longer here.

The Third Proposition.—The intensiveness, as well as the generality of the vertical social mobility, varies from society to society (fluctuation of mobility in space). This statement is quite evident also. It is enough to compare the Indian caste-society with the American society to see that. If the highest ranks in the political, or economic, or occupational cone of both societies are taken, it is seen that in India almost all these ranks are determined by birth, and there are very few "upstarts" who climbed to these positions from the lowest strata. Meanwhile, in the United States, among its captains of industry and finance, 38.8 per cent in the past and 19.6 per cent in the present generation started poor; 31.5 per cent among the deceased and 27.7 per cent among the living multimillionaires started their careers neither rich nor poor; among the twenty-nine presidents of the United States 14, or 48.3 per cent, came from poor and humble families.

The differences in the generality of the vertical mobility of both countries are similar. In India a great majority of the occupational population inherit and keep throughout their lives the occupational status of their fathers; in the United States the majority of the population change their occupations at least once in a lifetime. The study of occupational shifting by Dr. Dublin has shown that among the policyholders of the Metropolitan Life Insurance Company 58.5 per cent have changed their occupation between the moment of issuance of the policy and death.

My own study of the transmission of occupation from father to son among different groups of the American population has shown that among the present generation the shifting from occupation to occupation is high. The same may be said about the generality of the vertical economic mobility.

The Fourth Proposition. —The intensiveness and the generality of the vertical mobility—the economic, the political and the occupational —fluctuate in the same society at different times. In the course of the history of a whole country, as well as of any social group, there are periods when the vertical mobility increases from the quantitative as well as from the qualitative viewpoint, and there are the periods when it decreases.

Though accurate statistical material to prove this proposition is very scarce and fragmentary, nevertheless, it seems to me that these data, together with different forms of historical testimony, are enough to make the proposition safe....

The Fifth Proposition.—As far as the corresponding historical and other materials permit seeing, in the field of vertical mobility, in its three fundamental forms, there seems to be no definite perpetual trend toward either an increase or a decrease of the intensiveness and generality of mobility. This is proposed as valid for the history of a country, for that of a large social body, and, finally, for the history of mankind....

It is evident that the tendency to social seclusion and rigidity in the later stages of development of many social bodies has been rather common. While not trying to claim for this tendency a permanent trend, it is mentioned only to oppose the alleged tendency of an increase of social mobility in the course of time.

What has been said seems to be enough to challenge the alleged trend theories.

TALCOTT PARSONS

Talcott Parsons (December 13, 1902 – May 8, 1979) was an American sociologist who served on the faculty of Harvard University from 1927 to 1973. Parsons developed a general theory for the study of society called action theory, based on the methodological principle of voluntarism and the epistemological principle of analytical realism. The theory attempted to establish a balance between two major methodological traditions, that of the utilitarian-positivist tradition on the one hand and the hermeneutic-idealistic tradition on the other. For Parsons, voluntarism established a third alternative between these two. More than a theory of society, Parsons presented a theory of social evolution and a concrete interpretation of the "drives" and directions of world history.

Parsons analyzed the work of Emile Durkheim and Vilfredo Pareto and evaluated their contributions within the light of the paradigm of voluntaristic action. Parsons was also largely responsible for introducing and interpreting Max Weber's work to American audiences. Although he was generally considered a major structuralist functionalist scholar, in an article late in life, Parsons explicitly wrote that the term "functional" or "structural functionalist" were inappropriate ways to describe the character of his theory. For Parsons "structural functionalism" was the term of a particular stage in the methodological development of the social science; it was never a name for any specific school or specific direction. "Functionalism" itself was a universal method and again not a name for any specific school. In the same way, the concept "grand theory" is a derogative term, which Parsons himself never used.

THE STRUCTURE OF SOCIAL ACTION

The Structure of Social Action, (SSA) Parsons most famous work took form piece by piece. Its central figure was Weber and the other key figures in the discussion was added little by little as the central idea took form. One work, which became important for shaping Parsons idea of the central argument in SSA was when he unexpected around 1932 came over Elie Halevy, *La Formation du Radicalisme Philosophique,* (1901–1904) a 3 volume work, which he read in French. About Halevy work Parsons explained, "Well, Halevy was just a different world... and helped me to really get in to many clarifications of the assumptions distinctive to the main line of British utilitarian thought; assumptions about the 'natural identity of interest', and so on.

I still think it is one of the true masterpieces in intellectual history." Parsons first achieved significant recognition with the publication of *The Structure of Social Action* (1937), his first grand synthesis, combining the ideas of Durkheim, Max Weber, and Pareto, among others.

Parsons' Action Theory

Parsons' action theory can be characterized as an attempt to maintain the scientific rigour of positivism, while acknowledging the necessity of the "subjective dimension" of human action incorporated in hermeneutic types of sociological theories. It is cardinal in Parsons' general theoretical and methodological view that human action must be understood in conjunction with the motivational component of the human act. In this way social science must consider the question of ends, purpose and ideals in its analysis of human action.

Parsons' strong reaction to behavioristic theory as well as to sheer materialistic approaches derives from the attempt of these theoretical positions to eliminate ends, purpose and ideals as factors of analysis. Parsons already in his college student term-papers at Amherst criticized attempts to reduce human life to psychological, biological or materialist forces.

What was essential in human life, Parsons maintained, was how the factor of culture was codified. Culture, however, was to Parsons an independent variable in that it could not be "deducted" from any other factor of the social system. This methodological intention is given the most elabourate presentation in *The Structure of Social Action,* which was Parsons' first basic discussion of the methodological foundation of the social sciences. Some of the themes reaching a high point in *The Structure of Social Action* were presented in a compelling essay published two years earlier with the title: "The Place of Ultimate Values in Sociological Theory."

Relations to Cybernetics and System Theory

Parsons developed his ideas during a period when systems theory and cybernetics were very much on the front burner of social and behavioral science. In using systems thinking, he postulated that the relevant systems treated in social and behavioural science were "open," meaning that they were embedded in an environment consisting of other systems. For social and behavioural science, the largest system is "the action system," consisting of interrelated behaviors of human beings, embedded in a physical-organic environment.

As Parsons developed his theory it became increasingly bound to the fields of cybernetics and system theory, but also to Alfred E. Emerson's concept of "homeostasis" and Ernst Mayr's concept of "teleonomic processes." On the meta-theoretical level Parson attempted to balance psychologist phenomenology and idealism on the one hand and pure types of what Parsons called the utilitarian-positivistic complex, on the other hand. The theory includes a general theory of social evolution and a concrete interpretation of the major drives of world-history. In Parsons' theory of history and evolution, the constitutive-cognitive symbolization of the cybernetic hierarchy of action-systemic levels has in principle the same function as genetic information in DNA's control of biological evolution, except this factor of meta-systemic control does not "determine" any outcome, but rather defines the orientational boundaries of the real pathfinder, which is action itself. Parsons compares also the constitutive level of society with Noam Chomsky's concept of "deep structure." As Parsons writes, "The deep structures do not as such articulate any sentences which could convey coherent meaning. The surface structures constitute the level at which this occurs. The connecting link between them is a set of rules of transformation, to use Chomsky's own phase." These transformative processes and entities are generally (at least on one level of empirical analysis) performed or actualized by myths and religions but also philosophies, art-systems, or even semiotic consumer behaviour might in principle perform this function.

A Unified Concept of Social Science

Parsons' theory reflects a vision of a unified concept of

social science and indeed, of living systems in general. Parsons' approach differs in essence from Niklas Luhmann's theory because Parsons rejects the idea that systems can be autopoietic short of the actual action-system of individual actors. Systems have immanent capacities but only as an outcome of the institutionalized processes of action-systems, which in the final analysis consists of the historical effort of individual actors. While Niklas Luhmann became caught up in sheer systemic immanence, Parsons insisted that the question of autocatalytic and homeostatic processes on the one hand, and the question about the actor as the ultimate "first mover" on the other, was not mutually exclusive. Homeostatic processes might be *necessary* if and when they occur but action is *necessitating.*

It is only within this perspective of the ultimate reference in action that Parsons' dictum that higher order cybernetic systems during the course of history will tend to control social forms organized on the lower levels of the cybernetic hierarchy, should be understood. For Parsons the highest levels of the cybernetic hierarchy as far as the general action level is concerned is what Parsons calls the constitutive part of the Cultural system (the L of the L). However, within the interactional processes of the system specially attention should be made to the cultural-expressivistic axis (the L-G line in the AGIL). By the term "constitutive," Parsons generally referred to very highly codified cultural values especially religious elements (but other interpretation of the term "constitutive" is possible). Cultural systems Parsons maintained had an independent status from that of the normative and orientational pattern of the social system; the one system cannot be reduced to the other. For example, the question of the "cultural capital" of a social system as a sheer historical entity (that is, in its function as a "fiduciary system"), is not identical with the higher cultural values of that system; that is, the cultural system is embodied with a meta-structural logic there cannot be reduced to any given social system or cannot be viewed as a materialist (or behavioralist) deduction from the "necessities" of the social system (or from the "necessities" of its economy). Within this context, culture would have an independent power of transition, not only as factors of actual socio-cultural units (like Western civilization or China) but also in the way original cultural bases would tend to "universalize" through interpenetration and spread over large numbers of social systems as with classical Greece and Israel, where the original social bases had died but where the cultural system survived as an independently "working" cultural pattern, as in the case of Greek philosophy or in the case of Christianity as a modified derivation from its original seed-bed in ancient Israel.

TALCOTT PARSONS "AN OUTLINE OF THE SOCIAL SYSTEM"

A couple of things which might be helpful to know before I begin. Parsons is a FUNCTIONALIST, as big and nasty as they come. He is also heavily influenced by the writings of Durkheim and makes several references to the Big D in this essay, part. Elem Forms and DOL. Also, everything in this article, including all of the systems typologies and process schemas, are meant in the "analytic" sense. Parsons is primarily interested in how a social scientist can analyze a social system.

General Outline

This essay is an attempt by Parsons to outline an action frame of reference. This attempt is based on the conviction that there are two essential reference points for this type of systematic analysis; a classification of the functional requirements of a system and the arrangement of these with reference to processes of control in the cybernetic sense. Parsons posits that the most empirically significant sociological theory must be concerned with complex systems, that is, systems composed of many subsystems. The primary empirical type-reference is to society, which is highly complex. The basic functional classification underlying the whole scheme involves the discrimination of 4 primary categories: pattern maintenance, integration, goal-attainment, and adaptation, placed in that order in the series of control-relations. (Note Parsons order on this, which is L-I-G-A, the opposite order of what we're used to from Laumann's class.)

More generally, Parsons is also interested in making a fundamental distinction between the morphological analysis of the morphological structure of systems and the "dynamic" analysis of process. Neither has special priority over the other except that, at a particular level, stable structural reference points are necessary for determining generalizations about process. The old battle o f theory versus empiricism may be considered to be over. There is no longer a question as to the study of human behaviour as a scientific endeavour. Parsons theory is one of action, which goes beyond the old reductionist theories of social theory.

The concept of a social system is important for Parsons, and for the TS editors. To be clear, we must delineate the place of social systems within the action frame of reference. One aspect of this distinction, which can be taken for granted, is between the analytically defined individual and the systems generated by the process of social interaction. Social and cultural systems are also important for this discussion, but the two, however empirically intertwined, must be kept analytically distinct. Parallel to the social/cultural distinction, is that of nature/nurture in regards to developing the individual. This can be conceived of an the distinction between the individual organism and the organization of his behaviour. Finally, distinctions should be made between the functional subsystems of economy and polity within a society, even though they have often overlapped in the past. All of these distinctions can be seen as questions of boundaries fro both the individual and for systems.

With all of the above considerations in hand, Parsons moves on to offer a paradigm for the analysis of social systems. Parsons is a firm believer in interpenetration and mutual influence. This means, that however important logical closure may be for a theoretical ideal, empirically, social systems are conceived as open systems, engaged in complicated processes of interchange with environing systems. This concept of open systems implies, again, boundaries and their maintenance. A boundary means simply that a theoretically and empirically significant difference between structures and processes internal to the system and those external to it exists and tends to be maintained. Because of all of this, we need to define a set of interdependent phenomena as a system, so as not to confuse a statistical sample of the population with a true system.

Besides identifying a system in terms of its patterns and boundaries, a social system can and should be analyzed in terms of three logically independent-i.e. cross-cutting-but also interdependent, bases or axes of variability, or as they may be called, bases of selective abstraction.

1. The first of these is involves a distinction between the structural and the functional. The concept of structure designates the features of the system which can be treated as constants over certain ranges of variation in the behaviour of other significant elements of the theoretical problem. The functional reference diverges from the structural in the dynamic direction. Its primary purpose is integrative, mediating between the system's structure and that imposed by environing systems.
2. A fundamental distinction must also be made between the two dynamic processes of maintaining system equilibrium, and structural change in the system.
3. The hierarchy of relations of control. The basic subsystems of the general systems of action constitute a hierarchical series of such agencies of control of the behaviour of individuals or organisms.

Parsons returns to the 4 functional imperatives of any system of action, given in order of significance from the point of view of cybernetic control of action processes in the system under consideration.

L-The function of pattern maintenance. The function of pattern maintenance refers to the imperative of maintaining the stability of patterns of institutionalized culture defining the structure of the system. There are two distinct aspects of this function. The first concerns the character of the normative pattern itself; the focus lies in the structural category of values. The second concerns its state of institutionalization, which concerns the motivational commitment of the individual. A very central problem here is that of the socialization of the individual, taken as the processes by which the values of the society are internalized in an individual personality. Overall, systems do show a tendency to maintain themselves (inertia).

G-The function of goal-attainment. Goal-attainment becomes a problem in so far as there arises some discrepancy between the inertial tendencies of the system and its needs resulting from interchange with the situation. A goal is therefore defined in terms of equilibrium, and directional changes will tend to minimize the discrepancy between the two systems. Goal-attainment, or goal-orientation is thus, by contrast with pattern maintenance, tied to a specific situation. Systems often have a plurality of goals. For the social system as such, goal-orientation concerns, therefore, not commitment to the values of the society, but motivation to contribute what is necessary for the functioning of the system.

A-The function of adaptation. Adaptation is another consequence of goal plurality. A system has only so many set, scarce resources, and when goals are many, often one goal must be sacrificed so the resources may be used to attain another goal. This means that the system loses the benefits of the sacrificed goal. The sacrificed goal is chosen through the function of goal-attainment. Adaptation is concerned with providing additional disposable facilities independent of their relevance to any particular goal. More generally, at the macroscopic level, goal-attainment is the focus of political organization, and adaptation is the focus economic organization. Within a given system, goal-attainment is a more important control then is adaptation.

I-The function of integration. In the control hierarchy, integration stands between the functions of pattern-maintenance and goal-attainment. The functional problem of integration concerns the mutual adjustments of segmented units or subsystems from the point of view of their contributions to the effective functioning of the system as a whole. In a highly differentiated society, the primary focus of the integrative mechanism is found in the system of legal norms and the associated legal system. The system as a whole is concerned most with the allocation of rights and obligations. For any given social system, the integrative function is the focus of its most distinctive properties and processes.

Categories of Social Structure

Parsons conceives of social interaction as a structured affair. He provides a series of structural categories, given in ascending order as role, collectivity, norm, and value. These roughly cover the social structure from individual to social system. Role is the essential starting point for individual interaction (2 or more people) which occurs in such a way as to constitute an interdependent system (as distinguished from a social system). IN order for interaction to be stable, roles and actions must have meanings and be governed by understood, shared rules. Rules define goals and the consequences of ant given move by one player for the situation in which the other must make his choice. Thus, there is a temporal element to interaction. However, rules do not determine or prescribe any specific act. Facilities are provided, but they are generalized, and their allocation between players depends upon each player's capacities to take advantage of opportunities. The essential property is mutuality of orientation defined in terms of shared patterns of normative culture, known as values. When two individuals interact in the above ways, sharing a normative culture, and in so far as their behaviour is distinguishable from others by their participation and not others, they form a collectivity.

A role may now be defined as the structures, i.e. normati.ely regulated, participation of a person in a concrete process of social interaction with specified, concrete role-partners. Performing a role within a collectivity defined the category of membership, i.e. the assumption of obligations of performance in that concrete interaction system. Obligations correlatively imply rights. For any individual, there are many roles, and one role is only a sector in his behavioural system, and hence of his personality. In addition, in any given system, the concepts of role and collectivity are particularistic. Norms and values, in contrast with role and collectivity, are universalistic concepts. It may cut across all concrete collectivities in a given universe and apply to all roles of a given type. The universalistic aspect of values implies that they are neither situation-specific, nor function-specific.

To sum up: Structurally speaking, then, the role component is the normative component which governs the participation of individual persons in given collectivities. The collectivity component is the normative culture which defines the values, norms, goal-orientations, and ordering of roles for a concrete system of interaction of specifiable persons; the component of norms which define expectations for the performance of classes of differentiated units within the system-collectivities, or roles, as the case may be; and values are the normative patterns defining, in universalistic terms, the patterns of desirable orientation for the system as a whole, independent of the specification of situation or of differentiated function within the system.

We now have enough to outline a schematic ideal type for a complex social system. the main guiding line of the analysis is the concept that a complex social system consists of a network of interdependent and interpenetrating subsystems, each of which, seen as the appropriate level of reference, is a social system in its own right. (The infinitely repressible thing). The starting point is the concept of a society, taken to be relatively self-sufficient collectivity which cannot be said to be a differentiated subsystem of a high-order collectivity oriented to most of the functional exigencies of a social system. (All of these classifications are subjective, used and applied by an analyst.). The functional exigencies take shape in three distinct manners: differentiation, segmentation and specification.

There are several different modes of differentiation within societies. The most common, even universal, is differentiation among kinship lines. Kinship is essentially the point of articulation, i.e. interpenetration, between the structure of social systems and the relations involved in the biological process of reproduction. Biologically, there are 3 crucial structural components, (1) differences between sexes, (2) differences between old and young, mature and immature, and (3) the fact hat the sexual union of two specific individuals of opposite sexes is necessary to, and likely to result in, pregnancy and reproduction. These 3 factors set up the nuclear family unit, and other diversified family forms, around the conjugal bond of 2 people and its resultant offspring. Kinship structures are also clearly subject to important processes of functional differentiation, and have often become the locus for political and economic activities. Because of the connection of paramount societal collectivity organization and political function outlined, the functional differentiation of political from other structures also tends to come near the top of the social hierarchy. There are two preliminary steps. The first is to differentiate kinship units which carry high political responsibility, royals or aristocrats, from common kinship units. The other the differentiation of the political from the pattern-maintenace and integrative functions of the high-level units. Lower down, an important problem here concerns the restrictions on the mobility of resources imposed by the ascriptive aspect of kinship and its differentiation from political function. Even when bureaucracy and systems not directly ties to kinship are instituted, higher-level kinship units usually have an edge of advantage or resources. This imposes frustrating limits on lower units.

Parsons perceives the intertwining of political and economic functions as an ongoing problem, buried in many empirical examples. One must look closely, e.g. the function of a business firm is primarily economic; its goal is production, but its internal organization must be analyzed first in political terms. Economic function, as distinguished from the political, involves the production and allocation of disposable resources.

Traditionally, one of the main criterion of the values of economic resources is relative scarcity. The other most important one is general utility. The possibilities of generalizing about physical commodities and human resources is thus inherently limited. The utilization of scarce resources is dependent on the institutionalization of mechanisms which, independent of any prior knowledge or commitment, make it possible to gain access to wide ranges of different facilities as need for them develops. In known societies, there are in particular two highly generalized mechanisms of this type, namely political power and money. Both require the institutionalization of the disposability of facilities.

Money is not a commodity here, but a very special mode of institutionalization of expectations and commitments through communication. The usefulness of money as a much more generalized facility is dependent on a system of markets and adequate rules governing the continual flow of transactions through markets. Money has the primacy of economic function.

Power is defined as the generalized capacity, independent of specific conditions prescribed in advance, to influence the allocation of resources for the goals of the collectivity through invoking the institutionalized obligations of member units, utilizing such sanctions as are legitimized through these obligations and institutionalized roles involved in the power system. Power is necessitated by the effectiveness which is required for the political function. the mechanism of power are not nearly as structured as those of money. Power is a mechanism regulating the process of making actual commitments. Authority, on the other hand, comprises the general rules which govern the making of specific binding decisions. As used here, political and economic categories are generalized functional categories that permeate the entire structure of the social system. But it is a two-way street. Just as constraints on the commercial or competitive structure of markets are imposed by impinging non-economic factors, so in many collectivities there are constraints on the political primacy of their organization and orientation to situations.

No society can accept economic rationality as its most general societal value-orientation, though it can place the economic highest among its functional priorities. This statement also holds for other differentiated functional value-systems. The same basic principles of the relations between structure and function, apply to pattern-maintenance and the integrative functions, to the relations of the relevant structures to each other and to the economic and political. First, societies will differ in so far as structures with clear primacy of these functions have come to be differentiated from those whose functions are more diffuse. Second, relevant structures will be located at different levels on the scales of segmentation and specification, and may thus not be directly comparable with each other.

With respect to pattern-maintenance, as a functional category, it is not meant to have empirically static connotations. Analytically, specialization in both maintenance and change in values should be placed in this category. the primary area of concern here is the religion, placed within the realm of the cultural. Societal variance is great here, but even when a specific religion is not institutionalized, religious values will be. Also a primary component of pattern-maintenance is socialization of the individual, placed within the realm of personality. Socialization universally involves at least one kinship unit, usually the nuclear family, as the primary collective agent of early socialization. All more highly differentiated societies have developed non-kinship structures centering about the functions of formal education in which the higher-level patterns of normative culture and systems of objects are internalized in the personality.

Structures with integrative primacy must follow some normative code. Norms must be defined, interpreted, and implemented. The first imperative of a system of norms is internal consistency. Second, there s the specification of higher-order norms to levels where they can guide the action of the society's lower level structural units by defining the situation for them. A major functional problem of a normative system concerns the adjustments which occur because a social system is always involved in processes of interchange with a changing environment. There seem to be three basic types of processes of adjustment in these cases. 1. Keeping the regulatory norms at a sufficiently high level of generality so that much of the adjustment can be left to the spontaneous, unprescribed, action of the units themselves. 2. Altering the content of normative patterns to meet the varying functional needs without threatening the stability of higher level systems. 3. A third process which operates, short of major structural changes, in the areas where the other two are inadequate. (It is unspecified.)

A final aspect of social structure is stratification. Here, the focus of institutionalized stratification is legitimizing differential power and wealth, and more generally, access to valued objects and statuses. Social class is the most common basis of stratification.

The Dynamics of Social Equilibrium

The analysis of dynamic processes at the equilibration level must center around two categories of the system's components. The first are the resources which, starting from outside the system, go through various phases as they pass through the system, and at certain points are used in the system's functioning. The second are the types of mechanisms which mediate these processes of generation and utilization of resources and regulate their rates of flow, direction of use, etc. Money and power, as previously discussed, are the prototypes of these mechanisms. Parsons borrows the theoretical model of resources from economics because it is capable of generalization. In this model, there are four factors of production, namely, land, labour, capital, and organization. He is most concerned with applying the model's logical structure, because level of specification of resources and qualitative differences in resources make it difficult to apply the model directly to social systems theory.

None of the socially ultimate inputs consists in either actual physical objects or the physical behaviour of organisms. In an economic exchange, involving a physical commodity, what changes hands is not the commodity, but property rights in the commodity. Analytically, physical transfer of possession is a technological process, not a social systems process. Like a feeder chain, the ultimate resources of a society should comprise the ultimate outputs of the subsystems of the general system of action. Land is a special case because it is neither consumed in the production process, nor is it produced.

In the society as a system, the analog of land is the institutionalized normative culture. According to the paradigm, the inputs should be three: inputs respectively from the personality-capacity to socialize motivational commitments, the behavioural organism-plasticity which can be built into patterns of purposive response, and the cultural system-information. Generally, output corresponding too the input if institutionalized normative culture in the maintenance of the structure intact. The primary outputs of the other inputs are as follows: personality system: goal-gratification, behavioural organism: patterning of responses at the level of behaviour, and cultural system: validation. The resources complete this system as the thruput. They are consumed. Resource processing occurs in three phases: generation, allocation and utilization.

Parsons shows some heavy Freudian influences here when he speaks of the socialization of motivational capacity as an example of resource generation. He outlines the whole process of developing sexuality, complete with Oedipal complex. But then, its back to functionalism. Allocation is made to operative units of the system, to which resources are committed for use. The prototype for an allocative mechanism again comes from economics, it is the market. The market makes possible a relatively functional allocation without much centralized decision-making. It also allows for much differentiation. Another example can be seen in the power mechanism's allocation of power in a politically differentiated society.

Utilization is essentially a process of successively more particularized decision-making; action-opportunities, facilities, and responsibilities are allocated more specifically at each step. The most broadly defined stages are the allocation to the collectivity, to the role, and to the task. The function of the collectively is to define what is to be done; that of the role, to define who is to do it; and that of the task level, how it is to be done. Mechanisms controlling resource processes. Parsons again refers to power and money, the two most studied of the mechanisms. Money is simultaneously both a measure of value and a medium of exchange and it can function as both a facility and a reward. Power is a step above money in the hierarchy of control mechanisms because power can be used to control power, i.e. a government controlling its monetary system. Power allows for greater flexibility and effectiveness without prior knowledge or specifications. He also discusses real commitments, which I believe to be institutionalized role commitments, but I'm not sure. They seem to have a lot to do with contracts and legal agreements. Finally, there is integrative communication, which is also at the top of the hierarchy of control mechanisms. The operational focus of this type of mechanism is the motivational commitment of units of the system to the fulfilment of institutionalized expectations.

In a broad sense then, the problem of the dynamics of social systems is not so much a problem of transformation of energy as of the processing of information. Analyses of these processes are in an early stage right now.

The Problem of Structural Change

The processes of structural change may be considered the obverse of equilibrating process; the distinction is made in terms of boundary maintenance. The control resources of the system are adequate for its maintenance up to a well-defined set of points in one direction: beyond that set of points, there is a tendency for a cumulative process of change to begin, producing states progressively farther from the institutionalized patterns. As observed, structural change in subsystems is an inevitable part of the equilibrating process in larger system. Within this frame of reference, the problem of structural change can be considered under three headings: (1) sources of tendencies towards change, (2) the impact of these tendencies on the affected structural components, (3) possible generalizations about trends and patterns of change. Sources of change can be either exogenous or endogenous. Exogenous sources of change are changes in the environment or environing social systems. Their impact is made felt only through the endogenous tendencies to change which already exists in the units or subsystems of the social system in question. Endogenous change itself is often perceived as strain. A strain is a tendency to disequilibrium in the input-output balance between two or more units of the system. Strain can be relieved by being fully resolved, by being isolated or arrested, or by changing the structure itself. Since strain usually falls on relations between units of the system, structural change to relieve the strain is defined as alteration in normative culture defining the expectations governing that relation. Given structural inertial tendencies, strain should occur only when lower-level control mechanisms have failed. Sources of change may be myriad or multi-causal.

Disturbance in the system may result from the balance of inputs and outputs being thrown off. The impact of these forces for change will vary in accordance with their magnitude, proportion of system units affected, the strategic character of the affected unit(s), the degree to which the forces affect functionally different units or sectors, and resistance of system units. Empirically, it is hard to pinpoint these forces for change because they are diffuse and seldom operate discreetly. By present definition, a change in the structure of a social system is a change in its normative culture. At the most general level, it is a change in the paramount value system.

Change can also affect the interaction of different levels of the social system, e.g. normative culture and the personality system. However, symptoms of disturbance are common to processes which do and do not cause change. Structural change is only one possible outcome of strain.

The socialization of the child actually constitutes a process of structural change in one set of structural components of social systems, namely, the role-patterns of the individual-indeed, much of the foregoing paradigm has been derived from this source. The socialization of the individual does not, however, comprise change in the social system of society. This is a good illustration of Parsons' nested systems approach.

THE ROLE OF THEORY IN SOCIAL RESEARCH

In this short chapter, Parsons expresses his concern for what appears to be the complete divorce between the empirically-minded and the theoretically minded in which each does their type of research while degrading the work of the other.

For instance, Parsons says, "certain of the empirically minded are not merely not interested in attempting to contribute to theory themselves, they are actively anti-theoretical". He makes the same point of the theoretically minded. Although he is very sympathetic toward empiricists who do not like to structure their research on firm theoretical grounds, he argues the whether they would like to admit it or not, scientific endeavours cannot and do not make much contribution to scientific knowledge unless they are "guided by the logical structure of a theoretical scheme." Parsons sees the principle functions of analytical theory in research in the following four ways:

1) it provides a basis of selection for the important facts from the unimportant, given the wealth of miscellaneous facts we have
2) it provides a basis for organization of the facts
3) it reveals the gaps in the existing knowledge and their importance
4) it provides a source of "cross fertilization" of related fields.

The Place of Ultimate Values in Sociological Theory

Basically what Parsons says in this chapter is that people strive to achieve ends and they do so given the opportunities or means that are available to them (means-ends chain). However, people's "ultimate ends" as well as how they achieve them are not chosen randomly. Instead, the means by which people achieve their goals, etc., are defined and established by the group of which they are a part. Parsons calls this a "common system of ultimate ends." Actions are governed by normative rules of the group or institution. In other words, Parsons' concept of action is grounded in a normative framework.

The Action Frame of Reference

A frame of reference is the starting point for analysis and is determined by the particular vantage point and purposes. Mayhew says that "the grounding of the normative in the very concept of action as a necessary element of an action frame of reference, gives the study of norms a solid theoretical foundation'. Norms have special importance in social life; they provide an action frame of reference for analysing social structure and its functions.

Hobbes and the Problem of Order

Hobbes believed that people are guided by their passions. The good is simply what man desires. However, there are many limitations on the extent to which these desires can be realized. Therefore, in order to "control" people's desires, society has created a social contract that exists between members of society. Through this contract men agree to give up some liberties to the sovereign power and in return they receive security, or immunity, from aggression by the force or fraud of others. Through this authority, the desires and passions are held in check and order and security are maintained. Without it, men will attempt to achieve their ends in the most efficient means available, in other words, force or fraud. This will eventually lead to a state of war.

It is this social contract of Hobbes that is most interesting to Parsons. Hobbes' social contract is synonymous with Parson's normative framework. He says that an ordered social life cannot be founded on rational calculation alone; there must be a normative framework to establish criteria of choice that will provide for social control of disruptive conduct.

Pattern Variables

Pattern variables are "the principle tools of structural analysis outlining the derivation of these categories from the intrinsic logic of social action — the inherent dilemmas of choice facing actors". In this chapter Parsons argues that there are a strictly limited and defined set of alternatives or choices that can be made, and the relative primacies given to choices constitute the "patterning of relational institutions." These choices or alternatives are called orientation-selection.

There are five pattern variables of role-definition that Parsons discusses, although he says that there are many more possibilities. The first is the gratification-discipline dilemma: affectivity vs. affective-neutrality. The dilemma here is in deciding whether one expresses their orientation in terms of immediate gratification (affectivity) or whether they renounce immediate gratification in favor of moral interests (affective-neutrality). parsons says, "no actor can subsist without gratifications, while at the same time no action system can be organized or integrated without the renunciation of some gratifications which are available in the given situation".

The second set of pattern variables of role-definition are the private vs. collective interest dilemma: self-orientation vs. collectively orientation. In this case, one's role orientation is either in terms of her private interests or in terms of the interests of the collectively. Parsons explains, "a role, then, may define certain areas of pursuit of private interests as legitimate, and in other areas obligate the actor to pursuit of the common interests of the collectively. The primacy of the former alternative may be called "self-orientation," that of the latter, "collectively-orientation".

The third pair of pattern variables are the choice between types of value-orientation standard: universalism vs. particularism. Simply put, "in the former case the standard is derived from the validity of a set of existential ideas, or the generality of a normative rule, in the latter from the particularity of... an object or of the status of the object in a relational system". Example: the obligation to fulfill contractual agreements vs. helping someone because she is your friend.

The fourth pair of pattern variables are achievement vs. ascriptive role behaviour: the choice between modalities of the social object. Achievement-orientation roles are those which place an emphasis on the performances of the people, whereas ascribed roles, the qualities or attributes of people are emphasized independently of specific expected performances.

The final pair of pattern variables are specificity vs. diffuseness: the definition of scope of interest in the object. If one adopts an orientation of specificity towards an object, it means that the definition of the role as orienting to the social object in specific terms. In contrast, in a diffuse orientation, the mode of orientation is outside the range of obligations defined by the role-expectation.

Integration and Institutionalization in the Social System

Institutionalization: By institutionalization Parsons meant the integration of roles and sanctions with a generalized value system or normative framework which all members share. He states, "institutionalization is an articulation or integration of the actions of a plurality of actors in a specific type of situation in which the various actors accept jointly a set of harmonious rules regarding goals and procedures". Institutionalizing Roles: Parsons says that the social system of the institution must contain an allocative process by which the problem of who is to get what, who is to do what, and the manner and conditions under which it is to be done is made explicit. If this is not done, the social system will fail and will make way for another system. If it does occur, integration will be achieved. The function of allocation of roles, facilities, and rewards, therefore, must be established within the social system. Access to roles is determined by qualifications. Access to facilities is determined by position. One is given facilities to help to achieve the goals set forth by the duties of the position they occupy. The purpose of facilities is the fulfilment of role-expectations. Rewards have the function of maintaining or modifying motivations. Therefore, access to rewards is determined by achievement or how well one does her work.

The Integration of the Social System: Social integration of the social system takes place when members are governed by a common value-orientation, when the common values are motivationally integrated in action as a collectively, and when the people are given and take responsibility for their role-expectation in that they take responsibility for the definition and enforcement of the norms governing the allocative processes and take responsibility for the conduct of communal affairs.

Illness and the Role of the Physician

Parsons defines illness as a deviant behaviour because, as a sick person, whether mentally or physically, one is not able to perform the functions or obligations to society. He states, "behaviour which is defined in sociological terms as failing in some way to fulfill the institutionally defined expectations of one or more of the roles in which the individual is implicated in the society".

He deals with four issues here: the processes of genesis of illness, the role of the sick person as a social role, aspects of the role of the physician and their relation to the therapeutic process, and the way in which both roles fit into the general equilibrium of the social system. In the first issue, that of the processes of genesis of the illness, mental illness is assumed. Parsons suggests that the genesis of illnesses results from something that has gone wrong in a person's relationships to others during the process of social interaction. The support a person receives from those surrounding her in which she is made to feel a member of the group as well as the upholding of values of the group may be lacking resulting in the person becoming pathological.

In the second issue, the role of the sick person is considered a social role. First, the sick person is made exempt from normal social obligations. Then she is exempted from certain responsibilities of her own state. Third, given the role of the sick relinquishes one from the claim to full legitimacy. Fourth, being sick is defined as needing help; the sick person makes the transition to the additional role of patient and as such has certain obligations to fulfill.

The third issue, the aspects of the role of the physician and their relation to the therapeutic process are discussed. Parsons says that there are four main conditions of successful psychotherapy. The first is support which signifies the acceptance of the sick person as a member of a social group. The second is a special permissiveness to express wishes and fantasies which would ordinarily not be permitted in normal social relationships. The third is that the therapist does not reciprocate the expectations of the patient. The fourth is the conditional manipulation of sanctions by the therapist — the giving and withholding of approval. The final issue that Parsons discusses is how the illness/sick person, the physician, and well as the psychotherapy are built into the structure of society.

On the Concept of Influence

Ways of Getting Results in Interaction: Parsons argues that there are at least four ways of getting results in interaction. The first is through inducement of offering someone something that they want so that they will comply. The second is through deterrence of suggesting that by not complying something bad will happen to the person. The third means is through activation of commitment or suggesting to the person why it would be wrong, in the person's viewpoint, to refuse to comply.

Parsons defines influence as "a means of persuasion. It is bringing about a decision on alter's part to act in a certain way because it is felt to be a 'good thing' for him, on the one hand independently of contingent or otherwise imposed changes in his situation, on the other hand for positive reasons, not because of the obligations he would violate through noncompliance".

In other words, one has influence because of who they are, because they hold some title, etc., that makes people believe in them. Parsons states, "the same statement will carry more weight if made by someone with a high reputation for competence, for reliability, for good judgment, etc., than by someone without this reputation... It is not what he is saying... but what 'right' he has to expect to be taken seriously.". Persuasion is done in common interest. It is not in the interest of the persuader, but in the interest of the person being persuaded that the outcome would benefit. An example of this is a doctor and a patient. The doctor has influence because of who she is. She has a degree and training that gives credibility, and the aim she has is for the good of the patient.

Types of Influence. There are four types of influence: political, fiduciary, influence through appear to different loyalties, and influence oriented to the interpretation of norms. In political influence, there is a directly significant relation between influence and power. Fiduciary influence refers to the ability to allocate resources in a system where both collectivities and their goals are plural and justification of each among the plural goals is problematic. Influence through appeal to differential loyalties refers to commitments grounded in institutionalized values. It is a matter of justifying assuming particular responsibilities in the context of a particular collectively. The final type of influence, that of influence oriented to the interpretation of norms, refers to the interpretation of legal norms of the judicial process.

Evolutionary Universals in Society

Four features of human societies at the level of culture and social organization were cited as having universal and major significance as prerequisites for socio-cultural development: technology, kinship organization based on an incest taboo, communication based on language, and religion. Primary attention, however, was given to six organizational complexes that develop mainly at the level of social structure. The first two, particularly important for the emergence of societies for primitiveness, are stratification, involving a primary break with primitive break with primitive kinship ascription, and cultural legitimation, with institutionalized agencies that are independent of a diffuse religious tradition.

Fundamental to the structure of modern societies are, taken together, the other four complexes: bureaucratic organization of collective goal-attainment, money and market systems, generalized universalistic legal systems, and the democratic association with elective leadership and mediated membership support for policy orientations. Although these have developed very unevenly, some of them going back a very long time, all are clearly much more than simple inventions of particular societies.

Perhaps a single theme tying them together is that differentiation and attendant reduction in ascription has caused the initial two-class system to give way to more complex structures at the levels social of stratification and the relation between social structure and its cultural legitimation. First, this more complex system is characterized by a highly generalized universalistic normative structure in all fields. Second, subunits under such normative orders have greater autonomy both in pursuing their own goals and interests and in serving others instrumentally. Third, this autonomy is linked with the probability that structural units will develop greater diversity of interests and subgoals. Finally, this diversity results in pluralization of scales of prestige and therefore of differential access to economic resources, power, and influence.

SUGGESTIONS FOR A SOCIOLOGICAL APPROACH TO THE THEORY OF ORGANIZATIONS

Parson's version of sociological explanation of organizational theory. He attempted to define organization by locating it systematically in the structure of the society in relation to other categories of social structure. He defines an organization as "a social system oriented to the attainment of a relatively specific type of goal, which contributes to a major function of a more comprehensive system, usually the society".

(L) Its value system defining the societal commitments of which its functioning depends. This value system must be a subvalue system of a higher-order one, since the organization is always defined as a subsystem of a more comprehensive social system. From this concept, Parsons maintained two conclusions. First, the value system of the organization must imply basic acceptance of the more generalized values of the superordinate system. Secondly, on the requisite level of generality, the most essential feature of the value system of an organization is the valuative legitimation of its place or role in the superordinate system.

(A) Its mechanisms of resource procurement. The problem of mobilizing fluid resources concerns one major aspect of the external relations of the organization to the situation in which it operates. The resources which the organization must utilize are the factors of production as these concepts are used in economic theory; land, labour, capital and organizations.

(G) Its operative mechanism centering about decision making in the fields of policy, allocation, and integration. The policy decision meant decisions which relatively directly commit the organization as a whole and which stand in relatively direct relation to its primary functions. Parsons noted that the critical feature of policy decisions is the fact that they commit the organization to a whole to carry out their implications. The allocative decisions relate to the distribution of resources within the organization and the delegations of authority. From these points, there are two main aspects of the allocative decision process; one concerns mainly personnel, the other financial and physical facilities. The coordination decisions concern with the integration of the organization as a system.

(I) Its institutional patterns which link the structure of the organization with the structure of the society as a whole. The problem concern rather the compatibility of the institutional order under which the organization operates with other organizations and social units, as related to integrative exigencies of the society as a whole. This integrative problem can be generalized to both human agents and interorganizational integration.

The same basic classification of the functional problems of social systems was used to establish point of reference for a classification of types of organization, and broadest outline of a proposed classification was sketched. Then, Parsons suggested some illustrative cases by a rapid survey of some of the principal business, military, and academic organizations.

THE PROFESSIONS AND SOCIAL STRUCTURE

This chapter and the piece on age and sex can be seen as attempts to apply Parsons' theories to real life situations. In the case of business and the professions, he's looking at how our "society" as an organism, maintains itself. Two of Parsons' four functional needs of society-integration (coordinating system parts) and latency (managing tensions between parts and generating new parts)-are solved in this article by what he calls "functional specificity". (compare to Durkheim).

Parsons begins by wondering why the professions are so highly developed, and why there is such a highly refined division of labour nowadays. Three important elements distinguish our society from others and contribute to the unique importance of professions in our society.

1. In our society, scientific rationality-that is, not accepting traditional explanations just because they are traditional, and therefore searching for better ways and explanations-is "institutional, a part of a normative pattern." This is to say, scientific rationality is not just something that comes natural to all human beings.
2. Furthermore, certain people have authority in certain realms but in no others. For instance, regardless of their financial backgrounds or upbringing, doctors are given authority in the field of medicine because it is their specialty. This is what Parsons calls the "functional

specificity" of technical competence or authority. In contrast to commercial relations, which are functionally specific, kin relations are functionally diffuse. Your grandma has authority because she's your grandma, not because of their technical expertise. Parsons calls for a thorough study of functional specificity, since it is a product of our unique modern D of L.

3. Related to the last thing, there are two kinds of relations among people, universalistic and particularistic. The more contexts in which you know someone, like a relative or a friend, the less possible it is to abstract that person's personality from the particular role they play at one time. For instance, a person who has her elderly parent living with her will treat the parent much differently than she would treat a tenant who is a stranger. The mother is regarded as a particular individual, mom. The other tenant is regarded as any other tenant would be, by a "universalistic" rule for how landlords treat tenants.

But are professions and business really all that different? No, if we think of them both as having the goal of "success." People wish to succeed at whatever vocation their talent brings them to, be they doctors, scientists, painters or financial analysts. But this is only the case in the normal condition of society, a "well-integrated" situation. If achievement fails to bring recognition, or if you get recognition for doing nothing or the wrong thing, this causes strain. (Think of Merton) Strain leads to profiteering in the professions and shady practices in business.

It is not accurate to say that business folks are purely egoistic nor that professionals are purely altruistic. Both have the same sorts f motivation, and differences in normative behaviors are institutionally defined definitions of the situation. System is maintained by a complex balance of diverse social forces.

AGE AND SEX IN THE SOCIAL STRUCTURE OF THE UNITED STATES

This is another attempt to make Parsons' theories relevant. This piece deals mostly with the functional needs of integration and latency, where different age and sex groups can be seen as the different elements of an organism. To some extent, it deals with the question of how to reconcile individual with social needs. Parsons asserts that our society is unique in that our children of both sexes are treated alike, relative to other societies. The main reason for this similarity is that children are given education that focuses mostly on liberal arts rather than vocations.

In spite of the "conspicuous" exception that in the job world, men and women in this society share an underlying structural equality. Education through college is merit-based and there is little discrimination until you get to postgrad, where the strict focus on vocation leads to more sex-based discrimination. Elsewhere Parsons asserts that it is functional to have a woman at home raising the children and making the man's home life run smoothly, so he can dedicate himself to his career. Women need to be educated, he implies, because they need to life up to expectations which come with being the wife of a man of a certain status. He is where she gets her status.

If she isn't smart enough to find ways to entertain herself by following the "good companion" pattern, a women may choose to follow the glamour gal routine, going for clothes and makeup. Striving for success in these two realms is functional because these patterns keep women from competing with men. However, since these women have liberal arts educations, they may undergo such strain that it is no surprise that they often exhibit neurotic behaviour. This sex-based differentiation comes from adolescent "youth culture," where boys value things counter to adult male responsibility.

ROBERT K. MERTON

Robert King Merton (July 4, 1910 – February 23, 2003) was a distinguished American sociologist. He spent most of his career teaching at Columbia University, where he attained the rank of University Professor. In 1994, Merton won the National Medal of Science for his contributions to the field and for having founded the sociology of science. Merton developed notable concepts such as "unintended consequences," the "reference group," and "role strain" but is perhaps best known for having created the terms "role model" and "self-fulfilling prophecy". A central element of modern sociological, political and economic theory, the "self-fulfilling prophecy" is a process whereby a belief or an expectation, correct or incorrect, affects the outcome of a situation or the way a person or a group will behave. Merton's work on the "role model" first appeared in a study on the socializaton of medical students at Columbia. The term grew from his theory of a reference group, or the group to which individuals compare themselves, but to which they do not necessarily belong. Social roles were a central piece of Merton's theory of social groups. Merton emphasized that, rather than a person assuming one role and one status, they have a status set in the social structure which has attached to it a whole set of expected behaviors.

THEORIES OF THE MIDDLE RANGE

Middle-range theories, applicable to limited ranges of data, transcend sheer description of social phenomena and fill in the blanks between raw empiricism and grand or all-inclusive theory. In his plea for these kinds of theories Merton stands on the shoulders of Emile Durkheim and Max Weber.

Clarifying Functional Analysis

Merton argues that the central orientation of functionalism is in interpreting data by their consequences for larger structures in which they are implicated. Like Durkheim and Parsons he analyzes society with reference to whether cultural and social structures are well or badly integrated, is interested in the persistence of societies and defines functions that make for the adaptation of a given system. Finally, Merton thinks that shared values are central in explaining how societies and institutions work. However he disagrees with Parsons on some issues which will be brought to attention in the following part.

Dysfunctions

Parsons' work tends to imply that all institutions are inherently good for society. Merton emphasizes the existence of dysfunctions. He thinks that something may have consequences that are generally dysfunctional or which are dysfunctional for some and functional for others. On this point he approaches conflict theory, although he does believe that institutions and values CAN be functional for society as a whole. Merton states that only by recognizing the dysfunctional aspects of institutions, can we explain the development and persistence of alternatives. Merton's concept of dysfunctions is also central to his argument that functionalism is not essentially conservative.

Manifest and Latent Functions

Manifest functions are the consequences that people observe or expect, latent functions are those that are neither recognized nor intended. While Parsons tends to emphasize the manifest functions of social behaviour, Merton sees attention to latent functions as increasing the understanding of society: the distinction between manifest and latent forces the sociologist to go beyond the reasons individuals give for their actions or for the existence of customs and institutions; it makes them look for other social consequences that allow these practices' survival and illuminate the way society works. Dysfunctions can also be manifest or latent. Manifest dysfunctions include traffic jams, closed streets, piles of garbage, and a shortage of clean public toilets. Latent dysfunctions might include people missing work after the event to recover.

Functional Alternatives

Functionalists believe societies must have certain characteristics in order to survive. Merton shares this view but stresses that at the same time particular institutions are not the only ones able to fulfill these functions; a wide range of functional alternatives may be able to perform the same task. This notion of functional alternative is important because it alerts sociologists to the similar functions different institutions may perform and it further reduces the tendency of functionalism to imply approval of the status quo.

MERTON'S THEORY OF DEVIANCE

The term anomie, derived from Emile Durkheim, for Merton means: a discontinuity between cultural goals and the legitimate means available for reaching them. Applied to the United States he sees the American dream as an emphasis on the goal of monetary success but without the corresponding emphasis on the legitimate avenues to march toward this goal.

MANIFEST AND LATENT FUNCTIONS AND DYSFUNCTIONS

Manifest and latent functions are social scientific concepts first clarified for sociology by Robert K. Merton. Merton appeared interested in sharpening the conceptual tools to be employed in a functional analysis. Manifest functions and dysfunctions are conscious and deliberate, the latent ones the unconscious and unintended. While functions are intended (manifest) or recognized (latent), and have a positive effect on society, dysfunctions are unintended (manifest) or unrecognized (latent) and have a negative effect on society.

Functions

Manifest functions are the consequences that people observe or expect. It is explicitly stated and understood by the participants in the relevant action. The manifest function of a rain dance, used as an example by Merton in his 1967 *Social Theory and Social Structure*, is to produce rain, and this outcome is intended and desired by people participating in the ritual.

Latent functions are those that are neither recognized nor intended. A latent function of a behaviour is not explicitly stated, recognized, or intended by the people involved. Thus, they are identified observers. In the example of rain ceremony, the latent function reinforces the group identity by providing a regular opportunity for the members of a group to meet and engage in a common activity.

Peter L. Berger describes a series of examples illustrating the differences between manifest and latent functions: "...the "manifest" function of antigambling legislation may be to suppress gambling, its "latent" function to create an illegal empire for the gambling syndicates. Or Christian missions in parts of Africa "manifestly" tried to convert Africans to Christianity, "latently" helped to destroy the indigenous tribal cultures and this provided an important impetus towards rapid social transformation. Or the control of the Communist Party over all sectors of social life in Russia "manifestly" was to assure the continued dominance of the revolutionary ethos, "latently" created a new class of comfortable bureaucrats uncannily bourgeois in its aspirations and increasingly disinclined toward the self-denial of Bolshevik dedication (*nomenklatura*). Or the "manifest" function of many voluntary associations in America is sociability and public service, the "latent" function to attach status indices to those permitted to belong to such associations."

While Talcott Parsons tends to emphasize the manifest functions of social behaviour, Merton sees attention to latent functions as increasing the understanding of society: the distinction between manifest and latent forces the sociologist to go beyond the reasons individuals give for their actions or for the existence of customs and institutions; it makes them look for other social consequences that allow these practices' survival and illuminate the way society works.

Dysfunctions

Dysfunctions can also be manifest or latent. While functions are intended or recognized (manifest), and may have a positive effect on society, dysfunctions are unintended or unrecognized (latent) and have a negative effect on society. Manifest dysfunctions are anticipated disruptions of social life. For example, a manifest dysfunction of a festival might include disruptions of transportation and excessive production of garbage. Latent dysfunctions are unintended and unanticipated disruptions of order and stability. In the festival example, they would be represented by people missing work due to the traffic jam.

Medical Science Model

Broadly stated and here relying on the systems model first developed in medical science, an interrelated bundle of social structures (e.g., Zulu culture), treated as a social system, involves the parts (structural elements) acting in such a fashion so as to help maintain the homeodynamic equilibrium of the system of which they are an element. Manifest functions are the obvious and intended consequences a structural feature displays in the maintenance of the steady state of the system of which it is a part. Latent functions are less obvious or unintended consequences. Both manifest and latent functions contribute to the social system's unchanging ongoingness or stasis. In this very specific sense both may be interpreted as useful and positive.

In conducting a functional analysis, dysfunctions are consequences of structural elements that produce changes in their environing social system. The flame of the candle system flickers. The structural cause would be labelled dysfunctional. The candle's steady state has been disturbed or changed. The concept affords the only relief to structural-functionalism's inherent conservative bias. Dysfunction signifies the mechanism by which social change is evidenced within a social system. Whether that change is manifest or latent is a relatively simple empirical question. Whether that change is good or bad would seem to require interpretative criteria not afforded by a social scientific paradigm for functional analysis.

Quotes

- "... the distinction between manifest and latent functions was devised to preclude... confusion... between conscious motivations for social behaviour and its objective consequences"-Robert K. Merton, *Social Theory and Social Structure*, 1957, page 61
- "... I have adapted the terms "manifest" and "latent" from their use in another context by Freud...", ibid.
- "Emile Durkheim's... analysis of the social functions of punishment is... focused on its latent functions (consequences for the community) rather than confined to manifest functions (consequences for the criminal)", ibid.

MOHANDAS KARAMCHAND GANDHI

Mohandas Karamchand Gandhi (listen); 2 October 1869 – 30 January 1948) was the pre-eminent political and ideological leader of India during the Indian independence movement. He pioneered *satyagraha*. This is defined as resistance to tyranny through mass civil disobedience, a philosophy firmly founded upon *ahimsa*, or total nonviolence. This concept helped India to gain independence, and inspired movements for civil rights and freedom across the world. Gandhi is often referred to as Mahatma Gandhi. In India he is also called Bapu. He is officially honoured in India as the *Father of the Nation*; his birthday, 2 October, is commemorated there as *Gandhi Jayanti*, a national holiday, and worldwide as the International Day of Non-

Violence. Gandhi was assassinated on 30 January 1948 by Nathuram Godse, a Hindu Nationalist.

Gandhi first employed civil disobedience while an expatriate lawyer in South Africa, during the resident Indian community's struggle there for civil rights. After his return to India in 1915, he organised protests by peasants, farmers, and urban labourers concerning excessive land-tax and discrimination. After assuming leadership of the Indian National Congress in 1921, Gandhi led nationwide campaigns to ease poverty, expand women's rights, build religious and ethnic amity, end untouchability, and increase economic self-reliance. Above all, he aimed to achieve *Swaraj* or the independence of India from foreign domination. Gandhi famously led his followers in the Non-cooperation movement that protested the British-imposed salt tax with the 400 km (240 mi) Dandi Salt March in 1930. Later, in 1942, he launched the *Quit India* civil disobedience movement demanding immediate independence for India. Gandhi spent a number of years in jail in both South Africa and India.

As a practitioner of *ahimsa*, Gandhi swore to speak the truth and advocated that others do the same. He lived modestly in a self-sufficient residential community and wore the traditional Indian *dhoti* and shawl, woven from yarn that he had spun by hand himself. He ate simple vegetarian food, experimented for a time with a fruitarian diet, and undertook long fasts as a means of both self-purification and social protest.

SARVODAYA

Sarvodaya is a term meaning 'universal uplift' or 'progress of all'. The term was first coined by Mohandas Gandhi as the title of his 1908 translation of John Ruskin's tract on political economy, *Unto This Last*, and Gandhi came to use the term for the ideal of his own political philosophy. Later Gandhians, like the Indian nonviolence activist Vinoba Bhave, embraced the term as a name for the social movement in post-independence India which strove to ensure that self-determination and equality reached all strata of India society.

Origins and Gandhi's political ideal

Gandhi received a copy of Ruskin's *Unto This Last* from

a British friend, Mr. Henry Polak, while working as a lawyer in South Africa in 1904. In his *Autobiography*, Gandhi remembers the twenty-four hour train ride to Durban (from when he first read the book, being so in the grip of Ruskin's ideas that he could not sleep at all: "I determined to change my life in accordance with the ideals of the book." As Gandhi construed it, Ruskin's outlook on political-economic life extended from three central tenets:

1. That the good of the individual is contained in the good of all.
2. That a lawyer's work has the same value as the barber's in as much as all have the same right of earning their livelihood from their work.
3. That a life of labour, i.e., the life of the tiller of the soil and the handicraftsman is the life worth living.

The first of these I knew. The second I had dimly realized. The third had never occurred to me. *Unto This Last* made it clear as daylight for me that the second and third were contained in the first. I arose with the dawn, ready to reduce these principles to practice.

Four years later, in 1908, Gandhi rendered a paraphrased translation of Ruskin's book into his native tongue of Gujarati. He entitled the book *Sarvodaya*, a compound (samasa) he invented from two Sanskrit roots: *sarva* (all) and *udaya* (uplift) — "the uplift of all" (or as Gandhi glossed it in his autobiography, "the welfare of all"). Although inspired by Ruskin, the term would for Gandhi come to stand for a political ideal of his own stamp. (Indeed Gandhi was keen to distance himself from Ruskin's more conservative ideas.) The ideal which Gandhi strove to put into practice in his ashrams was, he hoped, one that he could persuade the whole of India to embrace, becoming a light to the other nations of the world. The Gandhian social ideal encompassed the dignity of labour, an equitable distribution of wealth, communal self-sufficiency and individual freedom.

Sarvodaya Movement

Gandhi's ideals have lasted well beyond the achievement of one of his chief projects, Indian independence (*swaraj*). His followers in India (notably, Vinoba Bhave) continued working to promote the kind of society that he envisioned, and their efforts have come to be known as the Sarvodaya Movement. Anima Bose has referred to the movement's philosophy as "a fuller and richer concept of people's democracy than any we have yet known." Sarvodaya workers associated with Vinoba, J. P. Narayan, Dada Dharmadhikari, Dhirendra Mazumdaar, Shankarrao Deo, K. G. Mashruwala undertook various projects aimed at encouraging popular self-organisation during the 1950s and 1960s, including *Bhoodan* and *Gramdan* movements. Many groups descended from these networks continue to function locally in India today.

NON-VIOLENCE & MAHATMA GANDHI

Mahatma Gandhi used the 'Non-Violence as a weapon' only against a most cunning adversary in a particular situation but it is really unfortunate that his name was made synonymous with Non-violence to make him irrelevant in the current scenario, when the concept of Terrorism is being patronized by a particular religion and without using some minimum force it can not be checked. I think the Gandhi's philosophy can offer very optimum solutions for such a situation, but it may not be 100% non-violent. I don't know why Gandhians examine any issue only on the basis of Violence & Non-violence only, when Gandhi always said that for prevalence of TRUTH, concept of Ahimsa can also be sacrificed. Considering the magnitude of Islamic Terrorism, minimum and optimum use of Violence can not be perceived as against the Gandhian principles & philosophy. Many people have only a little knowledge of history otherwise they would have been aware of the fact that Gandhi also approved the military action in J & K, when Pakistan invaded it in 1947/48.

Similarly such people must learn that the best tributes for the sacrifice of martyrs like Bhagat Singh / Rajguru / Sukhdev were offered by none other than Mahatma Gandhi himself. He was for all praise of their sacrifice but told that not enough such courageous young man are available in his country, therefore he opted the route of Non-Violence.

Moreover, where were the weapons in those days of 1920/ 30? Only a few Indian Royals had the Arms & ammunition, which were firmly behind the British Govt. The revolutionary party of Bhagat Singh was having only one or two pistols but certainly not a single gun. The coward & divided citizens of this nation never supported revolutionaries with money even in spite of their many heroic acts.

Therefore Non-Violence was also a compulsion for Gandhi. At the most it was only one aspect of Gandhi's versatile Hindu philosophy but always subordinate to TRUTH, as has been described by the Gandhi in following words:

Life and its problems have thus become to me so many experiments in the practice of truth and non-violence. By instinct I have been truthful, but not non-violent. As a Jain Muni once rightly said I was not so much votary of 'Ahimsa' as I was of truth, and I put the latter in the first place and the former in the second. For,, as he put it, I was capable of sacrificing violence for the sake of truth. In fact it was in the course of my persuit of truth that I discovered non-violence. Our scriptures have declared that there is no 'dharma'(law) higher than Truth. But non-violence they say is the highest duty. The word 'dharma' in my opinion has different connotations as used in the two aphorisms.

7

Paradigms of Sociological Thought

THE RISE OF THE FUNCTIONAL PARADIGM

In yesterday's address to the Ruby community, Dave Thomas invited Rubyists to fork Ruby, to freely research and experiment with new and interesting features. If this process is successful, many of these features will inevitably see their way back into Ruby's core, thus improving the language in leaps and bounds. And I feel he couldn't have been any more right. In fact, the whole industry is experiencing the trend of incorporating features developed in less common languages, research languages, "toy languages" if you prefer, within mainstream ones. Experimenting with these alternative languages is important because occasionally they themselves become widely used, and even when they fail to do so, they lend their insight to the world of software development, finding their way into other languages. This approach greatly accelerates the development of common languages for the good of their large user bases and the improvement of the software industry. It's a win-win situation for everyone involved and for the development community as a whole.

Pay attention to the development community online, and you'll quickly notice a few non-mainstream programming languages appear over and over again. I'm referring to languages like F#, Erlang, Haskell, Scala and Clojure. I'll admit to a certain selection bias, given that I tend to hang out in communities where hackers and developers actively pursue the betterment of their programming skills, beyond the stereotypical 9 to 5 requirements. But nevertheless, three or four years ago the average developer probably wouldn't have heard about any of them (at least the ones that existed at the time). And today all of these languages have active communities, books being published about them, and most programmers have at least encountered some of these names. They are all different languages, but their common denominator is the functional paradigm. Notice that I titled this post "The Rise of the Functional Paradigm" and not "The Rise of Functional Languages". In a sense the latter is true as well, since there's been much more attention towards functional programming languages lately. But there is a subtle difference. I don't expect purely functional languages to become the most used programming languages anytime soon. For the foreseeable future, I don't predict US companies to outsource Haskell jobs to India or China, like they do today for Java or.NET projects.

Yet these functional languages serve a higher purpose. Not only do they satisfy the needs of intellectually curious developers and companies looking for a competitive advantage, but they also have a great deal of influence on the rest of the development world.

We are seeing a convergence between these two groups of languages. Functional languages will strive to become as useful as possible, with libraries and tools that are more adequate for mainstream developers, while conserving their functional purity. Meanwhile, mainstream languages will slowly adopt powerful features found in these functional and other research languages, adding further expressiveness and capabilities to their largely adopted foundations. F#, the evolution of C# and the addition of LINQ should be enough evidence that this is the case at least for the.NET platform. And even C++0x and D are leaning towards the incorporation of some functional features (e.g. lambda expressions and closures). The two types of languages come from different directions but will reach a similar destination.

The ever increasingly popular Ruby, Python and JavaScript owe their success to several factors. And while they are considered multi-paradigm and were mostly aided in their popularity by their immediacy, simplicity, usefulness and a set of historical circumstances, they're all hybrid languages that adopt functional features. The functional paradigm is becoming so common, that it's hard to imagine seeing any new programming language rise to fame without including at least a subset of the features available in other functional programming languages. As developers, we've grown to expect the elegance of functional features in a language. No lambda, no party.

If the 90s were characterized by the rise of the Object Oriented paradigm, and this decade can be considered as a transition phase, then the future belongs to the functional paradigm. Whether developers prefer to mix this with other paradigms, like a powerful cocktail, or shoot it straight down (e.g. in purely functional languages like Haskell), the functional paradigm is here to stay.

AN ECOLOGICAL ORGANIC PARADIGM (EOP)

A modern version of the organic paradigm can be based on behavioural ecology, ecology being the study of the inter-relationships between an organism and its environment. To do this from the standpoint of behaviour and cognition the organic paradigm needs to coincide with our general levels of awareness or consciousness and be expressed in terms of our mental functional capacities. The modern ecological organic paradigm (EOP) being proposed thus will have the perspective of an ecology of cognition or an ecology of the mind or consciousness. It describes four general human mental functional capacities, in the context of evolutionary and psychological development, and loosely associates them to four general categories of experience with which we have to cope, adapt and inter-relate.

The four functional cognitive capacities are described as appetite, social conscience, reason and an interpretive capacity. The dimensions of experience to which they each primarily, but not exclusively, inter-relate are primal individual needs, society, the natural world in which we live and metaphysics. "Interpretation" and "metaphysics" are here being used as broad categories that represent integration, orientation, and narrative concerning meaning and purpose, and they represent our need for a coherent self and world in which we live. They have to do not so much with the natural world in which we live and of which we are a part, but with our individual and collective place in that world. This framework of analysis of four functional cognitive capacities and their inter-relationship to four general dimensions of experience will be referred to as the ecological organic paradigm.

The general framework of analysis that is being proposed is a modification of the work of Leslie Stevenson in *Seven Theories of Human Nature* (1987). In this work, Stevenson states that the best way to understand any philosophy or philosopher is to understand the assumptions being made concerning the nature of human beings, the nature of society, and the nature of the universe. Since the Copernican Revolution, however, assumptions about the nature of the universe have been increasingly divided into assumptions concerning the natural world in which we live and metaphysical assumptions about meaning and purpose that integrate our knowledge and create a narrative in space and time. One set of assumptions concerns the question *how*. The other set of assumptions concerns the question *why*. The ecological organic framework for understanding the dynamics of moral and political philosophy being proposed thus has four very general categories rather than the three described by Stevenson. These consider the assumptions concerning the individual, society, nature, and metaphysics. Our capacities of cognition that primarily relate to each of these categories are sequentially described as appetite, social conscience, logical reasoning, and an interpretive capacity of integration and narrative.

This modern ecological organic paradigm is derived in part from classical philosophy. It is also compatible, however, with some recent concepts that include both natural and cultural evolution (co-evolution) and some recent concepts of psychological cognitive development. This perspective not only includes both nature and nurture, but also sees an inter-relationship between them. There is freedom within form. Human nature is neither seen to be infinitely malleable by changing its social context, nor is it seen as only determined by evolution and genetics. James Q. Wilson, in *The Moral Sense*, wrote that, “two errors arise in attempting to understand the human condition. One is to assume that culture is everything, the other is to assume that it is nothing” (1993, 6).

At the human level, evolution in the broadest sense entails cultural history, but our cultural history in the broadest sense also entails evolution. Human history, in this perspective, did not begin 5000 years ago with the written word.

This framework can accommodate both descriptive and normative concepts of human nature, and it can accommodate both the individual and social dimensions of human knowledge and activity. In this framework moral and political philosophy are perceived to be dynamic, not only because human nature is multidimensional, but also because the experiences to which we relate change and are changeable. The different dimensions of our cognition, whether they be "gut reactions" or rational reflections, enable us to deal with both internal and external environmental complexity (Godfrey-Smith 1996). Because of these multiple factors one does not anticipate a convergence through reductionism such as one sometimes sees in the basic sciences (Flanagan 1997). Such reductionism has sometimes been referred to as physics envy. On the other hand, the logical implication of such a framework is not necessarily subjectivity, relativism, arbitrariness, or material utility, but more toward what Aristotle described as *phronesis* or practical wisdom. It should thus not be unexpected that the paradigm also is compatible with the categories of what is sometimes called a "folk psychology," which is based on introspection and accumulated experience. This framework of an ecological organic paradigm is not entirely new for it is based in part, for example, on Aristotle's sense of the composite whole and it addresses the problem of the one and the many. It is a reconsideration of an old and common idea.

ABANDONED IN PHILOSOPHY

The organic framework in its hierarchical Platonic form, along with such other metaphors as The Great Chain of Being, was used primarily to support the prevailing social structures and institutions of the times. For 1500 years such metaphors helped to provide support for the hierarchy in the Church and the State. King James I of England understood the importance and spectrum of such paradigms of thought when he was reported to have said "No bishop, no king". The Scientific Revolution challenged the assumptions of the past and the

Renaissance and the Reformation placed increased emphasis on the dignity and worth of each individual. The organic paradigm was thus eventually replaced in moral and political philosophy primarily by the concept of the social contract, which begins with the premise that all persons are born free and equal in a state of nature. The Stoic concept of equality, that we all have sufficient reason to understand a natural moral order, was always burdened in its challenge to hierarchy because the populace was illiterate and because in the Platonic framework of human nature reason was also used to justify hierarchy. The hierarchical social structures were more successfully challenged by Judeo-Christian concepts of equality based on ethical monotheism and love of one another with the best examples occurring when the particular religious beliefs were in a minority position. Moral and political concepts of equality, however, have been most widely accepted when they have been based on a concept of human rights that can be understood at the level of self-interest.

Moral theory also became more secular in what came to be widely perceived as a mathematical and mechanical universe. This view of an orderly world was also often accommodated and appropriated by a more natural theology. Such changes, it was thought, might also make possible a utilitarian determination of human well-being, not by seeking such uncertain principles as truth, goodness, beauty, and virtue, but by an egalitarian calculation of the consequence of actions in the terms of pleasure and pain.

Currently there are several reasons, however, why an organic paradigm should be reconsidered.

Developments in the biological sciences and medicine in the past one hundred years would tend to place a greater emphasis on a more balanced concept of human nature. Current scientific thought now considers feedback mechanisms and a system of checks and balances to be almost an essential part of the definition of a living organism. One example of a more balanced concept would be what Claude Bernard called the "internal milieu." This is the metabolic homeostasis of the internal environment or extracellular fluid in which our cells all live and which they monitor and help to maintain. Another example from medicine would be a current model used to evaluate pain (American Medical Association 1993, 307). The basis of even a utilitarian calculation of the greatest good, based on pleasure and pain, can thus be seen to depend on the categories of the older organic paradigm and folk psychology. These categories are compatible with those of a modern ecological organic paradigm and the framework need not necessarily be hierarchical.

As will be shown in an extended example to follow, the framework of analysis of the organic metaphor is even instrumental to a historical and analytical understanding of the social contract, the primary paradigm that replaced it. The general categories of the organic framework, but not their earlier hierarchical form, are instrumental to an understanding of the several aspects of equality on which United States constitutional democracy, as a social contract, is founded.

A central problematic or political issue of our time is the accommodation of pluralism. The ecological organic paradigm recognizes the multiple dimensions of human nature and, therefore, does not aspire to certainty or necessarily support any singular ideology. It does, however, provide a framework that at least has a capacity for accommodating pluralism. Recognizing even very broadly the multiple potentials of human nature can provide a rational basis for at least a threshold of values and conditions for the realization of those potentials as well as a basis for moderation and balance.

A barrier to learning in the past has often been the unavailability of information. A barrier to learning in the near future will be the difficulty of both selecting from an overabundance of information and associating such information in a meaningful way. A modern organic paradigm should be reconsidered because it can provide a useful framework for understanding the dynamics of moral and political philosophy. Folk psychology as an equivalent of the ecological organic paradigm has survived because it has provided some coherence. The ecological organic paradigm does not attempt to describe the specific anatomical mechanisms of perception and cognition. It provides coherence because it describes in a general way those cognitive functions that have progressively developed as coping mechanisms in both natural and cultural evolution. A new Darwinism, which recognizes both natural and cultural evolution, rejects the false exclusionary dichotomies of nature versus nurture, fact versus value, and nature versus free will (Arnhart 1995). If facts are not related to values, for example, the phrase "political science" is an oxymoron. In practice our perception of the facts usually has a very significant influence on our moral and political decisions. A more accurate description of the relationship would be that what we perceive to be the facts is not the sole determinant of our values. By recognizing the multiple dimensions of human nature, the ecological organic framework is able to accommodate what were previously sometimes seen as either/or dichotomies.

As a metaphor the ecological organic paradigm will remind us of the interrelationship between the character of the people and the character of the state. In his First Inaugural Address, George Washington stated that it was imperative "that the foundations of national policy be laid in the pure and inimitable principles of private morality." Aristotle, on the other hand, understood the central role of the *polis* or community in forming individual character. Our individual and social moral character has perhaps become the most significant factor in the survival of ourselves, our society, our environment, and intergenerational continuity.

Ecology changes. We live in a nuclear age that has seen defense strategies of mutual assured destruction and response times measured in minutes. We will be facing the moral problems of genetic engineering and population control under the conditions of limited resources and a threatened environment. Technology has markedly increased the possibilities of both totalitarianism and terrorism. Yet we live in a century that coined the word "genocide" and a century that will be identified with individual alienation. The general concern has been that our technological development may have exceeded the parameters of our biological adaptive mechanisms and our moral development. We also live in a time of pluralism in our own culture and in what is increasingly becoming a pluralistic global community. As the sociologist Max Weber described, this degree of pluralism usually requires societies to be based on legal authority, rather than traditional kinship-descent or charismatic social organization. These conditions point to the need for moral and political structures that both affirm life and can accommodate pluralism. They illustrate the need for limitations and moderation, but also the need for a model with a capacity for synthesis. A modern version of the organic paradigm should be reconsidered because it can provide a framework that has the capacity for affirmation, accommodation, moderation, adaptation, coherence, and synthesis.

The recurrent interest in a naturalized epistemology perhaps began in 1969 with a paper by W. V. Quine, "Epistemology Naturalized", in which he wrote that, "epistemology goes on, though in a new setting and a clarified status. Epistemology, or something like it, simply falls into place as a chapter of psychology and hence of natural science" (1996, 82). Psychology, however, is related to and needs to be understood in the context of the other biological sciences as well as the humanities and from the perspective of behavioural ecology. Toward the end of the *Origin of Species* Darwin wrote, "In the distant future I see open fields for far more important researches. Psychology will be based on the foundation... of the necessary acquirement of each mental power and capacity by gradation" (1936a: 373). Our cognitive capacities, our consciousness and ability to know, have in the past developed and continue to develop as part of an interaction with the complex world in which we live. The ecological organic paradigm can help to clarify the primary assumptions on which our thoughts and actions are based and take into consideration the contexts in which they occur.

In an article entitled "The Foundationalism in Irrealism, and the Immorality", the philosopher John F. Post states that "philosophers have tended to develop an image of themselves and their enterprise as largely independent of whatever the sciences might turn up." He quotes Wittgenstein as saying, "Darwin's theory has no more to do with philosophy than any other hypothesis in natural science" (1922, 4.1122). Post then writes, "But what happens when we consider concepts, language, and meaning not from the point of view of how they seem to us on reflection from within, but from the point of view of how they appear from without, in particular to biological science? By biological science I do *not* mean any of its possibly reductive subdisciplines, such as molecular biology or neuroscience, and certainly not any sociobiology. I mean the nonreductive, holistic biology of historically evolved living organisms in relation to their normal environments and to each other." He continues that "One of the key notions of such biology is that of the *proper function* of an organ, device or behaviour. For example, the proper function of the heart is to pump blood; to be a heart is to pump blood. Why?" He then sites Ruth Millikan in stating that the proper function of your heart is to pump blood because it was by pumping blood that past hearts (or enough of them) enabled containing organisms to survive and reproduce at rates higher than those without them. Post objects to language-game irrealism because it means that we who play the game are in charge only because of the rejection of relevant external constraints (Post 1996, 7-8). The ecological organic paradigm takes the concept of "selection" seriously, but at the human level applies this both ways in the interaction between humans and their environment. The framework is based in the biological sciences, but it also retains a place for interpretation and metaphysics broadly understood.

PARADIGM

The original Greek term (paradeigma) was used in Greek texts such as Plato's Timaeus (28A) as the model or the pattern that the Demiurge (god) used to create the cosmos. The term had a technical meaning in the field of grammar: the 1900 *Merriam-Webster* dictionary defines its technical use only in the context of grammar or, in rhetoric, as a term for an illustrative parable or fable. In linguistics, Ferdinand de Saussure used *paradigm* to refer to a class of elements with similarities. The word has come to refer very often now to a thought pattern in any scientific discipline or other epistemological context. The Merriam-Webster Online dictionary defines this usage as "a philosophical and theoretical framework of a scientific school or discipline within which theories, laws, and generalizations and the experiments performed in support of them are formulated; *broadly: a philosophical or theoretical framework of any kind.*"

Scientific Paradigm

The historian of science Thomas Kuhn gave *paradigm* its contemporary meaning when he adopted the word to refer to the set of practices that define a scientific discipline at any particular period of time. Kuhn himself came to prefer the terms exemplar and normal science, which have more precise philosophical meanings. However in his book *The Structure of Scientific Revolutions* Kuhn defines a scientific paradigm as:

- *what* is to be observed and scrutinized
- the kind of *questions* that are supposed to be asked and probed for answers in relation to this subject
- *how* these questions are to be structured
- *how* the results of scientific investigations should be interpreted

  Alternatively, the *Oxford English Dictionary* defines paradigm as "a pattern or model, an exemplar." Thus an additional component of Kuhn's definition of paradigm is:

- *how* is an experiment to be conducted, and *what* equipment is available to conduct the experiment.

Thus, within normal science, the paradigm is the set of exemplary experiments that are likely to be copied or emulated. In this scientific context, the prevailing paradigm often represents a more specific way of viewing reality, or limitations on acceptable *programs* for future research, than the more general scientific method.

A currently accepted paradigm would be the standard model of physics. The scientific method would allow for orthodox scientific investigations into phenomena which might contradict or disprove the standard model; however grant funding would be proportionately more difficult to obtain for such experiments, depending on the degree of deviation from the accepted standard model theory which the experiment would be expected to test for. To illustrate the point, an experiment to test for the mass of neutrinos or the decay of protons (small departures from the model) would be more likely to receive money than experiments to look for the violation of the conservation of momentum, or ways to engineer reverse time travel.

One important aspect of Kuhn's paradigms is that the paradigms are incommensurable, meaning two paradigms cannot be reconciled with each other because they cannot be subjected to the same common standard of comparison. That is, no meaningful comparison between them is possible without fundamental modification of the concepts that are an intrinsic part of the paradigms being compared. This way of looking at the concept of "paradigm" creates a paradox of sorts, since competing paradigms are in fact constantly being measured against each other. (Nonetheless, competing paradigms are not fully intelligible solely within the context of their own conceptual frameworks.) For this reason, paradigm as a concept in the philosophy of science might more meaningfully be defined as a self-reliant explanatory model or conceptual framework. This definition makes it clear that the real barrier to comparison is not necessarily the absence of common units of measurement, but an absence of mutually compatible or mutually intelligible concepts. Under this system, a new paradigm which replaces an old paradigm is not necessarily better, because the criteria of judgment are controlled by the paradigm itself, and by the conceptual framework which defines the paradigm and gives it its explanatory value.

A more disparaging term groupthink, and the term mindset, have somewhat similar meanings that apply to smaller and larger scale examples of disciplined thought. Michel Foucault used the terms episteme and discourse, mathesis and taxinomia, for aspects of a "paradigm" in Kuhn's original sense.

Simple common analogy: A simplified analogy for *paradigm* is a habit of reasoning, or "the box" in the commonly used phrase "thinking outside the box". Thinking inside the box is analogous with normal science. The box encompasses the thinking of normal science and thus the box is analogous with *paradigm.* "Thinking outside the box" would be what Kuhn calls revolutionary science. Revolutionary science is usually unsuccessful, and very rarely leads to new paradigms. However, when they are successful they lead to large scale changes in the scientific worldview. When these large scale shifts in the scientific view are implemented and accepted by the majority, it will then become "the box" and science will progress within it.

Paradigm Shifts

In *The Structure of Scientific Revolutions*, Kuhn wrote that "Successive transition from one paradigm to another via revolution is the usual developmental pattern of mature science."

Paradigm shifts tend to be most dramatic in sciences that appear to be stable and mature, as in physics at the end of the 19th century. At that time, a statement generally attributed to physicist Lord Kelvin famously claimed, "There is nothing new to be discovered in physics now. All that remains is more and more precise measurement." Five years later, Albert Einstein published his paper on special relativity, which challenged the very simple set of rules laid down by Newtonian mechanics, which had been used to describe force and motion for over two hundred years. In this case, the new paradigm reduces the old to a special case in the sense that Newtonian mechanics is still a good model for approximation for speeds that are slow compared to the speed of light. Philosophers and historians of science, including Kuhn himself, ultimately accepted a modified version of Kuhn's model, which synthesizes his original view with the gradualist model that preceded it. Kuhn's original model is now generally seen as too limited.

Kuhn's idea was itself revolutionary in its time, as it caused a major change in the way that academics talk about science. Thus, it could be argued that it caused or was itself part of a "paradigm shift" in the history and sociology of science. However, Kuhn would not recognize such a paradigm shift. Being in the social sciences, people can still use earlier ideas to discuss the history of science.

The Concept of Paradigm and the Social Sciences

Kuhn himself did not consider the concept of paradigm as appropriate for the social sciences. He explains in his preface to "The Structure of Scientific Revolutions" that he concocted the concept of paradigm precisely in order to distinguish the social from the natural sciences. He wrote this book at the Palo Alto Center for Scholars, surrounded by social scientists, when he observed that they were never in agreement on theories or concepts. He explains that he wrote this book precisely to show that there are no, nor can there be any, paradigms in the social sciences. Mattei Dogan, a French sociologist, in his article "Paradigms in the [Social Sciences]," develops Kuhn's original thesis that there are no paradigms at all in the social sciences since the concepts are polysemic, the deliberate mutual ignorance between scholars and the proliferation of schools in these disciplines. Dogan provides many examples of the non-existence of paradigms in the social sciences in his essay, particularly in sociology, political science and political anthropology.

Paradigm Paralysis

Perhaps the greatest barrier to a paradigm shift, in some cases, is the reality of paradigm paralysis: the inability or refusal to see beyond the current models of thinking. This is similar to what psychologists term Confirmation bias. Examples include rejection of Galileo's theory of a heliocentric universe, the discovery of electrostatic photography, xerography and the quartz clock.

Other Uses

Handa, M.L. (1986) introduced the idea of "social paradigm" in the context of social sciences. He identified the basic components of a social paradigm. Like Kuhn, Handa addressed the issue of changing paradigm; the process popularly known as "paradigm shift". In this respect, he focused on social circumstances that precipitate such a shift and the effects of the shift on social institutions, including the institution of education. This broad shift in the social arena, in turn, changes the way the individual perceives reality.

Another use of the word *paradigm* is in the sense of Weltanschauung (German for world view). For example, in social science, the term is used to describe the set of experiences, beliefs and values that affect the way an individual perceives reality and responds to that perception.

Social scientists have adopted the Kuhnian phrase "paradigm shift" to denote a change in how a given society goes about organizing and understanding reality. A "dominant paradigm" refers to the values, or system of thought, in a society that are most standard and widely held at a given time. Dominant paradigms are shaped both by the community's cultural background and by the context of the historical moment. The following are conditions that facilitate a system of thought to become an accepted dominant paradigm:

- Professional organizations that give legitimacy to the paradigm

- Dynamic leaders who introduce and purport the paradigm
- Journals and editors who write about the system of thought. They both disseminate the information essential to the paradigm and give the paradigm legitimacy
- Government agencies who give credence to the paradigm
- Educators who propagate the paradigm's ideas by teaching it to students
- Conferences conducted that are devoted to discussing ideas central to the paradigm
- Media coverage
- Lay groups, or groups based around the concerns of lay persons, that embrace the beliefs central to the paradigm
- Sources of funding to further research on the paradigm.

The word *paradigm* is also still used to indicate a pattern or model or an outstandingly clear or typical example or archetype. The term is frequently used in this sense in the design professions. Design Paradigms or archetypes comprise functional precedents for design solutions. The best known references on design paradigms are *Design Paradigms: A Sourcebook for Creative Visualization*, by Wake, and *Design Paradigms* by Petroski. In philosophy, C. S. Herrman applies the archetypal indication to methodology.

This term is also used in cybernetics. Here it means (in a very wide sense) a (conceptual) protoprogramme for reducing the chaotic mass to some form of order. Note the similarities to the concept of entropy in chemistry and physics. A paradigm there would be a sort of prohibition to proceed with any action that would increase the total entropy of the system. In order to create a paradigm, a closed system which would accept any changes is required. Thus a paradigm can be only applied to a system that is not in its final stage.

CONFLICT THEORY

Conflict theories are perspectives in social science which emphasize the social, political or material inequality of a social group, which critique the broad socio-political system, or which otherwise detract from structural functionalism and ideological conservativism. Conflict theories draw attention to power differentials, such as class conflict, and generally contrast historically dominant ideologies. Certain conflict theories set out to highlight the ideological aspects inherent in traditional thought. Whilst many of these perspectives hold parallels, conflict theory *does not* refer to a unified school of thought, and should not be confused with, for instance, peace and conflict studies, or any other specific theory of social conflict.

In Classical Sociology

Of the classical founders of social science, conflict theory is most commonly associated with Karl Marx (1818-1883). Based on a dialectical materialist account history, Marxism posited that capitalism, like previous socioeconomic systems, would inevitably produce internal tensions leading to its own destruction. Marx ushered in radical change, advocating proletarian revolution and freedom from the ruling classes.

The history of all hitherto existing society is the history of class struggles. Freeman and slave, patrician and plebeian, lord and serf, guild-master and journeyman, in a word, oppressor and oppressed, stood in constant opposition to one another, carried on an uninterrupted, now hidden, now open fight, a fight that each time ended, either in a revolutionary re-constitution of society at large, or in the common ruin of the contending classes. – *Karl Marx & Friedrich Engels The Communist Manifesto 1848,*

Two early conflict theorists were the Polish-Austrian sociologist and political theorist Ludwig Gumplowicz (1838-1909) and the American sociologist and paleontologist Lester F. Ward (1841-1913). Although Ward and Gumplowicz developed their theories independently they had much in common and approached conflict from a comprehensive anthropological and evolutionary point-of-view as opposed to Marx's rather exclusive focus on economic factors.

Gumplowicz, in "Outlines of Sociology" (1884), describes how civilization has been shaped by conflict between cultures and ethnic groups. Gumplowicz theorized that large complex human societies evolved from the war and conquest. States become organized around the domination of one group by another: masters and slaves. Eventually a complex caste system develops. Horowitz says that Gumplowicz understood conflict in all it's forms: "class conflict, race conflict and ethnic conflict", and calls him one of the fathers of Conflict Theory.

What happened in India, Babylon, Egypt, Greece and Rome may sometime happen in modern Europe. European civilization may perish, over flooded by barbaric tribes. But if any one believes that we are safe from such catastrophes he is perhaps yielding to an all too optimistic delusion. There are no barbaric tribes in our neighborhood to be sure — but let no one be deceived, their instincts lie latent in the populace of European states. – *Gumplowicz (1884).*

Ward directly attacked and attempted to systematically refute the elite business class's lassiez faire philosophy as espoused by the hugely popular social philosopher Herbert Spencer. Ward's "Dynamic Sociology" (1883) was an extended thesis on how to reduce conflict and competition in society and thus optimize human progress. At the most basic level Ward saw human nature itself to be deeply conflicted between self-aggrandizement and altruism, between emotion and intellect, and between male and female. These conflicts would be then reflected in society and Ward assumed there had been a "perpetual and vigorous struggle" among various "social forces" that shaped civilization. Ward was more optimistic than Marx and Gumplowicz and believed that it was possible to build on and reform present social structures with the help sociological analysis.

Durkheim (1858-1917) saw society as a functioning organism. Functionalism concerns "the effort to impute, as rigorously as possible, to each feature, custom, or practice, its effect on the functioning of a supposedly stable, cohesive system", The chief form of social conflict that Durkheim addressed was crime. Durkheim saw crime as "a factor in public health, an integral part of all healthy societies."

The collective conscience defines certain acts as "criminal." Crime thus plays a role in the evolution of morality and law: "[it] implies not only that the way remains open to necessary changes but that in certain cases it directly prepares these changes." Weber's (1864-1920) approach to conflict is contrasted with that of Marx. While Marx focused on the way individual behaviour is conditioned by social structure, Weber emphasized the importance of "social action," i.e., the ability of individuals to affect their social relationships.

Modern Approaches

C. Wright Mills has been called the founder of modern conflict theory. In Mills's view, social structures are created through conflict between people with differing interests and resources. Individuals and resources, in turn, are influenced by these structures and by the "unequal distribution of power and resources in the society." The power elite of American society, (i.e., the military-industrial complex) had "emerged from the fusion of the corporate elite, the Pentagon, and the executive branch of government." Mills argued that the interests of this elite were opposed to those of the people. He theorized that the policies of the power elite would result in "increased escalation of conflict, production of weapons of mass destruction, and possibly the annihilation of the human race."

One more recent articulation of conflict theory is found in Alan Sears' (Canadian sociologist) book *A Good Book, in Theory: A Guide to Theoretical Thinking* (2008):

- Societies are defined by inequality that produces conflict, rather than which produces order and consensus. This conflict based on inequality can only be overcome through a fundamental transformation of the existing relations in the society, and is productive of new social relations.
- The disadvantaged have structural interests that run counter to the status quo, which, once they are assumed, will lead to social change. Thus, they are viewed as agents of change rather than objects one should feel sympathy for.
- Human potential (e.g., capacity for creativity) is suppressed by conditions of exploitation and oppression, which are necessary in any society with an unequal division of labour. These and other qualities do not necessarily have to be stunted due to the requirements of the so-called "civilizing process," or "functional necessity": creativity is actually an engine for economic development and change.
- The role of theory is in realizing human potential and transforming society, rather than maintaining the power

structure. The opposite aim of theory would be the objectivity and detachment associated with positivism, where theory is a neutral, explanatory tool.

- Consensus is a euphemism for ideology. Genuine consensus is not achieved, rather the more powerful in societies are able to impose their conceptions on others and have them accept their discourses. Consensus does not preserve social order, it entrenches stratification, e.g., the American dream.
- The State serves the particular interests of the most powerful while claiming to represent the interests of all. Representation of disadvantaged groups in State processes may cultivate the notion of full participation, but this is an illusion/ideology.
- Inequality on a global level is characterized by the purposeful underdevelopment of Third World countries, both during colonization and after national independence. The global system (i.e., development agencies such as World Bank and IMF) benefits the most powerful countries and multi-national corporations, rather than the subjects of development, through economic, political, and military actions.

Although Sears associates the conflict theory approach with Marxism, he argues that it is the foundation for much "feminist, post-modernist, anti-racist, and lesbian-gay liberationist theories."

ETHNOMETHODOLOGY AND PHENOMENOLOGY

Phenomenological sociology holds that reality is an intersubjectively shared and socially constructed phenomenon. People act based on the meaning that events and others have for them. Drawing upon the understandings developed by Alfred Schutz (1962) phenomenological sociology focuses on describing the subjective reality understood to be reality by members of society. Schutz suggested that members= subjective experience is a shared reality which draws upon a common stock of knowledge-typifications, recipes and formulas for accomplishing particular tasks, and commonsense understandings and theories that are shared by members of a group. Through the processes of socialization, these typifications and understandings are internalized. In interaction, as we strive to produce meaningful accounts of the people and world around us, we apply these understandings in an attempt to order our experience. In doing so these understandings, and the objects to which we attach them, come to have the appearance of a reality of their own. The externalization of our shared intersubjective experience results in the objectification of the categories of understanding we have created (Berger and Luckmann, 1967). The interactionally produced explanations of deviance and normalcy, good and bad, right and wrong; interpretations of behaviors constructed as a means of making sense out of concrete situations, become "institutionalized versions of social reality...(operating) as controls over what we experience as real" (Pfohl 1994:355). Phenomenological analysis seeks to describe this shared, intersubjective reality as it is perceived and defined by societal members in the course of their everyday lives. To accurately do this, phenomenologists 'bracket' or suspend their own belief in the objective reality of the world around them.

Ethnomethodology goes further. The structures of "objective reality' are characterized as being far more fragile and malleable. For the ethnomethodologist there is no shared set of understanding and meaning which members attach to the world around them. There is no shared sense of "deviance" that can be called upon to order the strange and unusual behaviour of others. What members of a group do share are methods for making sense. Schutz's common stock of knowledge is reconceptualized as a shared set of interpretive procedures, sense making activities, that are invoked and employed continually in interaction. These procedures allow members to produce practical accounts of specific individuals engaged in specific activities in the context of particular situations. Deviance and deviants emerge as particular designations which provide practical understandings of everyday life situations. By constructing a sense that particular people and specific behaviour are "outside" the norm members produce a shared understanding of the reality of the norm.

By focusing on how deviant labels—symbolic meanings attached to behaviour, and norms are constructed through the interpretive work of individuals in everyday life situations, ethnomethodology, along with phenomenological sociology, can be seen as forming a foundation for other interactionist approaches to deviance. However, for ethnomethodologists the idea of an objective social structure (status, roles, groups, institutions and the cultural system of meaning, values and norms that support these elements) is no longer conceived of as a determinant of human behaviour. Ethnomethodologists suspend belief in (bracket) not only the objective reality of the world, but also the idea that members share symbolic meaning structures. Social structure—conceptualized as a moment-to-moment accomplishment, and its symbolic meanings are analyzed as emerging properties of human interaction. The process of continually negotiating the image of normative boundaries by accomplishing practical accounts of deviant behaviour that becomes the focus of the ethnomethodologist.

Significant within the ethnomethodological approach is a focus on how the constraints of the situational context, the biographies of the individuals involved, and the organizational demands placed upon the actors interact with the basic features of interpretive work to produce definitions of behaviour (deviance). There are a variety of interrelated processes that ethnomethodologists analyze in connection to the interpretive work of actors in everyday situations. The spiral of reflexivity and indexicality forms the core of their analysis. Specific interpretational procedures and guidelines such as retrospective interpretation, the rules of consistency and economy, and documentary interpretation are displayed as basic activities out of which understandings of deviance emerge.

Reflexivity

Once constructed, understandings of deviance become part of the context from which they emerged. The resulting typifications become explained within the context of common-sense theories. These theories, sometimes rooted in folk wisdom—sometimes rooted in science, focus attention on the relevance of specific features of situations as being keys to understanding behaviour.

Reflexivity expresses the ethnomethodologist's understanding of the ongoing (re)construction of meaning and the sense of continuity we maintain in our interpretive work.

Once defined, a situation or person "becomes" in our understanding the "type" we have constructed. The "objective reality" of this "type" thus created is paradoxically understood as a product of the features of the situation rather than our interpretive process (Pfohl, 1994: 357).

Theories of deviance, shaped within the historical context of understanding the deviant as simply bad, wicked, or evil—or the more contemporary conceptions of sickness and disease; structure our perceptions and allow us to recognize for the practical purposes at hand the meaning of individuals and their behaviour. Such understandings, couched in causal terminology, lead to the institutionalization of societal response to deviance. Whether the child molester is electrocuted, chemically castrated, or continually monitored via the Internet is dependent on the prevailing interpretive guidelines of the moment. When officials come to define tobacco as a drug millions of smokers >become= drug users, and a new campaign against drug use ensues.

Relevant here is the phenomenological concern with the subjective meaning behaviour has for the actor. Identity (a sense of order within the individual) is constructed and embodied in ways similar to the appearance of order "out there" in society. The individual actor may well become the deviant phenomenon. This social construction of reality produces the context of individual (and group) identity and behaviour out of which typifications and common-sense theories emerge.

Indexicality

The central concept of indexicality focuses attention on the (reflexive) sense we make of a particular situation or activity as being a product of our personal biographies (the experiences and expectations we bring to the situation) and the contingent elements of the situation. Smoking a marijuana cigarette 'means' one thing to the novice, another to an experienced user, and still another to a substance abuse counselor. The 'reality' of being high takes on different significance depending on whether one is entering a rock and roll concert or a calculus exam. Situational constraints and cues continually shape interpretational processes. Common-sense theories, constraints of time and place, appearances, and the practical demands of the moment organize an actor's response to particular situations. The construction of deviance is always from a particular point of view.

Sudnow (1965) describes how the broader context of the social organization of a public defender's office as well as the specific features of particular defendants intersect to "allow" attorneys to arrive at understandings of clients= behaviors as atypical and deserving of special handling, or typical—"normal crimes" which can be processed via a set of standard procedures and plea bargaining. The meaning of being a criminal is not contained within the act one commits but emerges from within the context through which one's act is interpreted.

The ongoing spiral of indexicality and reflexivity describes the central interpretive context through which typified understandings of deviance (labels) are produced and applied as practical accomplishments leading to reasonable accounts of particular individuals and their behaviour within the confines of specific situations. These accounts are seen as shaping social response that generates new contexts, both official and unofficial, and the process continues.

Through this process organizations emerge as definers and controllers of deviance, individuals come to be "understood" as deviant, and oftentimes the individuals come to see themselves as deviant. The important component here is that we typically fail to see, or at least forget, that it is through our "work" that reality and our sense of self is constructed. They come to take on a natural, taken-for-granted character.

Retrospective Interpretation

Retrospective interpretation details a particular process in this social construction of reality. The idea here is that the meaning of behaviour, in this case past behaviour, and the significance of past events, is continually being re-evaluated based on the exigencies of current situations and typified understandings. What was once perhaps confusing or even simply irrelevant for our understanding becomes seen in a new interpretive light.

Garfinkel's (1967) study of jury decision making processes suggests that jurors arrive at understandings of guilt or innocence through a variety of situational cues. Having arrived at this understanding the evidence presented in the course of the trial is organized to conform to the all ready arrived at conclusion. The image of rational decision making is maintained, but the "facts" are constructed to fit the conclusion. The point here is that once we arrive at a particular account (explanation) of a situation or person (decision making based on typifications and commonsense categories indexically tied to the context of the situation) we reflexively reconstruct our understanding of the process so that our decision or definition appears to us as normal, natural, and "real."

Sacks (1972) makes a similar claim in his analysis of how suicide threats are constructed out of crisis hotline telephone calls. Describing the process with his "consistency rule," information from the past, as well as newly encountered information, is interpreted as significant within the context of the now known threat; the individual's conversation is seen to have been leading up to the threat all along. Sacks extends his analysis with the associated interpretational process he calls the "economy rule" which suggests that once actors construct an organized understanding of a particular event they are hesitant to take into account competing explanations or constructions.

The power of these constructions when they are couched in an assumption of deviant behaviour can be so overwhelming as to shape an actor's identity and lead to his or her immersion within a world of deviance. The former identity, at best, receives the accent of mere appearance... What he is now is what, "after all, he was all along."

Erving Goffman (1963) discusses the process of retrospective interpretation as part of the "moral career" of those defined by deviance. The subjective understandings generated through current experiences allow for "turning points" during which...."the stigmatized individual may single out and retrospectively elabourate experiences which *(then)* serve for him to account for his coming to the beliefs and practices he now has regarding his own kind and normals". A disabling event can become reinterpreted as an opportunity to start on a new life path, or an inopportune disclosure that leads to an arrest becomes a "call for help." The individual may come to a new understanding of his or her past which then serves to (re)confirm the present. Out of the spiral of indexicality and reflexivity a sense of structure emerges. This structure is a practical accomplishment based on everyday interpretive processes and it serves to confirm and elabourate deviant identities—subjectively for the individuals involved, and objectively for the organizations which document and respond to these identities.

Documentary Interpretation

Documentary interpretation, a special case representing the indexical-reflexive structure of interpretational processes, refers to a procedure through which immediately given information (documents); appearance, police reports, past records, and other typifications are used to infer meaning and motive in the behaviour of others. "Not only is the underlying pattern derived from its individual documentary evidences, but the individual documentary evidences, in their turn, are interpreted on the basis of 'what is known' about the underlying pattern. Each is used to elabourate the other".

We selectively take bits and pieces of information, those presented informally in interaction and those that are part of the "official record," and construct a reasonable account of the individual that then seems to confirm the "reading" of the documents. Members work back and forth taking into account particular documents that then are seen as meaningful within the context of common-sense theories of behaviour. The theories direct our attention to particular documents, and as these contextual elements are taken into account, they become meaningful. Rosenhahn (1973) displays the workings of this process within the context of psychiatric evaluations. What would otherwise be seen as unremarkable statements about such things as occasional arguments and child spankings become interpreted as signs of an underlying mental disorder. The emerging significance of these statements develops based upon the assumption of the subject's underlying mental disorder.

Deviance, Negotiation, and Imputation of Motive

Sometimes behaviour is "normalized," explained away or even ignored. Members are likely to allow certain types of disrupting behaviour to pass assuming that clarification and understanding will come later. When clarification does not come or when behaviour is too problematic negotiation occurs. Actors do not always readily succumb to the process of being identified as deviant. The construction of a deviant identity often involves negotiation and bargaining. Information is selectively presented. Actors attempt to enable others to see the world from their particular point of view. Explanations are presented and evaluated. Actors may deny intentional activity, or present other rationalizing accounts; the drug user steals to feed his or her addiction, a victim may 'have had it coming to them," or an event may be presented as having been an accident.

How do we infer whether or not a specific act was planned and chosen by a particular individual? Intention is an important, though not specifically necessary, component in defining a person as deviant. Interpreting an actor's behaviour as being determined by forces outside their own control typically leads to more or less non-deviant designations (Jones and Davis,1965). In the context of modern medical (common-sense) theories of behaviour audiences are most likely to arrive at interpretations of sickness. On the other hand, if the audience can not come to accept the actors point of view, nor ascribe cause to external contingencies, then deviant intention becomes a defining characteristic of the interaction.

The "facts" established become part of the indexical reality of the situation and reflexively shape the definition constructed. Social response to the deviant, both formal and informal, is based upon the understandings that emerge from such interactions. If deviant definitions do not emerge, the actor in question may be reintegrated within the group. If understanding of the individual or behaviour as deviant develops, processes of exclusion, punishment, or treatment may ensue. Members act toward others based on the meaning constructed out of the situation at hand.

Organizational Context

The process of constructing images of deviance and deviants takes place at many levels of interaction. At the level of face-to-face interaction the construction of deviance allows members to account for behaviour viewed as problematic and to organize their daily lives. At the more formal level of social organizations, identification and control deviance becomes a practical activity embedded within the routines of organizational life. The rational demands for efficiency, calculability, predictability, and standardized control produce interpretive guidelines and categorical systems that further routinize the social construction of deviance.

At this formal level the process of negotiation is strained. The fixed categories and interests of the organization influence the decision making process. Viewed through the constraints of the organization a variety of behaviors are collapsed into standardized (surveys of illicit drug use which define use during 20 of the past 30 days as daily use and do not distinguish "daily use" at this level from multiple use throughout the day). Once confirmed within a certain type, the action of the control agent toward the "deviant" is determined by the prescribed routines of the organization of social control. Based on this analysis, the accounts of deviance provided by official agencies of social control are not viewed by ethnomethodologists as information on the reality of deviant behaviour, "...but as indicators and reflections of organizational properties and routines".

Phenomenology-Ethnomethodology And Family Discourse

Ethnomethodology, an approach developed by Harold Garfinkel, emerged out of social phenomenology as a reaction against Parsonian functionalism. Ethnomethodology refers to people's (ethno) methods for making sense of their world. Although building upon a phenomenological foundation, ethnomethodology extends the phenomenological concern for explicating what constitutes an experience to an analysis of how an experience is accomplished. This subtle shift in focus moves ethnomethodology away from an analysis of experience per se to an analysis of how people make sense of their experience. The end result of such a shift is that ethnomethodologists focus on everyday language use and examine how everyday language in use both constitutes its context and is constituted by its context.

For ethnomethodologically inspired scholars, the study of familial experience becomes the study of how *family* is produced through language use or discourse. Family emerges whenever it is talked about, whenever the discourse constructs social relations as familial. Enacting family through talk does not mean one can make family any way she pleases. Rather, family discourse always depends on context and is sensitive to the situation. Therefore, scholars must carefully examine how the social organization of the context within which family discourse is evoked conditions the use of family discourse and also how family discourse serves to construct the context itself. Understanding family as a discursive production enables scholars to examine family as an organizationally embedded social reality. Family can be studied wherever family discourse occurs. Through this approach, family scholars have examined how family is enacted in family therapy clinics, nursing homes, the judicial system, and a wide variety of organizational settings. Although future developments in phenomenological studies of family life are likely to occur, phenomenology remains an underutilized theoretical resource in the study of the family. It holds great promise for assisting scholars in understanding various aspects of familial experience and how family realities are constructed through language use in a wide variety of contexts. In particular, phenomenological approaches can facilitate a greater understanding of the cultural diversity of familial experience that characterizes social life at the beginning of the new millennium.

SOCIAL EXCHANGE THEORY-MAJOR CONTEMPORARY CONCEPTS

The major exchange concepts can be classified as falling into the following broad categories:

Rewards, costs, and resources. Exchange theories make use of the concepts of rewards and costs (which were borrowed from behavioural psychology) and resources (which were borrowed from economics) when discussing the foundation of the interpersonal exchange. Rewards and resources refer to the benefits exchange in social relationships. Rewards are defined as the pleasures, satisfactions, and gratifications a person enjoys from participating in a relationship. Resources, on the other hand, are any commodities, material or symbolic, that can be transmitted through interpersonal behaviour and give one person the capacity to reward another (Emerson 1976). The costs of social exchange relationships can involve punishments experienced, the energy invested in a relationship, or rewards foregone as a result of engaging in one behaviour or course of action rather than another (Blau 1964). *Satisfaction with exchange relationships: outcomes and comparison levels.* Satisfaction with an exchange relationship is derived, in part, from the evaluation of the outcomes available in a relationship. Outcomes are equal to the rewards obtained from a relationship minus the costs incurred. Although it is generally the case that the higher the level of outcomes available, the greater the satisfaction, these concepts are not equivalent. To account for satisfaction, both the experiences of the outcomes derived from the relationship and the expectations that individuals bring to their relationships are taken into account.

The concept of Comparison Level (CL) was developed by Thibaut and Kelley to explain the contributions that previous experiences and expectations make to the determination of how satisfied an individual is with a relationship. Individuals come to their relationships with an awareness of societal norms for relationships and a backlog of experiences. The CL is influenced by this information and, thus, reflects (a) what individuals feel is deserved and realistically obtainable within relationships, and (b) what individuals feel is important for them to experience within a relationship. When the outcomes derived from a relationship exceed the CL (particularly highly valued outcomes or ones that are important to individuals), global assessments of a relationship are likely to be high.

Relationship stability: comparison level for alternatives, dependence, and barriers. According to exchange theorists, satisfaction with a relationship alone does not determine the likelihood that a relationship will continue. Thibaut and Kelley (1959) developed the concept of comparison level of alternatives (CLalt), defined as the lowest level of outcome a person will accept from a relationship in light of available alternatives, to explain individuals' decisions to remain in or leave a relationship. The CLalt is an individual's assessment of the outcomes available in an alternative to the present relationship. When the outcomes available in an alternative relationship exceed those available in a relationship, the likelihood increases that person will leave the relationship.

Hence, staying in or leaving a relationship is not simply a matter of how rewarding that relationship is. Relationships that are rewarding are more likely to be stable because a high level of outcomes reduces, in terms of expectations, the likelihood of a better alternative existing. Unsatisfactory relationships, in turn, may remain stable for the lack of a better alternative. These relationships have been conceived of as *nonvoluntary relationships* by Thibaut and Kelley (1959). Married individuals who stay in violent relationships can be thought of as participating in a nonvoluntary relationship—that is, the relationship stays stable in spite of the violence because of the absence of better alternatives (Gelles 1976).

The CLalt is also related to the experience of dependence. Dependence is defined as the degree to which a person believes that he or she is subject to or reliant on the other for relationship outcome. The degree of dependence evidenced is determined by the degree to which the outcomes derived from a relationship exceed the outcomes perceived to be available from existing alternatives. Dependence may be experienced as one of the costs of participating in a relationship, but this is probably determined in part by the level of satisfaction experienced with the relationship. Dependence, in other words, is tolerated in highly rewarding relationships.

Dependence is further influenced by the barriers that increase the costs of dissolving an existing relationship (Levinger 1982). Levinger proposes the existence of two types of barriers—internal and external—that discourage an individual from leaving a relationship by fostering dependence even if attraction is low. Internal barriers are the feelings of obligation and indebtedness to the partner that contribute to dependence by increasing the psychological costs of terminating the relationship. Internal constraints might involve the moral belief that a marriage, for example, is forever or that children should be raised in a home with both parents present. External barriers are things like community pressures, legal pressures, and material or economic considerations that foster dependence by increasing the social and economic costs of terminating a relationship.

Norms regulating exchange relationships: exchange orientations and rules. Exchange relationships are governed by both *normative* and *cognitive* exchange orientations that delineate acceptable and appropriate behaviour. Normative orientations refer to the societal views on acceptable and appropriate behaviour in relationships. These norms refer to the broader consensus that exists within a culture about how exchange relationships should be structured.

Cognitive orientations represent the beliefs, values, and relationship orientations that an individual associates with various types of exchange relationships (McDonald 1984). These orientations serve as the standards for interpersonal behaviour that an individual brings to his or her personal relationships. Among the more prominent of the cognitive orientations discussed in the exchange literature are the norms of distributed justice, or fairness, norms of reciprocity, and norms of equity. Each of these has to do with the expectation that within a close and intimate relationship, the rewards experienced by partners should be more or less proportionately distributed. When these norms are violated, as when housework is unfairly distributed within a marriage, people are apt to complain more about the relationship and pressure their partners to restore a more just and fair pattern of exchange.

Bibliography

Aho, J. A.: *The Things of the World: A Social Phenomenology.* Westport, CT: Praeger, 1998.

Bitton, T.: *Introductory Sociology*, London: Macmillan Press, 1996.

Bottomore, Tom: *A Dictionary of Marxist Thought,* Cambridge, Harvard University Press, 1983.

Bruun, Hans Henrik: *Science, Values and Politics in Max Weber's Methodology*. Copenhagen: Munksgaard, 1972.

Callinicos, A.: *Social Theory: A Historical Introduction*. New York University Press, 1999.

Cohen, B.: *Developing Sociological Knowledge: Theory and Method*. Nelson Hall, 1989.

Comte, A.: *The Positive Philosophy*. New York: AMS Press, 1974.

Crotty, M.: *The Foundations of Social Research: Meaning and Perspective in the Research Process.* Thousand Oaks, CA: Sage, 1998.

Durkheim, E.: *The Rules of the Sociological Method*. New York: The Free Press, 1982.

Giddens, A.: *Social Theory and Modern Sociology*. Broadview, 1987.

Giorgi, A.: *Phenomenology and Psychological Research.* Pittsburgh, PA: Duquesne University Press, 1985.

Grant, G. P.: *Philosophy in the Mass Age*, Copp Clark, Toronto, 1959.

Gyford J: *The Politics of Local Socialism*, London, George Allen and Unwin, 1985.

Haralambus, M and Holborn, M.: *Sociology: Themes and Perspective*. London; University Tutorial Press, 2002.

Heilbron, Johan: *The Rise of Social Theory*. Cambridge University Press, 1995.

Hoggett, P.: *The Politics of Decentralisation*, Basingstoke, MacMillan, 1994.

John Akula: *Law and the Development of Citizenship*. Ph.D. dissertation, Harvard University, 1973.

Jonathan H.: *The Structure of Sociological Theory*, Belmont, Ca., Wadsworth, 1991.

Kewal Krishan: *Materialism in Indian Thought,* Munshiram Manoharlal Publishers, New Delhi, 1974.

Kincaid, Harold: *Philosophical Foundations of the Social Sciences: Analyzing Controversies in Social Research*. Cambridge University Press, 1996.

Larson, C.J.: *Pure and Applied Sociological Theory: Problems and Issues*. Harcourt, 1993.

Levesque-Lopman, L.: *Claiming Reality: Phenomenology and Women's Experience*. Totowa, NJ: Rowman & Littlefield, 1988.

Norman Birnbaum: *Social Structure and the German Reformation*. Ph.D. dissertation, Harvard University, 1958.

Rainer Carl Baum: *Values and 'Uneven' Political Development in Imperial Germany*. Ph.D. dissertation, Harvard University, 1968.

Ray, L.: *Theorizing Classical Sociology*. Open University Press, 1999.

Richard W.: *Sociological Theory: An Introduction to the Classical Tradition*, Peterborough, Broadview Press, 1997.

Ritzer, George: *Sociological Theory*, New York: McGraw-Hill, 1992.

Robert Nisbet: *A History of Sociological Analysis,* New York, Basic Books, 1978.

Sydie, R. A.: *Natural Women Cultured Men: A Feminist Perspective on Sociological Theory,* Toronto, Methuen, 1987.

Tong, Rosemarie: *Feminist Thought: A Comprehensive Introduction*. Boulder: Westview Press, 1989.

Index

❑❑❑